Remarkable Ramona Park

A Passionate History of a Much Beloved Place

RAMONA

THE · RENDESVOUS · OF · REFINED · AMUSEMENT · SEEKERS

Gail Marie Snow

Printed by Color House Graphics

ISBN 978-0-615-82344-7

Remarkable Ramona Park: A Passionate History of a Much Beloved Place
© 2013 by Gail Marie Snow

Publisher: Gail Marie Snow

Printed in Grand Rapids by
Color House Graphics
Grand Rapids, MI
www.colorhousegraphics.com

First Edition, First Printing

Library of Congress Control Number: 2013910100

From the History Room, East Grand Rapids Library

Dedication

This book is dedicated to the many institutions around the country which are responsible for preserving history. Libraries, museums, archives and historical and genealogical societies, most often working with an overwhelming lack of funds, continue to provide public access to materials which make it possible to produce works like this book. Volunteers within these institutions are also vitally important in processing and making the respective collections known to the public through indexing and internet exposure.

It is the hope of the author that readers of this book will consider showing appreciation for the importance of such institutions by donating time, funds and/or items of historic importance.

Learning about the past enriches our understanding of the present.

Ryerson Library Archives

These boxes contain items donated by people and organizations: photographs, letters, diaries, records, brochures, maps, clippings, booklets and other ephemera. The carefully controlled environment of this room protects these treasures so they will be available for research for many years to come.

Ryerson Library, Grand Rapids, Michigan, 1909

Acknowledgements

Thomas R. Dilley, of course you realize that if you hadn't bought a postcard from me back in 2008, I would probably never have met you, and this book would not exist! Besides providing the initial spark, you kept the flame burning with your encouragement, wisdom and guidance, and finally, your endorsement.

The Local History Room at the East Grand Rapids Public Library was the place where I started my search, aided by **Mary Dersch** who absolutely loves everything to do with Ramona Park and Reeds Lake. **Tim Gleisner**, as head of the local history department and archives of the Grand Rapids Public Library, your enthusiasm for all things Grand Rapids and your eagerness to create a friendly and helpful environment for all researchers, have provided for me an invaluable platform for my own research. Also, **Bill Cunningham**, your tireless efforts to preserve Grand Rapids History through the City Archives provide a great service to this community. People of this city are also very fortunate to have you, **Alex Forist**, to oversee the collections and photo archives of the Grand Rapids Public Museum.

Dr. Dan Arsulowicz, during my annual visit to your office, I casually mentioned the project to you. You stopped testing my eyes and enthusiastically phoned a friend to suggest he needed to interview me to get the word out. **Tom Rademacher**, I'll never forget your visit when we discussed Ramona Park and you mentioned that your last official day as a full-time employee of the Grand Rapids Press was that very week. I couldn't forget the jump start caused by that July 4th, 2009, column which caught the eye of so many readers. A veritable landslide of contributions resulted.

Warren "Hap" Hecker, you contacted me after reading that article and told me stories about the years when you worked at Ramona. You have continued throughout the process to be a rich source of information and interesting ideas as well as enthusiastic affirmation. **Dick Ryan**, although most of your work at Ramona was on the boat, your memories of your varied jobs in the concessions have added seasoning. Likewise **Jim Chrysler**, you were another young worker in the park during the days when grown men weren't available for hire because of the war. Your continuing interest in the "park layout" has added much to the reconstruction of "the way it was." Even though it was so long ago, you have supplied many great details.

Mary Ellen Miklas Siegel, teen dancer at the theater, what a great collection of photos you shared along with playbills from those war-year productions and tales of working in the theater. **Donna Kruizenga Boelema**, you told me your dad, Dick, had the best job of any in the park, running the merry-go-round. The photos taken by your parents will bring to mind many fond memories for readers. **Karin McElwee Westdale**, granddaughter of John McElwee and keeper of family memorabilia, you were a wonderful source of photos of the Derby Racer and Carousel and background information on your remarkable ancestor.

John Kamstra, your interest in Grand Rapids history caused you to become a collector, and you generously provided me with some fantastic one-of-a-kind photos and scans of interesting ephemera. **Gordon Hubenet**, also an avid collector concerned with preserving history, you came through with some very interesting treasures.

Diana Barrett, you have continued to supply me with fascinating newspaper articles you encountered as you pursued your own research for the Grand Rapids Historical Commission. You and **Shirley DeBoer** encouraged me to speak at the 34th Annual Great Lakes History Conference sponsored by Grand Valley State University. **Rich Hubbard**, because you attended that conference in November of 2009, you invited me to speak to the Westminster Presbyterian seniors, which snowballed into many presentations to many Grand Rapids area organizations. Besides opening up future engagements, Westminster introduced me to **Margaret Kimber** who shared some outstanding photographs.

Through my hours and hours spent at the library microfilm machines, I met many fellow history researchers. **Kim Rush**, my work has been so enriched by your continuous contributions of information about theater productions and dance bands. **Carl Bajema**, our mutual interest in Ramona, Reeds Lake and the Railways has enhanced the research efforts of both of us. I look forward to your next book with great anticipation.

Dan Rogers, besides the great conversations we've had about the Ramona train, and the opportunities you provided for up-to-the-minute photographs, everyone owes you a debt of gratitude for continuing to care for the little train. Thanks to you, we who rode it at Ramona can ride it once again, and introduce our grandchildren to the experience.

Susan Mozley, you were truly a Godsend! I'm sure you didn't realize what you were getting into when you told me you'd be glad to proofread this book. Your service was invaluable. Likewise, members of the **Writers' Group of the Western Michigan Genealogical Society**, you have listened patiently to my research tales month after month since the very beginning of this adventure. Your comments and suggestions through these years have aided me greatly. **Chris Byron** and **Tom Wilson**, I do so appreciate your sharing your knowledge of this whole book-producing process gained from your own very successful ventures.

My first interview was with **Ken Ellis**, one-time employee of the park who sadly has passed on before the publication of these pages. Likewise, **Nancy Loeschner**, with whom I spent many joyful hours uncovering the mysteries of Point Paulo. May you both rest in peace.

And back to you **Tom Rademacher**. During these past four years, your own pathway has changed but you keep on giving to the people of this community. I feel very honored that you have, once again, supported this project with your kind words.

Many more people than those mentioned above have contributed to this effort, but no amount of help would have been sufficient were it not for my patient and loving spouse. **Chuck Snow**, you accompanied me on so many occasions into myriad adventures in discovery, provided assistance with editing and making decisions and encouraged me even though I spent countless hours on this endeavor.

Ramona park is owned and operated by the Grand Rapids Railroad company for the enjoyment of Grand Rapids citizens, the city's visitors and western Michigan residents. It is one of the few remaining amusement parks in the country that has a "free" gate. As a member of the National Amusement Park association, Ramona has the highest rating for its high class entertainment, clean amusements, safety and management. For years Ramona has been the summer mecca for those who enjoy clean theatrical productions, wholesome amusements and concessions that offer thrills and enjoyment with safety.

Grand Rapids Herald, May 22, 1931

Foreword

Like too many unfortunate others, I was but a tot when they closed Ramona Park, and so I have not a single direct memory of the whirlwinds this storied attraction created, its many elements standing tall and proud for more than half a century on the shores of Reeds Lake in East Grand Rapids.

But I can go there now, more than 60 years after its last vestiges were carried off piece by piece. And so can you – so can we all -- thanks to this delightful history penned by Gail Snow, who has been delving into Ramona's ghosts for nearly half a decade.

Her painstaking research put her face to face with everything from 9,000 newspaper clippings to interviews with old-timers who gave her first-person accounts of what Ramona looked like, felt like, smelled like. And with her gifted pen and eye for detail, she's cornered it all and tucked it between two covers.

For a generation cutting its social teeth on screens and pushbuttons, this keepsake book is nothing less than a primer on how people used to amuse and be amused, and the relevance of human play and interaction.

For the rest, each turn of the page will no doubt prompt "Ahhhhh" moments, the sort that pays homage to nostalgia and good old-fashioned whimsy.

To take in what once was Ramona Park is to absorb these days a quiet yacht club, a cozy restaurant, and further west a warren of condos and shops and parking lots.

But there was a time when the same space bustled with the air of a carnival, wowing wide-eyed patrons with the likes of C.B Clarke as he and his motorcycle cheated fate each time he roared around the inside of the "Globe of Death" on the Ramona Theater stage.

There was the Jack Rabbit Derby Racer, a wooden rollercoaster featuring an 80 percent drop, and it lorded over a landscape that at times swelled with thousands of visitors to the Park below. In 1914, The Grand Rapids Press Newsboys convened for a picnic – all 1,400 of them.

A dance pavilion lured music lovers to the now-legendary sounds of Tommy Dorsey, Bob Crosby and Glen Miller. Couples swooned to time spent in the Mystic Chutes and Tunnel of Love. And a theater on the grounds played host to the likes of Jack Benny, Will Rogers, Fannie Brice, Bill "Bojangles" Robinson – and others who flourished during the long-gone days of silent films, vaudeville, burlesque.

I'm tempted to write more, but I don't want to further your delay into a savory feast that stars another icon: Yesteryear.

Enjoy.

Tom Rademacher

(Author's Note) Tom Rademacher worked full-time more than 31 years as a reporter and columnist with The Grand Rapids Press. He now serves as a storyteller and strategist with RTM Ltd., with offices in Rockford MI and New York City.

People waiting in line at the Derby Racer

Preface

I remember going to Ramona Park. I don't even recall how many times I went or with whom. Images in my mind are, at best, fleeting. But, I do remember my favorites, the Fish Pond and Tilt-A-Whirl, a few of the Fun House features and the fact that I was never tall enough to drive a bumper car. I have no trouble remembering that I loved Ramona Park. Funny how seeing an old photo of a beloved place can bring to mind something long forgotten.

When I needed a topic on which to present a fifteen-minute talk for the O-Wash-Ta-Nong Questers, "Ramona" just came to me. Once I started doing the research, I couldn't stop, I had to know more and more. It was exciting but frustrating because information was scattered around in so many places, even within one location. In gathering stories and images, I have become a repository of Ramona Park information, so to speak.

Tom Dilley encouraged me to put this research into a book. My own goal in doing so has been to provide an opportunity for bringing back enjoyable memories. It is my hope that for those readers who attended the park, good memories will return over and over. For those who went to other parks around the country, perhaps various images will cause the same pleasant recollections. And, just maybe, for readers who never attended Ramona, a journey through the book will produce the feeling that they had actually been there.

Initially I expected to make the book about both Ramona Park and Reeds Lake since the two merge easily together in people's recollections. However, I have amassed so much material that to do so would have meant eliminating too much that is important. This way I can include interesting little side tidbits in both volumes. It will not take me as long to put together the Reeds Lake book because most of the research is done. At the end of this volume, I have included some photos of topics from that book.

The story of Ramona Park since its closing has previously only been told in bits and pieces in magazine and newspaper articles, and in an occasional reference in history books. The complete story can never be written for it is too vast and some of its secrets will always be locked away. Facts were recorded in countless documents, newspapers, photographs, and people's memories, waiting to be uncovered by relentless research.

The major source for this volume has been old newspapers. This may seem puzzling to people in the 21st century when most of us are suspicious of the validity of information published in current issues. Newspapers carried a different importance in the 19th and early 20th centuries. For many decades they were the only source of news for the average household, and for some, the only reading material. Even so, I have attempted to substantiate information by comparing different newspaper articles and consulting other sources. I cannot guarantee that I haven't made any errors, but I have taken great pains to try to avoid inaccuracies. As a result, some of the information in this volume will be in disagreement with other writings about Ramona.

I will probably continue to collect Ramona Photos and facts as long as I am able to draw a breath. I expect that once this publication is in the hands of other Ramona Park lovers I will be contacted with offers of new items. There is nothing that says there couldn't some day be another book with additionally discovered material!

Gail Marie Snow

A Reeds Lake Steam Engine
1881-1892

Contents

Remarkable Ramona Park

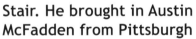

What was remarkable about Ramona Park? It was just one of dozens upon dozens of amusement parks that existed in major cities around the country in the early twentieth century. Grand Rapids was certainly not a major city, and East Grand Rapids was virtually unknown.

The setting for the park was in itself remarkable. The natural beauty of Reeds Lake had drawn people to its shores for decades before the amusement park came into being. The many resorts that developed around the lake added to its appeal to visitors from Grand Rapids and surrounding areas. To people who recall the Ramona Park experience, there is no separation between the park itself and Reeds Lake. The swimming beaches, the boats and steamers, the athletic park, taverns, dance halls, hotels and other resorts all blend together.

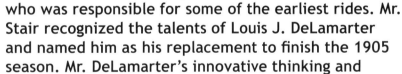

The specific people involved in its origination and ongoing operation also made this park remarkable. At first, it was just a theater called, *"Ramona,"* but it grew in significance under the management of theater-man Orin

Stair. He brought in Austin McFadden from Pittsburgh who was responsible for some of the earliest rides. Mr. Stair recognized the talents of Louis J. DeLamarter and named him as his replacement to finish the 1905 season. Mr. DeLamarter's innovative thinking and business acumen kept the park on the leading edge of amusement advancements and he established the theater as a nationally acclaimed vaudeville venue. The McElwee brothers installed one of their carousels at Ramona in 1909. Their association with Fred Ingersoll through Detroit's Electric Park, brought the Derby Racer in 1914. The McElwee brothers were responsible for many major amusements, and their involvement at Ramona lasted until its final year, 1954.

THE WHIRL-A-GIG

RAMONA
REED'S LAKE

While many of the amusement parks around the nation were operated by railway companies, the Grand Rapids company which owned Ramona was exceptional in its ongoing policies. Making its presence felt in the early 1880s, the company established its reputation as the provider and

protector of family amusement. The policy of offering entertainment appropriate for children and ladies was adhered to throughout the life of the theater and the park. The *Journal of the Michigan State Medical Society* stated in the August 1915 issue, *"Seldom, if ever, has nature provided a location where so many attractions, natural and otherwise, can be offered the*
refined amusement seeker, as at Ramona Park and seldom, if ever, has park management been more conscientious in providing for patrons than at Ramona."

Ramona Park, in its setting on Reeds Lake, was not just a place for simply indulging in amusements and spending hard-earned coins. It was a place

where people went to celebrate. Families held picnics to celebrate life by being reunited with long-lost relatives. Companies rewarded employees by treating them to a day-long picnic, providing everything needed for the glorious occasion. Organizations held picnics to celebrate their heritage, emancipation,
immigration. Holidays were times of special balloon ascensions, fireworks, concerts, speakers and parades. The theater provided a grand arena for youngsters receiving certificates of accomplishment as they left one phase of education and moved on to another.

People made life-long friends at Ramona, some resulting in marriage. Young men got their first jobs working at the park or on the boats. Teenagers spent hours dancing to the best bands in the nation, or roller

skating with friends or strangers who became friends. Society ladies held theater parties, men attended ball games. A person could arrive alone and leave with a crowd. Youngsters who lived near the park or were fortunate enough to have parents who worked there, could spend all day amusing themselves with a baby-sitter named

Ramona. Those not so fortunate either walked from home or took a streetcar or bus, carrying a sack lunch and a few saved-up pennies, and spent the whole day having a good time. For years, especially during the time of war or depression, the springtime slogan was, *"Cheer Up! Ramona is open!"*

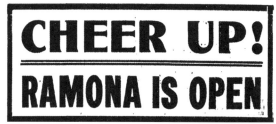

The strong appeal of Reeds Lake and Ramona Park, in some cases, caused problems. One gentleman filed for divorce citing that *"his wife spent a large portion of his money at Reed's Lake and left him at home to get his own meals and wash his own clothes."* In another divorce court testimony, a man states that he objected to his wife going to Reeds Lake because of the company which she kept. Other incidents were reported in which young boys stole money and then spent it all riding the Derby Racer. The more honest types worked for money which was immediately donated to the roller coaster.

Amusement parks were a popular theme for early post card pictures. But the images of Ramona Park that have been preserved on postcards only show individual amusements. There was no entry fee or entry gate, no big sign that identified it to visitors. Besides aerial views, the closest thing to a picture of all of Ramona Park is a double card from around 1906 that shows most of the amusements available at that time, because they were all visible from the south where the streetcars entered. After that, the park spread northward into the trees, making a whole-park view no longer possible. Pictures of the Derby Racer, the Ramona Theater, the Ramona Gardens dance hall, and the octagonal carousel building can be found on old postcards as well as many scenes around and on Reeds Lake.

A visit to Ramona Park involved all five of the senses. The ears picked up screams from roller coaster passengers, music from the carousel, bells and chimes from the games, voices from the crowds, the whistles of the miniature train and steamboat and the buzzing of electric sparks from the Skooter's bumper cars. Coming to recollection are visions of multicolored lights, smiles on the hundreds of faces moving from one attraction to another, animals in cages, and ornate doorways that enticed people to enter the exhibits and games within. The nose detected the smell of cigars or the distinct fragrance of freshly cooked french fries, the memory of which still teases the taste buds. The flavors of cotton candy, ice cream, Cracker Jacks and Pronto Pups were also a part of the experience, especially when all mixed together. And, no one could forget the feeling of the wind in the face and hair while racing along in a roller coaster car or whirling around on the Ferris wheel or rocket planes. Plummeting down the 80 foot incline of the Derby Racer generated a queasy feeling as did spinning on the Tilt-A-Whirl or Whip. Driving a bumper car and smashing into another vehicle without any consequences except the anticipation of revenge on the part of the victim, created electrifying excitement. The sensation of the hairs standing up on the back of the neck came about while on the ride through the scary Pretzel or in anticipation of the blast of air blowing the skirts or pant legs in the Fun House. All of this was a part of the totally remarkable Ramona Park experience.

Ramona Chronology

1875	Grand Rapids and Reeds Lake Street Railway completes track to the lake
1881	Conversion to steam dummy Railway purchases 10 acres of property in Boynton Judd Lake Add
1882	First railway pavilion opens
1883	First merry-go-round is set up on railway property
1888	Switchback roller toboggan is running
1892	Conversion to electric streetcars
1893	Second railway pavilion opens
1894	First Newsboys' picnic
1897	Second railway pavilion burns Third pavilion, a theater, built Theater receives the name, "Ramona"

1903	Railway resort becomes an amusement park with
	    Figure-eight roller toboggan
	    Carousel in the octagonal building
	    Laughing Gallery, House of Trouble, Cave of Winds

1904	Old Mill ride opens
1906	Miniature Train opens Midway receives the title, "Circle"
1909	McElwee carousel opens Point Paulo established First exhibition of baby incubators. Return in 1911, 1912
1910	Major revisions to theater, roof garden, balcony Cottages built at Point Paulo
1912	Round-roofed dancing pavilion is opened
1914	Derby Racer opens; Old Mill, Laughing Gallery gone
1916	Derby Racer receives the title, "Jack Rabbit"
1921	Mystic Chutes opens
1922	First Glidden miniature railroad built
1923	First Marcus Girls appearance
1924	Fun House opens
1925	Dancing pavilion receives the title, "Ramona Gardens" Slides added to Fun House
1931	Mystic Chutes burns, is not rebuilt
1937	Glidden locomotive "5001" introduced
1942	Ramona Gardens becomes skating rink
1955	Ramona Park razed Ramona Gardens building moves to Plymouth Glidden train moves to Lowell
1963	Ramona carousel organs rescued
1967	"The Place" opens in old skating rink
1974	"Ramona Gardens" Plymouth building razed
1998	Mini train moved to Burley Park at Howard City

Background

Long before Ramona Park existed, resort activity at Reeds Lake flourished.
The history of the amusement park itself actually begins with the story of the railway presence at the lake, and the development of its property.

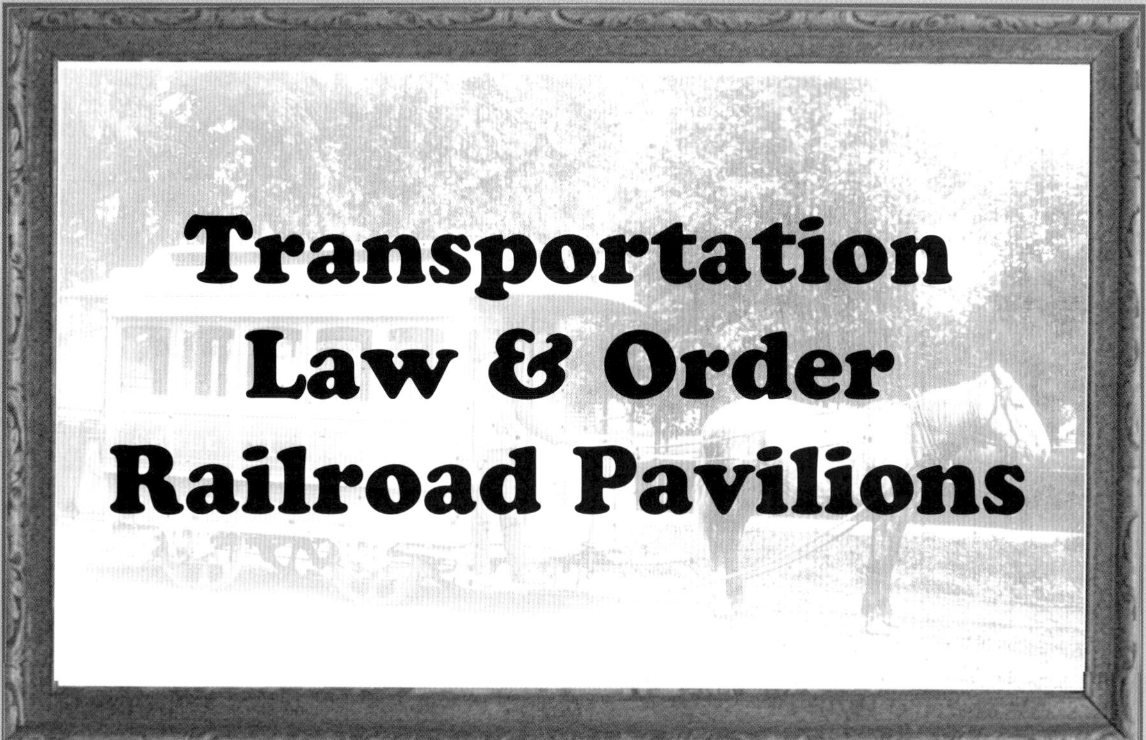

Transportation
Law & Order
Railroad Pavilions

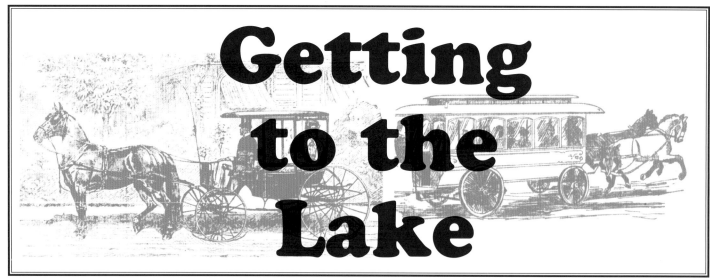

Getting to the Lake

To the Lake. Back from the Lake. In the 1800s and early 1900s, such references were always to Reeds Lake. It was the closest lake of any size to the city, it was where people went to get away, and they did so by any means they could. If there hadn't been a Reeds Lake, would there have been a Ramona Park in East Grand Rapids? In fact, if it weren't for Reeds Lake, would there have been an East Grand Rapids? It is certain that there would not have been a Ramona Park were it not for the railway company, for the park was established and maintained by the transportation business for its entire lifetime.

Known initially as Grand Lake, Reeds Lake attracted settlers Ezra and Lewis Reed, brothers, their nephew Porter Reed, and Ezekiel Davis, in 1834. By 1855, the rest of the land around the lake had been purchased from the Federal Government, and the name, Reed Lake, honored the pioneers. Through the years the name was spelled Reed's Lake and Reeds Lake, the latter being the version that has triumphed.

The distance from the lake to the edge of the city of Grand Rapids in the 1870s, was a little over 3 miles. From the earliest times there were roads that led eastward from the city to the north and south sides of the lake. The challenge was to find the means to make the journey from the city. Of course, people living in the city of Grand Rapids had easy access to the Grand River without need of conveyance. But, the desire to get away from town was strong, even back then.

Other than actually trekking the distance on foot while lugging a load of picnic or fishing paraphernalia, people had to rely on horses for transportation. Most people living in the city did not need to own a horse or any of the appurtenances required to transport humans. This meant either renting a rig or taking some form of public conveyance to go outside the city. The various alternatives required more money than some segments of the population could easily afford.

J. M. Kennedy livery, one of the places in town where people could rent transportation to go to the lake.

This photo from the late 1890s shows rigs that brought people to the lake for a day of pleasure. Even bicycles can be seen parked near the trees.

The *GR Democrat* in 1875 provided this description of a trip to the lake:

"Whoa, boy! Jump in; and away we roll out of the city, leave behind us some of the worst paved streets in the world, reach Lake Avenue with its hard gravel road-bed, and spin merrily along by 'fresh woods and pastures new.' There is a whirr and rush of wheels by us, for everything, from the latest and nobbiest carriage to the rattling one-horse milk-cart, seems to be in requisition this afternoon for a ride over the road. Here comes the 'Queen of the West,' drawn by four horses, and conveying a load of laughing, rosy school children to Miller's Landing. We are passed by two of the local fast nags, drawing skeleton wagons, and trying each other's speed and endurance over this excellent drive."

The Furniture City Barge was an omnibus or carry-all.

In 1874, the Lake Park resort, on Pioneer Club grounds on the north side of the lake, ran its own omnibus shuttle to town, which cost 20 cents each way.

Captain George E. Judd, who attained his rank in the Civil War, lost an arm in battle. This didn't stop him from serving his country as his tour of duty lasted until 1868. He was a Grand Rapids grocer who eventually dealt in hardware. He was also a commandant of the Soldiers' Home in his later years and was made a Colonel at that time. In 1872 Capt. Judd started a different business venture. He, along with Jeremiah W. Boynton, purchased 80 acres of land between the western shore of Reeds Lake and southern shore of Fisk Lake and within a week began selling off the newly platted lots. In the 21st century, this land is still known as, **"Boynton & Judd's Lake Add."** Capt. Judd kept some of the choice lots bordering Reeds Lake and later erected a pavilion and boat landing.

By this time, there were boat liveries on the south side of the lake at Miller's Landing, and Paul's Landing. Also, the new association, Pioneer Club had formed on the north shore. Capt. Judd, no doubt realizing that public transportation would be a boon to his future business, set out to raise funds to bring the street railway out to the lake from the center of the city, via the fair grounds. This endeavor had been tried before, unsuccessfully. Although sufficient funds were raised very rapidly through subscriptions, the other necessary arrangements did not come together in 1872.

Right, June 1872

Below, 1876

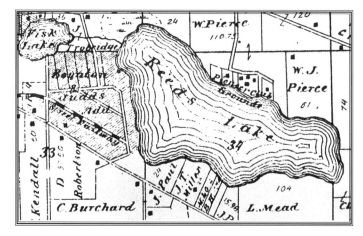

The Street Railway

Jeremiah W. Boynton was the man who finally achieved success in bringing the street railway to Reeds Lake. A colorful figure to say the least, he had what it took to get the job done. The first trip of the horse-drawn streetcar to the lake occurred on July 29, 1875. A few days later, it was reported in the *GR Morning Times* that,

"The cars of the street railway company were crowded to their utmost capacity, and carried 2,800 persons during the day. They were well managed, and the trips over the road were speedy, and no accidents occurred. Had they been capable of carrying twice as many passengers they would not have been too large. No sooner did a car reach either end of the road than it was immediately filled up, and hundreds were left standing at points along the route."

Because of the street railway, more people were able to make the trip to the lake. The fare was 5 cents to the city limits, 5 cents more to go all the way to the lake. A reporter from the *GR Morning Telegram* made this perceptive observation:

"The poor man can now enjoy the pleasures of the lake with the rich. Heretofore a trip to the lake has involved an expense that but few could afford, and hence it has not been generally frequented. Now the poor man with his family, the small salaried clerk, the apprentice, the laborer and the representatives of all classes can enjoy the pleasure of boat riding, fishing and picnicking under the grand old oaks that encircle the lake. In the construction of this road, Mr. Boynton and his associates are entitled to be ranked as public benefactors, and their enterprise should be rewarded with liberal patronage."

This photo shows the type of car that first took passengers out to Reeds Lake. Horses pulled the cars along the track.

What Was a Street Railway?

The difference between a street railway and a railroad had to do with the ownership of the property on which the rails were laid. While the railroad company had to purchase the land and construct the rail bed, the street railway company had to acquire permission or a franchise to use an existing street from the municipality in which the street lay. To do this, the request from the railway company had to specifically mention the route to be taken, and then the governing body voted to accept or reject it. Once the franchise was granted, the company could proceed to lay tracks in the designated street or streets.

While this is not the Reeds Lake line, the photo shows tracks in the street, the condition of the dirt street, and repairs being made under the street.
This photo was made after the automobile entered the transportation scene.

Railway Horses

One of these newspaper articles indicates the perils to the horses and the other tells of the importance of horses to the early railway company.

Two HORSES fell dead on the Reed's lake road yesterday. They were attached to carry-alls, and were probably overworked. At last accounts the carcasses had not been removed, but lay by the roadside as a reminder to horsemen not to attempt to draw a car load of humanity on a road wagon.

1878

This picture of Consumers' Ice Company stables is a reminder that horses needed to be fed, groomed and housed.

"THE most important factor in our business," said a gentleman connected with the Grand Rapids Street Railway company this morning, "is the propelling power. The company now has for its various lines 385 horses, and as this part of our equipment is considered the most necessary and at the same time most perishable, the care and good judgment necessary in buying suitable animals can be readily seen.

"Our manner of buying horses is somewhat unique and yet we have been wonderfully fortunate. We buy chiefly of Grand Rapids dealers, buy a carload at a time and generally without any special examination of the animals. Of course it would not do for us to buy of strangers in this manner. A short time ago we gave Mr. E. S. Morse, whom everybody knows in Grand Rapids as one of our very best and perfectly reliable horse dealers, an order for a carload, unsight-and-unseen. Mr. Morse knows as well as we the animals that are suited to our needs and he makes his purchases accordingly. This lot of animals cost us on an average $180 apiece, and so far the lot has proved to be worth the big money paid for it."

1888

The Dummy Line

The demand of patronage far exceeded the capacity of the little street railway with its horse-drawn cars, almost from the beginning. Complaints about its inadequacy abounded, some coming from the fact that people were left stranded at the lake after the last "train" to the city pulled away.

In 1881, roadbeds were improved and the rails were replaced by heavier rails in order to handle the weight of a steam engine and larger cars. Its institution allowed faster round-trips with greater carrying capacity, thus multiplying the number of people transported to the lake by rail. The operation of this dummy line was seasonal, late April or early May until after Labor Day, depending on the weather.

Even though the introduction of the dummy line increased business considerably, it wasn't long before even that service was deemed inadequate. This is evidenced by this quote from the *GR Daily Democrat* just after the July 4th holiday in 1884:

"The Street railway company took over 4,000 people to the lake and was wholly unable to care for all the business offered—many were compelled to walk to the Sherman Street barn. Some of the trains hauled by the dummy consisted of five cars and were loaded to their utmost capacity. The carryalls and private conveyances were plentiful and all filled."

This situation was repeated many times over the next few years, especially during the heart of the resort season. Various attempts were made to increase loads, number of trains and speeds in order to remedy this problem. In 1884, the street car company was unsuccessful in obtaining permission to install double tracks on the lake route. This would have allowed cars to run every five minutes during peak times. In 1889, a petition was drawn up requesting that the dummy be allowed to increase its speed to 10 miles an hour.

What Was Meant by Dummy?

There are various explanations for the term "dummy" when applied to a locomotive, or even a railway line. The reason for using the term for the Reeds Lake train is a matter of conjecture.

One big problem with early steam engine use in cities for passengers was the noise and steam that were generated. This would scare horses on the street which were drawing vehicles of various sorts. Disguising a steam locomotive to look more like a streetcar by enclosing the engine in a wooden box was done occasionally. It was thought that by resembling a street car, the locomotive would be less likely to frighten horses. Doing this also quieted the engine. Of the three engines used by the Reeds Lake line, one was so built.

In the late 19th and early 20th century, across the country, there were dozens of lines carrying passengers that were referred to as dummy lines. Most were short lines that connected suburbs to a city. Another characteristic was that the branch only went to one place and then came back. Any of these is a plausible reason for the use of the term in the case of Reeds Lake.

The Reeds Lake steam dummy train. On this occasion, besides the regular car, two trailers were added to handle the crowds.

Electric Cars

In the years from 1890 to 1892, several changes took place in the railway transportation business in the Grand Rapids area, and the line to Reeds Lake. The many individual companies were merged into the Grand Rapids Consolidated Street Railway Company. The conversion from horse and steam to electricity was instituted. The route to the lake was changed from Sherman street to Wealthy street, cutting out nearly a half mile of travel. At the lake terminus, a loop of track was put in on company property. This interesting description was written in the *GR Evening Leader* in April, 1892:

"We are making a new terminus which will give better accommodation to the public and greatly facilitate travel. Heretofore we have run into the little station in the rear of the Lakeview house and the trains have been compelled to switch. This year we have put in a loop upon our own property and built a new terminus near the pavilion. Trains will not switch there now as the loop turns them around. This will be a great advantage in handling a crowd and will also avoid all delays. Ladies who wish to go out for a ride in the afternoon or evening can ride to the lake and back without changing their seats, and without riding backwards."

The opening of the 1892 season at Reeds Lake was a test of the new railway route and streetcar facilities. The glowing report in the May 30th *GR Eagle* stated that the company had ample power and more speed. General Manager Chapman of the Consolidated Street Railway Company was quoted, as saying,

"I am well pleased with the way things went yesterday. The traffic to the lake was very large, more than double that on any other line. We had sixteen motors and sixteen trailers running on that route. We did all the work on all the lines with one pair of engines. We did not start up either of the summer engines, though we have had one ready for several days. This proves that we have ample power even for the maximum demand that may be made upon it."

Unprecedented Horse Sale.
On Saturday, May 14, at 10 o'clock a. m., the Consolidated Street Car company will put up at auction fifty of its best horses, all of which will be positively sold to the highest bidder. The sale is made to dispose of stock which is rendered useless by the recent operation of West Side lines by the electric method. These horses are all in prime condition, are sound in wind and limb, are good travelers, and were bought with reference to performing the severe service of street car service.

As the street railway system changed over to electric power, horses were no longer needed by the company. Thus, the above announcement of the sale from the *GR Herald*, May, 1892

The Fate of the Last Dummy Engine

With the coming of the electrified cable system, there was no use for the old dummy engines. The GR Eagle reported on the fate of the last one in August 1892:

"The last old dummy which used to run on the Reed's Lake line, has been fitted up, repainted and is ready to be shipped to Milwaukee, where it will run on the Milwaukee & Wauwatosa railroad, a road running to Milwaukee's chief suburban village."

The *GR Press* newsboys' picnics involved so many youngsters that it took much scheduling ingenuity to transport them to the lake. This photo shows a gang of street cars arriving for one of these events.

A 1904 photo along the loop at Ramona. The figure-eight roller toboggan and its ticket house are visible in the background.

Ramona Pavilion, Reed's Lake, Mich.

This postcard shows passengers alighting from the streetcars. These were known as open cars, used in the summer. People could step directly from their respective seats onto a type of running board.

12

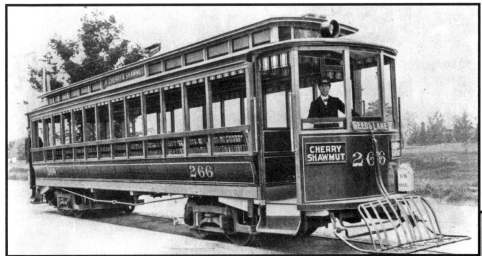

An electric car put on the Reeds Lake route. This car has been opened up for the summer season.

Postcard showing a streetcar in the loop, the merry-go-round building, the fountain, the covered waiting platform and the red theater roof.

Postcard showing a busy afternoon about 1910. People lounging on the lawns of the pavilion are enjoying the view and the outdoors. Note both automobiles and horse and buggy rigs parked in the street. Also showing are the Lakeside Club in the background, *The Hazel A.* at the dock, and a loaded *Major Watson* in the distance.

Front of the special streetcar named in honor of Charles A. Lindbergh.

The Lindbergh car seen June 19, 1927 in "the loop" at Ramona. The Ramona Athletic Field is in the background.

Buses

The evolution of the amusement park on company property is told in the story of the railway pavilions. Through the years, the company had to increase transportation service to Reeds Lake to accommodate the crowds by adding cars and trailers and by providing faster and more powerful engines. The amusement park supplied a great deal of additional revenue for the company over and above the fares, which remained reasonable throughout the history of the park.

The use of electric powered vehicles on tracks lasted until 1935. That was the year that all the electric street cars in the city ceased to run having been replaced by buses. Also, by then, many families owned an automobile, and drove themselves to Ramona. Space had to be made available on Ramona grounds for increasing numbers of cars to park. Of course, even before the horseless carriage, space to park horses and rigs still had to be arranged.

Photo from about 1950 of the loop and wait area for the city buses.

Prompt Bus Service Promised for Ramona on 4th Holiday

"To expedite service to Ramona park for the 4th of July celebration, the GR Motor Coach Co. will place all extra motor coaches in service. Coaches will run to the park at 5 minute intervals beginning at 12:30 pm. Officials promise busses at 3 minute intervals later in the afternoon. All available coaches also will be lined up and waiting at night after the fireworks display to take patrons home."
GR Herald, July 4, 1939

14

You "pay as you enter" leaving Ramona Park now You drop your fare in the box. pass through the turn-stile, and board the car. It's an improvement toward safety and convenience. This is one of the turn-stiles, with Claud Tubbs in charge.

1922

Left, 1922 picture of newly installed turnstile for more orderly access to railway cars.

Above, photo taken before 1949 of the turnstile at the bus entrance to the park. The porch of the theater can be seen in the park behind the gate. A wire fence is just visible on either side of the entrance. Entry to the park was always free, this was the method used to control the crowds as people emerged from the bus.

Right, Mr. Louis J. DeLamarter by the ticket booth of the Derby Racer. He retired as the Chairman of the Board of City Coach Lines Inc. He was involved in Ramona Park management from 1906.

Managers for Ramona Theater and Ramona Park were in the employ of the transportation company. Other individuals leased space from the company for the various concessions. These people maintained the rides or booths, paid the company a percentage of the profit and paid tax on the concession to East Grand Rapids. It was the ingenuity and enthusiasm of many remarkable people that made Ramona Park such a remarkable success over the years. And, of course, there was Reeds Lake.

Law & Order

When the railway company engaged itself in the resort business at Reeds Lake in 1882, it made strong promises about keeping the peace on the grounds. When the pavilion opened, its statement was to the effect that an officer would be present to prevent undesirable individuals from visiting. The goal was to provide the kind of environment in which families would be safe and comfortable.

By the early 1880s, many places of business around Reeds Lake offered opportunities for obtaining intoxicants, and the crowds freely availed themselves. By the time the railway made its appearance in 1875, laws were already in effect to prevent liquor from being sold on Sundays. However, these were usually ignored by the saloon keepers outside the Grand Rapids city limits. In one instance in 1878, the township constabulary attempted to close down Sunday business in the hotel and saloons at the lake. The *GR Daily Democrat* reported, *"They did close but were mad althrough and declared that if they could not do business in their own way, others should not. They declared that the cars and steamboats should not run if they could not keep open. Names of parties visiting the lake, car drivers and others were taken with the threat that they would be prosecuted."* This was not actually carried out but illustrates the level of desperation that law enforcement met.

In essence, the company had created problems for itself. Making it possible for increased patronage to the lake also encouraged more saloons to open. Keeping law and order at Reeds Lake was a tall order, but the railway company was up to the challenge. The persons who patrolled the property were either from the sheriff's department and assigned to the railway, or deputies hired by the railway, or, as in the early 1900s, deputized railway conductors.

The most common infraction and reason for arrest was disorderly conduct, usually attributed to drinking. Under the influence of liquor, people became contentious and picked fights, teased and annoyed women, or freely used profanity. Occasionally, when groups of inebriated souls engaged in such provocations, the arresting officer was assaulted by one or more friends of the perpetrator.

Such an incident occurred in the spring of 1887 when Deputy Sheriff Gilden attempted an arrest and was struck by the offenders. Being worthy of his position, Gilden managed to bring the three men to jail to await trial. When interviewed by a *GR Eagle* reporter, railway superintendent Andres Bevier stated, *"I don't propose to have such a scene repeated at the lake, if I can prevent it. We want the best of order there, so that the best citizens will be glad to go to the lake, and if necessary, we shall take the strongest possible repressive measures as to the saloons and bars at the lake. Two or three such troubles as that of yesterday, will spoil the Lake as a resort for good citizens and respectable people. The public may rest assured that disgraceful rows and fights and obscenity and other offensive acts or words, will not be permitted at Reed Lake."*

HAD GOOD EFFECT

Crusade Against Rowdyism at the Reeds' Lake Resort.

Disorderly conduct at the lake was one thing, but such activity on the streetcars was also inhibited by these stalwart officers. Posted at the platform at the lake, the officer in charge observed the demeanor of entering riders and at times would decide to get aboard himself to further attend to someone. It was then possible that the deputy would put someone off the car who comported himself in an unseemly fashion. An officer at the platform late in the evening might also need to keep order while large crowds attempted to board for the ride home.

CELEBRATE TOO FREELY AT REEDS LAKE; ARRESTED

Seven persons were arrested at Reeds Lake Saturday night by deputies who considered that the men celebrated too freely by imbibing alcoholic liquors.

It should also be noted that it wasn't always men nor drunken men who were the perpetrators of mischief. Occasionally a hussy from the city might ride out to the lake and mingle with men who were intending to have a good time within the limits of proper decorum. Said gentleman might be unaware of the intentions of the female and himself become sirenized and fall captive to the meshes of said women. Such an association might result in unseemly behavior of the pair of them landing both parties in the overnight lock-up.

Disorderly conduct due to drink ceased to be a problem in 1918 as this statement from the *GR Press* indicates:

"A new and improved condition now prevails at Reeds lake as elsewhere throughout Michigan. On May 1, Miss Prohibition took a little journey around the lake, pulled down all the old beer signs, silenced the clink of the ice in the pitchers and substituted lemonade and various denatured drinks. Since that time the park policemen have found life to be 'one grand sweet song' and Manager Louis DeLamarter, who by strenuous effort and nerve wracking vigilance, used to succeed in keeping Ramona park 'safe for decency' as well as for democracy, now goes home early and 'lies down to peaceful dreams.' He has nothing more to worry about."

Theft was another crime for which the officer needed to be on the lookout. Pickpockets found the crowds at Ramona a fertile field from which to pluck the awaiting quarry. Using various methods of the trade, these light-fingered looters could do very well at the larger events in a relatively short period of time. This happened not only at the park, but on the streetcars leaving the park. On one occasion, the artists were a pair of ladies who "befriended" the victim while at the lake. They boarded the car together after midnight, and before long the pocketbook containing $175 was discovered missing from the gentleman's vest. His confrontation of the two ladies resulted in the purse being tossed out a window and the women rapidly departing the car. The next day, detective Peter Viergever of the Grand Rapids Railway Company's special force not only hunted for and recovered the stolen money, but apprehended the ladies at the lake where they had planned a repeat performance. These special officers had to be ready for all manner of duties.

Officers of the law not only had to be on the lookout for theft at Ramona, but the park itself attracted thieves for another reason. On many occasions, youngsters who were in the habit of lifting funds from any place they could be successful, would head out to the park with their new wealth to enjoy the fruits of their labors. In 1905, one such lad, who was an accomplished thief at age 9, rifled the attic of a house being built in town going through the workmen's clothes.

"With the money he went to Reed's lake, rode around on the steamer, the merry-go-round and the figure eight, and filled up with peanuts, soda water and candy. He also bought a pair of trousers, a shirt, a belt and a cap. His total expenditures amounted to $2.50; the rest is unaccounted for."

THIRTEEN-YEAR-OLD THIEF IS CAPTURED

Frank Brusky Steals $6 and Proceeds to Have Good Time.

Another lad stole $20 from the purse of his mother's visitor and invited his chums to accompany him to the park to help relieve him of the funds. Not knowing the source of his wealth, the youngsters went along. When questioned later and asked about the fate of the dollars, the perpetrator reported they spent it for popcorn, candy and other knickknacks. Yet another young man stole a purse on the way to church and altered his destination to Ramona instead of sacred realms. When apprehended later, he was found to have spent all but a small amount of the money. He said he had ridden eight times on the Derby Racer at Ramona and that he enjoyed the sport very much.

HE BORROWED A CAR.
The Wild Night Ride of a Man Who Wanted to Go to the Lake

A more bizarre theft occurred not aboard a streetcar, but the theft of a streetcar itself, in 1896. Wanting to go to the lake, the hero of the story was distraught upon discovering that the line had finished its last run for the evening. The *GR Press* provided this account:

"...was surprised when the car reached the Wealthy avenue barns to be told that it went no further. The conductor and motorman jumped off to take the car in and the unknown sprang up and gave the switch seven points. The car buzzed down the track and the astonished crew got out another car and gave chase. They did not catch the runaway, but they did find the car at the lake safe and sound. The thief evidently knew how to run a car, but that is all the comfort that the company can obtain from the affair. The man is still unknown."

17

Lest anyone believe that patrolling Ramona Park after dark was a job that could be handled by just anyone, the story of what happened to night watchman Thomas Stachowiak, in June, 1925, refutes the claim. The essence of the story was that five safe crackers managed to get the drop on him, tie him up at gunpoint in the theater office, and blow the safe to bits. The charge was sufficient to shoot a piece of the safe door across the room and cause it to penetrate a wall eight feet away. Some $2,000 was lifted from the premises, which constituted the days' receipts from the dance hall and theater. The watchman was not seriously hurt.

These patrolmen not only successfully stemmed criminal behavior over the years, but in 1913 performed another type of protective service.

Special police force detective Peter Viergever along with William VandenBerg, a clerk from Benjamin Hanchett's office, managed to squelch a fire that started on the roof of the theater. While watching the crowds who were viewing fireworks on the lake front, Viergever turned his eyes toward the roof, remembering the dry condition of the wooden shingles. His alertness caught sight of a stray spark that began to kindle a flame on top of the big pavilion. The detective rushed toward the building and placed a ladder for his ascent. VandenBerg saw this and followed in order to offer assistance. The clerk, wearing rubber soled shoes was able to scale the steep slant of the slippery roof, and between the two, they succeeded in tearing up the burning shingles and beating out the flames.

Crowd control was a big part of the Ramona law enforcement crew, particularly during special events like Kiddies' Days, shown on the left, Newsboys' Picnics and Holidays.

Photo of street railway men who were deputized by the sheriff for special park duty. Second from right is Darius Kimber, conductor and electrician for the company. This photo was probably taken in 1904.

Railway Company Pavilions

The natural beauty of Reeds Lake enticed people to travel out from the city. When boats were offered for rent, people could go fishing and enjoy the far reaches of the lake. Then resorts came into being drawing more people for a variety of reasons. Once the street railway was extended to Reeds Lake, crowds of people could travel at a lower cost, and when the faster and stronger dummy engine made its appearance, the number of visitors multiplied greatly. The Grand Rapids and Reeds Lake Street Railway Company purchased its own land in the Boynton & Judd's Lake Addition in the Fall of 1881. They did this in part to have some control over the activities of rowdies who brought disrepute to the lake. The railway company built a pavilion for the pleasure of families and other decent folk. Over the years, the main focus of the pavilion changed, but not the standards.

First Pavilion

The new building, which made its debut in early June, 1882, was described as being of the Elizabethan style. Its main salon was twenty-four foot square with twenty-foot wings on the north, east and south sides. A twelve-foot wide piazza extended around the sides and front. The building was located in a grove of hardwoods, oak, butternut, walnut, hickory and maple trees and it provided a good view of the lake. Several thousand dollars were expended by the company on this new resort which was considered to be an experiment in order to supply what was termed a *long-felt want,* that being a respectable resort at the lake. Before the building was open to the public, the *GR Eagle* published this statement:

> Beer and spirituous liquors and undesirable people will be excluded from the grounds, and an officer will be kept in charge of the grounds to prevent intrusions of unpleasant visitors.

Glimpse of the veranda of the first railway pavilion when it was still one level. Chairs and benches invited visitors to view the lake and grounds.

Seats and tables were situated in the grove to the north of the building, and swings and other "paraphernalia" enhanced the area for picnickers. At one time, Judd's Grove stood on this property with a boat dock and dance pavilion. Miller's Landing on the western shore of the lake was between the railway pavilion and the water, which was a good arrangement for both businesses. The end of the rail line was just a short distance from the building to the south.

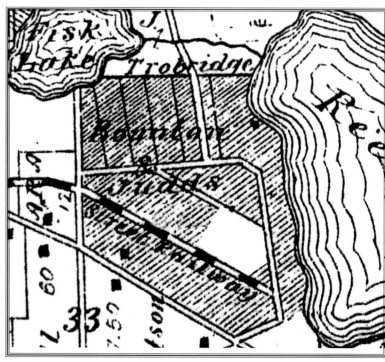

The 1876 map to the right shows Boynton & Judd's Lake Add. The white block is the railway property in 1882, bounded on the south by Michigan (Wealthy) on the east by Lake (Lakeside) and the north by Barnard (gone). The grey triangle to the southeast of the property was the location of the Lakeview House hotel, not owned by the railway company.

The facility was put to the test its first season when the Old Residents had their annual picnic which started out in the grove. A rainstorm drove them to the pavilion where the group of nearly 1,000 filled every nook and cranny.

The first manager of the pavilion was an experienced caterer rather than a businessman. People were invited to bring their own picnic lunches but they could also purchase or rent everything they needed for a picnic. They were offered cigars, various temperance drinks, tea and coffee and cold lunches. The restaurant aspect of this resort expanded over the years, offering full hot meals at all times of the day.

The railway company resort was so successful that it was expanded from year to year, both the building itself and the attractions offered to the public. In 1883, an addition was added to house the manager and staff. In 1887, the pavilion was enlarged to two stories in height and a dance floor was put on the north side.

This 1888 photo view of the south side of the expanded pavilion, shows the addition on the south for dining and manager's residence, the second level, and the veranda with its chairs and benches. Off to the left of the building, the switchback ride is just visible.

In 1885, the railway company initiated a series of sacred concerts on Sunday afternoons. This endeavor drew a lot of people to the resort and was such a success that in 1887 a bandstand was built on the shore of the lake directly in front of the pavilion. Two of the organizations that performed regularly at the lake were, Remington's Brigade Band and Wurzburg & Bronson's Band, later to become Wurzburg's Band.

Most of the additions and changes to the pavilion were to accommodate the growing patronage of people who came to eat. One example of the kind of food offered is seen in the description of a clam bake from August, 1887, to the right.

Below, an 1888 picture of the railway company's bandstand on the lakeshore. Immediately to the right of the structure is the landing for the boats rented out by the railway company. To the right of that, the dock with the crisscross, is Miller's Landing.

THE CLAM BAKE.

A Feast for Gods Enjoyed by 250 Men and Women at the Lake Last Night.

The bake at Ramona park last night given by Manager Swetland as a feature of the closing season was an immense success. Upward of 250 persons, ladies and gentlemen, amateur and experienced clam eaters, were there and partook of the feast, and it was a very enjoyable affair.

A hole is dug in the ground and a layer of hard-head rocks are arranged in the bottom. A fire is then built and when the stones are throughly warm the place is swept out, sea weeds are strewn on the hot stones and then the clams, with lobsters, chicken, green corn, sweet potatoes and fish, are dumped in and the pile is closely covered with weeds and sand. In a couple of hours the "bake" is baked and the clams and other things are served up steaming hot to the hungry and water mouthed crowd in waiting.

Business went so well at the railway resort on Reeds Lake that General Manager James R. Chapman of the Consolidated Street Railway Company decided it was time to build a bigger pavilion. In September, 1892, after eleven seasons, he engaged an architect to design a building to be ready for the next resort season. Mr. Chapman told the *GR Eagle* reporter,

"We have asked for drawings for a very handsome pavilion, modern in all its appliances. If built, it will be on the ground now occupied by the old pavilion, only of course it will be much larger and improved in every way. It will be somewhat higher than the present building and will be three or four steps from the ground. Running out from in front will be a bridge, over the present road, carrying people to a large covered platform or veranda facing the lake, of course, and giving a splendid view of it. In every way it will be a credit to the city, and will make a much better resort of Reed's Lake."

It was difficult to decide whether to commit to this because a lot of money would be involved, and the building would only be used for one fourth of the year. However, since the fare to the lake was still only 5 cents per person from the city limits, it was apparent that the additional money from patrons of the pavilion would pay in the long run.

In two months time the old pavilion was removed and excavation for the new building begun. The basement was to be for storage and contain the heating plant for the pavilion.

Second Pavilion

On the top is a panoramic photo of the second railway pavilion, which opened for the 1893 resort season.

The drawing in the middle is a better view of the walkway that went down to the veranda at the beach.

The photo on the bottom is a view from the water, also showing Miller's Landing.

Billed as a magnificent monument to the liberality and business sagacity of the street railway company and its management, the new pavilion was opened for business at the end of May, 1893. The dining room was dedicated at the banquet of the Hesperus Club on May 25th. This grand building had a tower reaching above the trees and a promenade that crossed Lake Avenue, leading to a veranda at the water's edge.

The manager of the pavilion continued to be well-known culinary artist, Warren Swetland, noted confectioner from the city. The fruits of his talent were enjoyed through three summers until he went on to head up the new Lakeside Club, selling his interest in the railway pavilion. The baton was passed to Charles S. Jandorf, also a caterer and businessman of renown.

The popularity of the food in the pavilion and the magnificence of the facilities drew large groups to hold banquets here. The building was often referred to by the name of the caterer instead of the railway company.

A SUMMER THEATER

To Be One of the Attractions at the Reed's Lake Pavilion.

REED'S LAKE . . .
Jandorf's Pavilion.

Daily band concerts, sponsored by the pavilion, continued afternoons and evenings. Besides the Wurzburg Band, the Evening Press Newsboys also performed there. Then in 1896, G. Stewart Johnson, general manager of the railway company, had a large stage built inside the pavilion. The music performances continued, but high class vaudeville attractions were also brought in to entertain the crowds that season.

The 1896 season was a roaring success for the railway company and for the people of Grand Rapids. City people now had two elegant places at the lake where they could go to get away from town, have a multi-course meal and be entertained, namely, the Reeds Lake Pavilion and the flourishing Lakeside Club.

This 1894 view of the western shore of Reeds Lake shows from left to right: Capt. John Poisson's house and dock with awning and lunch counter and the stern of the "Major Watson"; Miller's Landing on the shore; The Railway Pavilion with walkway and observation tower; Railway Company Dock with the "Hazel A"; The old O-Wash-Ta-Nong building, at that time occupied by the Grand Rapids Boat and Canoe Club.

A familiar story in the early days of resortdom at Reeds Lake was total destruction by fire. That glorious building, so new, so well received, so promising, went up in smoke in the wee hours of George Washington's birthday, 1897. Ironically, Mr. and Mrs. Jandorf were occupying the residence quarters for the winter to keep a watch on the building. Asleep in the northwest corner of the second story, and directly over the area of the basement housing the furnace, the Jandorfs were awakened by the smells and sounds of fire. They hastily dressed and exited the building to alert the railway representative quartered at the lake. By the time

the Grand Rapids steamer from the Madison Avenue firehouse responded, there was no hope for the building. In a way, fortune was smiling on the town because even though this occurred during a blizzard with high winds, the force came out of the northeast. This kept the flames from igniting the new building of the Lakeside Club and Ross' Pavilion which were directly across the road. It was also what saved the Jandorf's by giving them time to escape.

Third Pavilion

When interviewed at the scene of the fire, as dawn was breaking and the extent of the destruction could be viewed, Manager Johnson of the railway company declared that the pavilion would be rebuilt. *"We shall doubtless begin on the new structure just as soon as the ruins get cold. The building destroyed, I believe, cost about $17,000. The new one will be along the same lines of architecture, but will be a little more elaborate in the way of theater appointment and orchestra accommodations."*

On March 6th, just a dozen days after the fire, this headline appeared in the *GR Press*:

THAT NEW PAVILION

It Will Be a Thing of Beauty and Will Cost Like Sixty.

Architect William G. Robinson was already at work on the plans for the third railway pavilion which would be the grandest yet. During the last season of the second building, the response of the public to the vaudeville shows appearing there was sufficient to steer the direction of the new building. This would not be just a pavilion, but a full-blown theater with all the accommodations needed for "high-class" productions.

As soon as weather permitted, workers cleared away the rubble from the fire and set out to begin the masonry work for the new building. The company had decided to use their own men rather than contract out the work. Railway carpenters put in extra effort to have the building ready for a June opening and dedication. As the big day approached,

the newspapers advertised that the new pavilion needed a name, and offered $5 to the person who submitted the winner. The committee that made the selection had one member from the *GR Evening Press*, the *GR Herald* and the *Daily Democrat*.

The Ramona Name

Author Helen Hunt Jackson wrote the novel "Ramona" which was published in 1884. It was the story of an orphan girl living in Southern California whose heritage was both Scots and American Indian. According to the New York Herald-Tribune, "the novel was devoted to setting forth the wrongs done to the Mission Indians in California." The critics of the novel compared it in impact and stature to "Uncle Tom's Cabin."

The great success of the book was evidenced by the use of the name, "Ramona," around the country, including Reeds Lake. Grand Rapids newspapers tried to assign the name to the lake area in 1887, and it is found in articles about the resort business then. This movement was quashed by the Old Residents' Association in 1890 during their annual picnic at the lake by making this declaration:

"The name of these old pioneers
Abideth with thee yet –
For such men history reveres –
And lest we should forget
Along thy whispering shore shall run
The name that was an honored one.

. . .

And as each cycling year succeeds,
Still be thou ever known as Reed's."

When the name Ramona was chosen for the new pavilion in 1897, its association with the railway company resort was official.

The big day arrived and the pavilion was ready to meet her public. The announcement of the new name, *Ramona*, was made during the dedication, so it wasn't even printed on the program.

All the dignitaries in town were a part of the preparation and ceremony for the inauguration of the Ramona Theater on the afternoon of June 19, 1897. On the new stage were musicians from the Wurzburg's Military Band and the Evening Press Newsboys' Band. Also, assorted musical numbers were performed, such as from "Master Georgie Welsh." The address was given by the Hon. Thomas F. McGarry.

The musical part of the program was repeated again that evening, and it was estimated that nearly 10,000 people visited the grounds that day.

Right, the back of the dedication program, naming the people involved.

RECEPTION COMMITTEE.

MAYOR L. C. STOW,	J. C. SPROAT,	E. G. STUDLEY,
GEN. I. C. SMITH,	E. J. ADAMS,	THE HON. W. J. STUART,
W. R. SHELBY,	J. W. McCRATH,	JOHN A. VERKERKE,
GEN B. R. PIERCE,	W. B. WESTON,	GEN. B. M. CUTCHEON,
P. C. CAMPBELL,	C. DYKEMA,	U. DEVRIES,
POSTMASTER T. F. CARROL,	GEO. LAMBRIX,	HENRY SPRING,
GEORGE FORRESTER,	MR. HOPP,	C. E. PECK,
COL. W. T. McGURRIN,	W. W. HYDE,	COL. C. H. ROSE,
WARREN H. GIBSON,	CHARLES F. PIKE,	CAPT GEORGE E. JUDD,
SAMUEL M. LEMON,	CHARLES M HEALD,	FRED SAUNDERS,
WALTER PIERCE,	THE HON. PETER DORAN,	E. P. MILLS,
DAVID FORBES,	ROBERT LOGIE,	E. F. SWEET,
COL. C. G. SWENSBERG,	WM. H. ANDERSON,	C. PHILLIPS,
F. M. DAVIS,	W. STOUGHTON,	E. H. STEIN,
MILES G. TEACHOUT,	DR. J. B. GRISWOLD,	M. H. SORRICK,
CLAY HOLLISTER,	JOHN BENJAMIN,	CHAS. HILTON,
BURT THOMPSON,	LEO A. CARO,	COL. C. W. CALKINS,
WM. H. KINSEY,	F. W. WILCOX,	COL. J. C. HERKNER,
JOSEPH EMMER,	JOHN H. HOSKEN,	CAPT. E. W. JONES,
THE HON. E M. BARNARD,	JOHN A. COVODE,	COL. FRANK WILLIAMS,
DR. J. LINDSAY HOAG,	COL. J N. MURRAY,	GEN. L. W. HEATH,
PETER VAN HEKKEN,	JEREMIAH H. ANDERSON,	CAPT. C. E. BELKNAP,
JUDGE E. A. BURLINGAME,	GEN. L. G. RUTHERFORD,	COL. GEORGE G. BRIGGS,
CLARK E. SLOCUM,	CAPT. POISSON,	LEUT. ED. HOYT,
C. L. HARVEY,	MAJOR J W. LONG,	MAJOR J. K. COWES.
JOSIAH TIBBETTS,	THOMAS DORAN,	

USHERS.

J. M. CROSBY,	WILLIAM WURZBURG,	IRVING W. BARNHART,
HARRY MAISSE,	L. L. SKILLMAN,	TERRY HEATH,
JOHN L. BOER,	B. M. CORWIN,	MORRIS WHITE,
W. A. MARTINDALE,	W. HERBERT WOOD,	L. P. CODY,
W. B. JARVIS,	PERCIVAL B. GARVEY,	VAN WALLIN,
HENRY STONE,	HOWARD O. THORNTON,	WILLIAM WILLIAMSON,
HUGH BLAIR,	L. E. TORRY,	JOHN DUFFY,
CHARLES McQUEWAN,	CARROLL PERKINS,	H. D. JEWELL,
M. B. HAZELTINE,	E. E BLISS,	SCHYLER EDDY,
FRED McR. DEANE,	HEBER KNOTT,	WALTER C. WINCHESTER,
W. J. LANDMAN,	JOHN B. MARTIN,	EDGAR HUNTING.

View of pavilion as seen when looking north on Lake (Lakeside) Avenue

Unlike its predecessor, this railway pavilion did not offer up the best in cuisine to patrons since its emphasis was to offer up the best in vaudeville. Only refreshments were available at first. The picnic grove on the railway grounds to the north side continued to provide the beautiful natural setting for people who brought their own meals. For the annual outing of the Old Settlers at the end of June 1897, the picnic grounds and pavilion were reserved for the exercises. The attendance went way beyond expectations and due to inclement weather that day, they sought refuge in the new building. A grand old time was had by all.

Even though nothing special was done for the first season of its existence, the success of the vaudeville shows in the pavilion was great enough to warrant changes for the next year. The railway company hired managers for the theater and for refreshments. The stage was slightly remodeled, and the best seats in the house were converted to opera chairs placed on a floor that was raised. Those 600 seats became reserved seating for people who paid the 10 cents in advance. Other people could attend for free, but they either stood up or sat in the less comfortable seats. Since the east and south sides of the building were open to the elements, performances could be enjoyed by anyone standing in the vicinity.

The inside of the newly opened Ramona Theater before the opera seats were added and before the ice cream parlor was outfitted.

Note the cigar stand, far left, and the refreshment area to the left of the stage.

PAVILION AT REED'S LAKE BEING IMPROVED.

While this section deals only with the buildings and not the activities on the stage, it is important to note that the response to the shows actually caused changes to be made in the building. The manager who brought fame to this enterprise beyond the local area, was Mr. Orin Stair, hired in 1899. Mr. Stair's prior accomplishments included ownership of several newspapers, such as The Detroit Free Press, and management of various establishments in the entertainment world. At the time he was hired to manage Ramona, he had experienced great success with both the Powers and Grand opera houses in Grand Rapids. His many contacts around the country allowed him to pull in the very best vaudeville performers for Ramona.

The public response to the shows at the Ramona pavilion exceeded both the expectations of the railway company officers and the capacity of the building. So, architect Robinson was brought in again to work on revisions to the building. Assisting him was a theatrical architect and acoustics specialist from Detroit. Changes had to be made to the theater room of the pavilion to comfortably accommodate many more patrons and improve the auditory features. When the theater opened for the 1900 season, it had been transformed.

26

The stage was lowered and increased to a 42 foot opening making it the largest in the city for that time. The floor in front of the stage was redesigned with more slope. Sixteen boxes were installed at the sides of the main floor, each holding six people. More opera chairs were added to accommodate 1,200 people. The ceiling was enclosed above the stage and extended out over the audience area, providing a sounding board to improve the acoustics. Colonnades and arches were added to the sides of the auditorium.

Artist's conceptual drawing.

Interior view of the remodeled theater shows the proscenium arch and ceiling, colonnades on the sides, and raised seating.

Henry C. Rehn, a renowned theatrical scene painter, was brought in from Philadelphia to paint stage settings for the modernized theater. He rigged up a temporary studio in the Wealthy Avenue Streetcar Barn, the only space where sufficient room and light could be found. He was quoted in the *GR Press* as saying, *"When a theatrical scene painter, or a scenic artist, as he would prefer to be called, sets out under orders from a national manager to paint a series of scenes for a play, there is not half the demand for artistic abilities as for a thorough understanding of the opinion of the man who pays the freight."*

View of front, or east side of the Ramona Pavilion, which faced the lake. Steps went up the bank from Lake (Lakeside) Ave.

View of south side of Ramona Pavilion where bicycle parking was allowed. Note the firehose building, people on the porch.

View of Michigan (Wealthy) Ave, the south side of Ramona Pavilion, street car loop, and figure-eight roller coaster, far left.

View of the Ice Cream Parlor located in the theater building. In 1910, a soda fountain was added which cost $ 2,000. Note glimpse of theater stage, far right.

Cigar Stand, also located in the theater pavilion, decorated for a Japanese Fete.

Photo taken along Lake (Lakeside) Ave., between 1903 and 1909.
The merry-go-round building is on the left
with refreshment stand nearby.
The Lakeside Club is behind the trees on the extreme right.

View of south side of theater taken at the same time.
On the left, the east end of the Figure-Eight waiting area with a
glimpse of the porch of the Palace of Mirth. The Lakeside Club is seen
through the trees and on the extreme right is the refreshment stand.

NEW RAMONA WILL SURPRISE WITH STRIKING FEATURES

In 1906, the management of the theater was turned over to Louis J. DeLamarter. He was very successful in continuing to pull in top-notch entertainment from around the country. As a result, in 1910 the theater had to be remodeled again, but this time with major renovations. The reason for this effort was not only to accommodate more people, but to broaden the scope of the type of entertainment which could perform there. With two sides of the auditorium open to the outdoors, not only had the weather intruded, but also noise. By this time, the theater was surrounded by a full-blown amusement park and the hullabaloo associated with it. So, one major change was to completely enclose the theater portion of the pavilion.

Another feature of the "New Ramona" theater was a balcony installed in the rear of the auditorium. The seating in the balcony included eighteen more boxes around the front with tiers of regular seating behind. This increased the total capacity to 1,500. There were two stairways leading up to the balcony from the main floor.

On the night of the opening of the newly remodeled theater, inclement weather provided the opportunity for patrons to appreciate the fact that it was now fully enclosed. Those that came by rail were able to go from the theater to the railway platform in comfort since a covered walkway was another of the improvements.

NEW COVERED STREET CAR STATION AT RAMONA.

INTERIOR VIEW OF REMODELED RAMONA THEATER.

At right, from "GR Herald" June 1910

Banishes Ad Curtains

Manager DeLamarter has inaugurated a reform at Ramona that might be followed by every Grand Rapids theater manager to advantage. It consists in the banishment of all so-called advertising drops and curtains. The effect is decidedly pleasing. The elimination of the signs removes an affront to the eyes of playgoers and adds to the "class" of the theater.

In vaudeville it is a regular thing to drop before the eyes of the audience at times a street' or olio drop that is plastered over with ugly, inartistic signs. Manager DeLamarter came to the conclusion that these advertising plastered curtains were an imposition upon his audiences and detracted to a certain degree from their enjoyment of the performance. Therefore he resolved to eliminate them, even buying up existing contracts in order to carry through the reform.

From the balcony, patrons could access the new roof garden which was perched above the curvaceous front porch of the theater. The *GR Herald*, on the 15th of May, 1910, gave a good description of this feature below:

Not all the changes, however, have been made inside. Outside, the crescent shaped roof which extends around the dome and covers the promenade has been transformed into a roof garden, or "sundeck." The heavy tar and gravel roofing has been covered over with neat hardwood gratings, a handsome rail has been built along the outer edge, and above has been erected a tubular iron framework over which, in rainy weather, can be stretched a storm proof canvas covering. At intervals along the rail there have been built artistic flower and plant boxes, while close up to the dome are the small tables at which refreshments will be served. This roof, or "sundeck," is worthy of high commendation and will be a great boon. Entrance to it is had from the balcony of the theater and it is fitted with two fire escapes, one at either end. It commands a fine view of the lake and is large and roomy, and will no doubt become one of the most popular features of Ramona.

View of the roof garden above the curved porch on the east side of the theater.

31

Enjoying Leisure Time

The covered walkway from the streetcar loop provided shade and a place to view the lake.

The pavilion's gently sloping lawn was available for people to lounge about and enjoy the scenery. Note the angle-parked vehicles in the street.

The Searchlight

In these two pictures – the upper from a postcard taken before 1910, the lower after the roof garden addition in 1910 – the eye settles upon the device mounted on the roof. This was a searchlight, installed atop the great theater to illuminate the darkness. It served to draw attention to the park, but also to enhance the viewing of such things as nocturnal balloon ascensions. The beams would follow the balloon on the way up, and the parachute with its precious cargo on the way down.

In order for the light to follow a moving object, it had to be directed by a human. For the 1909 season, this was done by young Gerald Kerwin, *"the operator who stands up there high above the heads of the moving throngs several nights of the week, humped up with the cold, shivering in the chilly night atmosphere."* At that time, the light was not just used for special events, but to entertain observers by revealing the secrets of the dark. *"It is great sport to watch him flash the long, white ray over the shadowy corners of the park, the unfrequented bypaths, and throw out in strong relief some spooning couple, who supposed they were far removed from interruption. It's funny to watch the surprised pairs scramble for cover."* It was also strong enough to light up boats on the lake.

FOLLOW THE BEACON SEARCHLIGHT TO
RAMONA
—ACRES OF FUN—

In 1928, a much stronger searchlight was installed. Originally "borrowed" for testing purposes from the Grand Rapids airport, this light was then purchased for use at Ramona. It became the heart of the slogan, **"Follow the Beacon to Ramona."** Referred to as a revolving beacon, the beam could traverse its path 40 times a minute, and was visible for 20 miles.

The Roof

Pictures on colored postcards show that the roof of the Ramona Theater was sometimes green, sometimes red. Initially the roof was covered with wooden shingles. But in 1916, Reynolds asphalt and granite surfaced shingles were installed. It took 500 squares of "red rock" shingles and three-fourths of a ton of nails. A motor truck took two days to haul the shingles to the lake. It was very fortunate that this was done because in 1918, the huge O-wash-ta-nong Club, just across the street from the theater, went up in a roaring conflagration. At least the roofing company believed that its shingles protected the roof of the theater from **"the rain of fire-brands,"** as attested to in the advertisement published the very next day after the fire.

RAMONA STILL STANDS!

It is roofed with Reynolds' Shingles and they successfully resisted the rain of fire-brands

"Reynolds' Shingles Mean Protection From Fire"

In the 1840s, roofing material was created by saturating felt with coal tar. A gritty substance, such as sand or gravel, was applied to the surface for protection. Mr. Herbert Morton Reynolds began his roofing business in Grand Rapids in the late 1860s. In 1873, he was listed in the city directory as a "Felt, Gravel and Composition Roofer." In 1903, he started hand cutting the rolls into individual shingles, making installation easier. Mr. Reynolds has been credited with producing the first asphalt shingles.

Postcard view of the south side of the theater showing the improvements made in 1910, including details of the porch.

A view of the Ramona Theater pavilion as it looked around 1920 from the company dock.

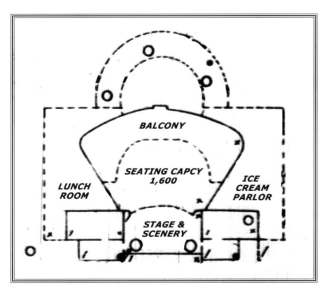

Theater shown in the 1930-1950 Sanborn Fire Insurance Map. The small circles represent water hydrants.

Aerial view of theater building in the early 1930s.

Early view of crowd on the front porch. Note the many small trees. Also, note the fire extinguishers.

Over the next 39 years, the Ramona Theater rose to great heights in popularity, and then fell into the depths of neglect. It was on a theatrical roller coaster, but the good days were the most remembered and written about. Over those years, the stage offerings varied in type, and from local to international stars. The details of that part of its history are told elsewhere.

According to Mr. Louis J. DeLamarter when interviewed in 1949, Ramona Park would undergo an *"orderly abandonment"* in the next few years, and the theater would be the first to go. He said the company felt the community would welcome a residential development in place of the amusement park. He told that operators of the park, under lease, had suffered losses for several years, and in recent years, revenues in general had been declining. East Grand Rapids mayor, John A. Collins, stated that, *"With full appreciation of the benefits of recreational facilities afforded by Ramona park to the people of west Michigan for more than one-half a century, we feel that with the expansion of new homes in East Grand Rapids, the status of the park has now materially changed."*

Unlike most of the beautiful pavilions that graced the shores of Reeds Lake, the Ramona Theater did not burn down.

Ramona Theater near the end.

The Final Curtain

The west side, or back,
of the theater

Through these portals passed
multitudes seeking great
entertainment

The north side of the grand front porch,
scene of many gatherings of all ages.

The roof structure for the circular
front porch, towering above the
remains of the balcony.

South side of the theater.
Note the doorway to the
ice cream parlor.

The hallway of the dressing rooms.
Behind these doors, performers
readied themselves for an
appearance on the stage of the
great Ramona Theater: local
girls from dance studios, the
glamorous Marcus Girls, famous
comedians, singers, musicians,
animal trainers. What stories
those walls could tell!

Interesting and curious reminders
of those vaudeville days.

Last glimpse of the stage before the walls came tumbling down.

Ghostly view of the carousel building through the opened wall of the theater.

Right, exit stage...
Last, but not least.

Below, dying
a dusty death.

Nothing left but photos, souvenirs and memories.

Entertainment

People could attend concerts and theaters in downtown Grand Rapids from the very earliest days. But a trip to Reeds Lake offered much more in the way of entertainment.

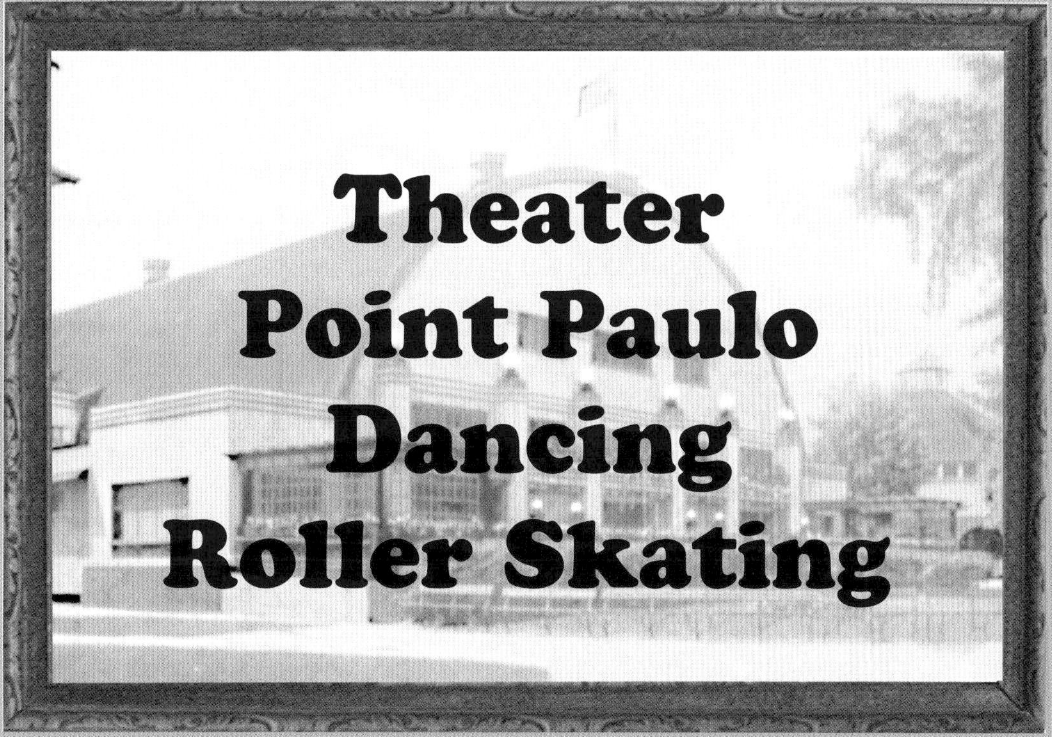

**Theater
Point Paulo
Dancing
Roller Skating**

That's Entertainment

People from the city were attracted to Reeds Lake. Making that trip eastward rewarded travelers with cool breezes, serenity and the chance to enjoy nature. At first, this was entertainment enough for pleasure-seekers. When resorts entered the lake scene, so did other forms of entertainment. Competition for business resulted in special events like balloon ascensions and various performing artists to attract people away from the other resorts.

One of the first venues that offered stage performances at the lake was the unlikely setting of a baseball stadium. After a flurry of construction feats, the stadium was transformed into an opera house. There was already a grandstand, so all it needed was a stage area around the outfield with canopy. The performances were put on by the Casino Opera Company, which traveled around from city to city.

The first operetta that was presented was actually not in the new "opera house," but on board the side-wheeler *Belknap*. This was appropriate because the production was "H.M.S. Pinafore," most adaptable to the setting of an actual ship. After that, for two months, the company performed various operettas, including "La Mascotte," "Giroffe" and "Merry War."

Another early location at the lake where stage

performances were held was the first O-Wash-Ta-Nong Club building. Although the club was formed to promote rowing and boating, it also furnished other entertainments for the wealthy class. The building, opened in 1886, had a second story which provided for evening amusements. Here was located a large hall, called a "theatorium" with a stage and seating capacity of 600, having arrangements for musical or dramatic programs. It also included three reception areas and dressing rooms.

Entertainment provided by the O-Wash-Ta-Nong Club and its successor, The Lakeside Club, was local talent and mostly musical. Professors Wellenstein and Lawson were favorites along with the Schubert Club and several of the Wurzburg bands.

Mr. Charles Godfroy, who became proprietor of the Lake View House in 1885, also brought entertainment to the lake. He built a bandstand for concerts and unusual entertainments such as a one-man-band. With the success of his ventures, Mr. Godfroy expanded his theatrical offerings to include vaudeville shows, performed in the extension to the hotel which he added in 1892.

One of the acts that appeared at Godfroy's Theater was "Little Lulu." **Lulu Beeson**, before she was 10, won the title, "champion buck and wing dancer of the world." Her parents were also vaudeville performers. Later, she married actor-comedian George O'Hanlon (Sam Rice). Their son George went on to become the neighbor of William Bendix' in "The Life of Riley" and the voice of George Jetson. Another son, James, wrote screen plays for movies like "Calamity Jane" and wrote for TV shows such as "Maverick" and "77 sunset Strip."

Godfroy continued to present vaudeville shows at the lake, even after the magnificent Ramona Theater was built. This didn't seem to affect the attendance at the grand Ramona, however. In 1905, Godfroy's theater was renovated and increased in size. A nine-piece orchestra was engaged and it was ready for a season with two performances a day. However, it seemed that most of the activity at Godfroy's had migrated to the realm of athletics and not the typical vaudeville theater it set out to be.

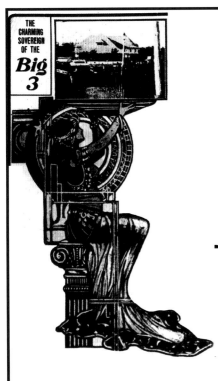

THE·RENDESVOUS·OF·REFINED·AMUSEMENT·SEEKERS

With a span of 53 years running, the stories of this institution could fill a book. In fact, they did. The book is called, *"Ramona Theatre : a descriptive account of a successful resort/amusement park theater at Reeds Lake, East Grand Rapids, Michigan, 1897-1949"* by Deborah Lynn Kerr. Thus, the following account of Ramona Theater productions will be highlights of the myriad offerings from this glorious venue.

The Ramona Theater, built and established in 1897, had a slow start. Even so, audiences were most responsive. The first show: Wurzburg's Band, Burnette, baritone soloist; La-Petit Inez, the smallest dancer in the world. One of the last shows of that season was The young ladies of the Grand Rapids Turn-Verein society giving exhibitions of Club Swinging and Spanish Dances in appropriate costumes, and then the season was finished out with concerts.

There was no manager dedicated to bringing in talent for the theater that first season, but for 1898, the railroad company hired Mr. William Darnbrough. It was his intent to offer regular shows, light opera, minstrel and vaudeville. Indicative of this policy was the schedule of programs like The McKay Opera Company, Barlow Brothers' Minstrels, Akimato Japanese Troupe, and novelties like, The Harmans' Revolving Ladder act, Carter, the magician, who was *"entertaining every minute. His versatility leads from spirit rappings to optical illusions, and local talent."*

Not exactly in the realm of novelty, but rather innovation, preaching by a local minister was the bill of fare for a couple of weeks. Rev. Leslie W. Sprague of All Souls' Church was engaged to deliver discourses on "The Life Worth Living?" and "Rational Amusement." These occurred before the regular entertainment, and although surprisingly well received, not repeated in subsequent weeks.

Another pioneering event for a summer theater to offer was a Cornish wresting match. Whether manager Darnbrough had anything to do with this is not known but arrangements were made by the railway company for the use of the pavilion. It was the first time Grand Rapids people witnessed this type of sport, and a large audience was gathered for it. It was characterized by the wrestlers wearing tough jackets enabling them to gain better grip on their opponent.

THE SIGN OF GOOD SHOWS

Also, during the second season of the Ramona Theater, Manager G. Stewart Johnson of the railway company got involved in the programming as a result of being told by an employee that the music being offered didn't cause the audience to get excited. The three weeks remaining in that season were devoted to musical experiment where the Wurzburg Band played a wide variety of ditties. Music which was popular in "The East" won out over Wagner.

The opening of Ramona Theater for the 1899 season marked the beginning of its steady rise to fame, due to the efforts of Orin Stair, contracted by the railway company to *"take care of the amusement features."* Mr. Stair was already manager of the Grand and Powers opera houses in town. Eventually he became the first manager of the Majestic Theater. For Ramona, the mandate was given to offer a mixture of theatrical, vaudeville, circus, minstrel, acrobatic and operatic features, and to promote afternoon attendance with programs suitable for children and families. Another important request was to have amusements outside as well as in the theater. It was possibly due to this plan that the amusement park was eventually developed.

41

The opening program under Mr. Stair fit into most of the directives for entertainment at the Ramona Pavilion. The Great Hanner Combination came to town and for a week entertained record crowds both inside the pavilion and outside. The program featured Hanner, the Aeronaut; Mlle. LeVoy's *"Great Slide for Life"* down an inclined cable, from the top of the water tank to the ground, suspended by her hair; a 60 foot high dive into a canvas net by man and dog; aerial cyclists and gymnasts on high wire, and the usual, juggler, trapeze artist, marksman, knife thrower, etc.

This and subsequent programs soon filled the big pavilion beyond capacity even though additional chairs were added. Overflow crowds could still hear the performances through the two open sides. Obtaining tickets for seats inside caused such congestion at the theater that another office was opened downtown for advanced sales.

Louis J. DeLamarter

Grand Rapids born Orin Stair and his brother, E. D., expanded their theater involvement beyond this city to such an extent that Orin relinquished his relationship with Ramona in favor of the up-and-coming Louis J. DeLamarter. Long associated with the theater and the Stair brothers, Louis was brought into the Ramona realm first as a ticket taker, then assistant manager, then acting manager at the end of 1905. His first year of full involvement was in 1906.

By this time, not only was the manager of the theater in charge of booking its entertainment, but the full-blown amusement park was under his auspices as well. Mr. DeLamarter began with the conviction that each year would be better than the previous. Rather than booking acts from independent agencies, he enlisted with the Western Vaudeville Manager's Association, the western branch of a large nation-wide vaudeville syndicate. The executive head of the circuit, J. J. Murdock, stated, *"[Ramona] is the only park theater that is receiving the direct attention of the heads of the association. The smaller theaters are of course handled by us, but they take in most cases cheaper acts which are booked by the agents. I am delighted with my visit here and surprised at the size and attractiveness of Ramona resort and the beauty of Reeds lake."*

In 1909, the great Orpheum circuit out of New York took over the bookings for the Ramona Theater. Mr. DeLamarter stated, *"By having our booking done there we have a chance of picking up all the leading features that are coming this way, and also to secure a large number of fresh acts that have been appearing over the so-called united time in the east."*

For the next ten years, the Ramona Theater presented the best acts in vaudeville. As a change to the norm, the year 1921 offered a whole season of light opera with the Ralph Dunbar Company.

While Louis DeLamarter was escalating Ramona Park and its theater into fame and fortune, he was also working his way upward in the railway company business beyond Ramona, and in 1922, enlisted help with the theater. Producer and stage director Jerry Cargill became theater manager and Danny Boon managed the park, both answering to DeLamarter. In 1923, W.S. Butterfield was hired to manage the theater and his booking manager was C.S. Humphries. The traditional vaudeville was replaced by musical comedy that year. It was when A.B. Marcus entered the Ramona scene. The plan was, *"If the Ramona patrons take kindly to musical comedy, other organizations will be booked. If the patrons prefer vaudeville, he will have Keith acts booked from the Chicago office all ready to send in."*

Audiences must have dwindled during these two years, for in 1925, once again Louis DeLamarter took the helm with the assistance of Danny Boon. Vaudeville type entertainment was reinstated to the Ramona Theater, but in future seasons, the A. B. Marcus shows were interspersed. During the next few years, acts were booked through Keith, Keith-Albee and R-K-O-Keith offices. Other managers of the theater were John McElwee, Arthur S. White, F. A. Wurzburg, American Attractions Inc. and Fred Barr. One year, 1932, the theater turned exclusively to second-run motion pictures managed by Goodrich and Murray, who also ran the Savoy Theater in downtown Grand Rapids.

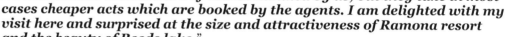

1925 GR Herald cartoon

The term vaudeville might call up visions of straw hats and canes and soft shoe dancing to folks born after the first few decades of the 20th century. Actually it included everything from the ridiculous to the sublime. That could very well be a description of the acts presented on the vaudeville stage. Ridiculous as in outlandish, peculiar, unique or eccentric. Some of the acts had descriptions that just called out to the theatergoer to attend out of curiosity. Sublime as in sophisticated, refined, elegant or cultured. The Ramona Theater always promised high-classed entertainment even if some of the acts sounded ridiculous.

Performances seen on the vaudeville stage were not unlike those seen at a circus. In fact, some people would bounce between the circus and stage depending on scheduling. Some circus acts needed more height and floor space than could be found within a theater, and some vaudeville acts required acoustics not found a tent or out in the open air. Song and dance artists, musicians, acrobats, cyclists, and people with bizarre talents found their way to the stage. But those who were headlined had to be outstanding. An example of this was **Signor Travato**, the "Filipino Virtuoso" who was acclaimed to be an exceptional violinist, would play two violins at once, or he played serious numbers on a violin held between his knees. When asked why he did this, he stated, *"One must do a stunt in vaudeville."*

UNTHAN
The Armless Wonder.

"**Plays the Violin With His Toes**" was the billing that drew people in to see **Carl Unthan** perform. He had to play with his toes because he had no arms. What may appear to some as a side show attraction was to others an inspiration. When Carl was born in Prussia in 1848, the nurse didn't believe he should be allowed to live. His father took matters in hand and nurtured his son to use his toes in place of fingers. This "Armless Artist" could not only play the violin but the trumpet, shoot a rifle,

shuffle cards, smoke, and do almost anything normally done with fingers. Swimming was a specialty of his, and while at Ramona, he swam around the lake with James Rose, thanking him later in the postcard pictured below. During the first World War, Carl joined the German Army and traveled to various hospitals to inspire men who had lost limbs in the war.

Another out-of-the ordinary musician was **Mrs. Alice Shaw**, billed as 'The Coloratura Whistler," who performed at Ramona in 1900. Ten years prior to that engagement, she gave an exhibition of her talent before the Czar in St. Petersburg. This Detroit native, finding herself in circumstances where she needed to do something to support herself and her twin daughters, perfected the talent she exhibited as a child. She claimed that as a whistler, she was born, not made. As an adult, she studied singing and voice production to enhance her particular gift. She cultivated this talent in her daughters who performed with her. Early in her vaudeville career, audiences initially thought her performance was comedy, but were soon convinced otherwise. A great composer once said of the lady whistler that she had every known reed instrument in her mouth.

Moon and Morris were known as "simultaneous dancers" or "eccentric dancers" who did the "two-in-one dance" or "double dancing." They worked so hard to be unique, even though other dance acts tried to do the same thing, they actually succeeded in having their moves patented and copyrighted. They were quoted as saying, ***"We received many bruises and kicks while working these dances out, but we feel that the reward we nightly receive in the form of applause from the audience is ample reward for our efforts."***

While ballet was performed in the best of theaters, versions were developed for the vaudeville stage. In 1907, Ramona featured the **Grigolat Aerial Ballet**. Brought to America by the Ringling Brothers, this so-called ballet was done in the air, literally, through the use of wires. The ballerinas wore a corsets of wood and were attached to invisible wires. They performed their poses in mid-air, sometimes clad with wings appearing as birds. At Ramona, fifty white doves were released at the back of the auditorium and then took their places on the heads and arms of the flying young women. Besides the ladies on stage, it took nine people to handle the mechanics. It cost the Railroad company $750 to book the act for one week, but it proved well worth the investment.

A PRIESTESS OF FIRE   **AMETA**   **THE MIRROR DANCER**

In Wonderful Spectacular Electric Dances.

Dancing was another popular type of vaudeville act, another area where the innovations provided variety. Miss **Lydia Lange** from Grand Rapids, who called herself "**Ameta**," was known as a mirror dancer and fire dancer. She was aided by electric effects, special costumes and a series of mirrors. She was the only person to appear in her act and yet she required the accompaniment of a carload of properties and four electricians. While some dancers who did the fire dance actually set fire to their costumes, Ameta's fire dance was done with lighting and fabrics for she would appear as a sylph whirling about in a cloud of drapery that looked like flames. In a video on Youtube, she appears with two large squares of white fabric attached to poles held in her hands. Moving these flag-like implements while performing an exotic style dance made her look almost birdlike. She finished off the dance within a spiral of fabric covering her body. Newspapers of the day described her dancing through prismatic sets, fiery sets (fabric) and water fountain sets (with real water). She was most famous for a 'mirror dance' amidst eight enormous plate-glass mirrors.

The "Fantastic Phantoms" appear first as a set of dancing skeletons, the effect being decidedly weird. Then eight pairs of bodyless legs go through terpsichorean movements. Finally the phantoms materialize as seven young women and two young men, who execute pretty dances and vary the program with acrobatics that are startling yet graceful.

PHANTASTIC PHANTOMS

Article from the May 16, 1908, a *GR Press* description of the act produced by Ned Wayburn, who became the choreographer for The Ziegfield Follies

Bicycles were an artistic "vehicle" often employed by vaudevillians. From aerial acts to acrobatics to weird bicycles, the range was boundless. One of the most noted such acts at Ramona was the **Charlie Ahearn Bicycle Troupe**. He used up to 35 different sorts of vehicles, all operated like bicycles. This included a pedal-propelled bathtub, bike-giraffe and airship. Mr. Ahearn went from a professional bicycle rider to performing, adding comic variations to the act as he stretched his imagination. But a big "break" came about as a result of a train wreck when his precious cycles were mangled. He repaired the grotesque wheels only to the point of operating, and a new comedy routine was born.

Juggling acts were plentiful, so the more outlandish the act, the more attractive to audiences. **Paul Spadoni**, who performed at Ramona in 1907, was said to have perfected a number of feats never attempted by others. He was known for juggling cannonballs, but he also performed a stunt with the barrel of a cannon. It was propelled into the air by a see-saw and he would catch it behind his neck with his shoulders and back. He was more than a juggler, he was a strong-man and balancer. For example, he balanced a chair on his chin while his assistant was sitting in it! Other balancing acts were also very popular. **The Bremens** had an act in which they used unsupported ladders like children's stilts, skipping rope and climbing up and down. The **Ishikawa Brothers** were called hand equilibrists, the climax being when the brother, who started a one-hand stand on top of a staircase, did a series of hops to descend the stairs, lowered his legs to horizontal and returned to the vertical without touching the floor.

GLOBE OF DEATH
"Will Be the Talk of the Town."

Add a motor to the bicycle and the thrills are multiplied. One of the biggest names in motorcycle stunts was Charles Clarke Bunting, known as, "**Dr. C.B. Clarke**." He began to do death defying stunts in 1903, after he became a practicing physician. When a circus came to town that featured the "loop-the-loop," he signed up as an understudy for "Diavolo." While at Ramona in 1906, he performed the "Globe of Death" stunt in a great transparent sphere made of a network of steel wires, about half the width of the stage. Inside the sphere, the rider guided the vehicle – at great speed – in all conceivable directions. In his own words, *"In the globe, I have to depend upon a motor cycle and everyone knows how cranky a gasoline engine is."*

View of a Globe of Death from around 1930, not at Ramona, but the same type and size as was there in 1906.

One of the most bizarre acts of the balancing type was performed by "**The Patty Brothers**" or the "Upside-Down Head Walkers." One of them would balance upside down on the head of the brother and in that position they would juggle, play musical instruments, or eat lunch. This was peanuts compared to the rest of the act. Each of the brothers could propel himself across the stage, upside-down on his head, by merely bouncing. Not only that, this feat was performed on a flight of steps. When the brothers were performing at Ramona in 1906, the Ringling Brothers Circus was in town. A member of the circus visited Ramona and immediately signed on the brothers. It was said in later years that one of the Pattys would have seizures and savagely attack his brother for no "apparent" reason.

Dog & Pony Shows

While the phrase has become a slogan for an ostentatious display designed to garner attention, back in the glory days of vaudeville, many stage acts were dogs and ponies. Those two groups of animals performed together successfully in production numbers that amazed and amused audiences. Varieties of trained animal acts constituted a significant segment of vaudeville theater offerings around the time of Ramona's beginning. The more difficult the "tricks" or the more bizarre the animals, the greater the attraction. Some of the more interesting or more famous animal acts that came to Ramona are mentioned here.

Dogs

Trained dog acts abounded but the presentations differed greatly. There were those who did the prescribed stunts, leaping, tumbling, hind-leg walking, acrobatics, etc. But perhaps one of the most interesting dog troupes to visit Ramona was "**Merian's Canine Actors**." It consisted of some 30 intelligent dogs of various types and sizes. The words "intelligent" and "educated" were used early on to indicate that animals were highly trained. These dogs actually put on a drama called, "**The Elopement of Salome**." They played all the parts in the play's seven scenes without humans appearing on stage at any time. This behind the scenes description was presented in the *GR Press*. It could have been written about a play with humans.

"Interesting as is the view of the dog-acted drama from the side of the audience it is just as interesting, but in a different way, as seen from the wings of the stage. All about is the paraphernalia used in the play, the automobile, the costumes of the dogs, their trappings and the various properties. The dogs themselves, with shoes on and garbed in the costumes they wear in their first appearance, await their cues in their own special places in half a dozen open crates placed at convenient points near the entrances. Some of the stars are permitted to stay outside the crates, but each has its own place and they never stray.

"Five men assist Prof. Merian in handling the dogs. These travel with the troupe and are in addition to the regular stage hands who handle the scenery. They dress the dogs, fit them out with their properties and send them on the stage at the proper moment. After the dogs are on the stage they know just what to do themselves, and they do it."

View of a typical educated dog act on a vaudeville stage.

Ponies and Horses

Several different pony acts appeared on the stage over the years. In 1902, **Leon Morris' Educated and Comedy Ponies** visited with an act that included two "wrestling" ponies. These equines furnished a comedy sketch in which they wrestled with a human opponent.

Howard's Musical Ponies and Comedy Dogs

Howard's Ponies and Dogs performed several times between 1899 and 1917. The act changed performers, but always included comedy in the title. In 1899, the description in the *GR Press* said, *"The work of these equine performers is really wonderful and the intelligence displayed is equally surprising. Singly, in pairs, and quartets, the ponies march, trot, gallop and dance through a large and varied list of accomplishments, including skipping the rope, wrestling and a realistic game of leap frog between a pony and a big St. Bernard dog."* In 1917, Prof. Howard invited children to a reception on the stage after the show, and then took them out for pony rides.

According to **Mlle. Olympia Desvall**, whose act contained both dogs and ponies, *"Horses are more easily trained than dogs, and they remember longer. They must have temperament, too, in order to make good performers. A dog is flighty. He is here one minute and away the next. A horse is more steady and sure."*

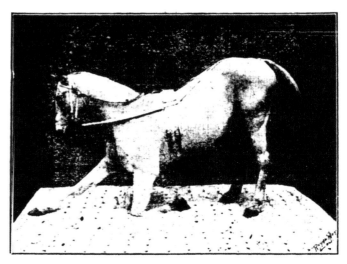

Rose Royal's posing horse, Chesterfield

A unique horse act was called, "**Rose Royal and Her Statue Horse Chesterfield**." The beautiful snow-white horse was trained to hold poses which, it was stated in Variety Magazine, *"would tax the ability of most any human being."*

The Great Fillis Family presented a type of circus act with four horses prancing about on the stage while their riders performed stunts. Those horses also were dancers, garnering favor with audiences when they swayed to rag-time music.

Lions

When the Ramona Theater was just emerging as a viable vaudeville venue in 1898, **Madame Pianka** thrilled audiences with her trained lions. The description of the performance in the *GR Press* creates interesting images in the imagination.

"The four lions sat at table in their cage, off in one corner of the big stage at the Ramona Theater. They drank milk from bowls, ate ice cream from a spoon and raw meat from a fork, while the great male lion, carried his napkin under his chin with all the dignity of a Chesterfield. They rang dinner bells with their teeth, jumped over sticks held high in the air, played dead, arranged themselves at the word of command in groups on the floor, while the Madame reclined on top of them, formed tableau effects, and finally the great male opened his mouth and Madame inserted her head." After the performance, they were each fed ten pounds of raw meat!

In 1915 **Havemann's Lions** came to Ramona to perform on the stage, and created quite a stir upon their arrival. As their animal cages were being wheeled in, the lions gave out with tremendous roars when they spotted the little caged bears on the midway. Tigers and leopards were also a part of this troupe, all of which were born in captivity.

PIANKA
"THE LADY OF LIONS"

The appeal of the animals was so great that Havemann was secured for an extended period. The iron cages used on the stage during the performance were set outside on the picnic grounds to the west of the resort, and visitors could peer at the animals at close range. These animals returned to Reeds Lake after the summer vaudeville season and stayed on... in Fred Paulo's new garage! Mr. Havemann enjoyed the area so much that he came back to wait until the cold weather set in.

47

Elephants

It is rather difficult to imagine elephants performing in the grand Ramona Theater, but they did! Thompson's Elephants, one of the early performing elephant acts was one of the most well-known at the time. The trainer was **Eph Thompson**, born in Ypsilanti, and at 14 years of age, while working in Lansing, joined Adam Forepaugh's Circus. Starting out carrying water to the elephants and working his way up through various tasks he was eventually given charge over all of the Forepaugh elephants. When he was 23, he left the circus business and struck out on his own, entering vaudeville with his animals. Seeking out theaters in Europe, he spent twenty years in the major cities there, and when he returned to the United States in 1906, just prior to coming to Ramona, he could speak five languages. The animals could understand them as well!

Mr. Thompson stated to a *GR Press* reporter,

"I have my own way of training the elephants. I study the animals and learn their character. Animals have different dispositions as well as persons. One elephant can do what another can't. I study them out, find out what they can do, and then train them to do it. They know the meaning of every motion I make. They understand what I say, too. I don't have to use a hook to pull them about with. They obey intelligently and willingly, because I know them and they know me."

He was widely known as an exceptional trainer but another notable thing about Eph was that he was "colored."

Minnie The Elephant became a favorite with the children of Grand Rapids. During her "Peanut Receptions," children could feed her and even get a ride. She performed with **Max Gruber's Animals** at Ramona and other venues in town. Besides Minnie, in the act were other animals, ponies, dogs and even ferocious felines.

Max and his wife Adele became residents of the Muskegon Actor's Colony, Bluffton, along with Minnie who appeared now and then in city parades.

Max Gruber is astride the horse in the photo. Joe and Myra Keaton are riding Minnie in a parade celebrating Joe's birthday.

The photo and poster come from the Muskegon Actors' Colony website where stories of the inhabitants are told. The Keaton family also owned a place in the colony. actorscolony.com

Monkeys

"A Night in a Monkey Music Hall"

Monkeys in cages were often placed in the midway at Ramona, but highly "educated" monkeys were also seen on the theater stage. The monkeys of **Maud Rochez** performed in 1910 an act called, "**A Night in a Monkey Music Hall**" given on a miniature stage. It had a monkey orchestra in a tiny pit, complete with a monkey conductor. The monkey acts included a weight lifter, juggler, trapeze and comedy sketch. An observer reported, *"The solemn monkey conductor, at the ring of the stage-manager's bell, turns over his music, raps loudly with his baton upon his music-desk, and then proceeds to conduct his monkey orchestra with a look of bored indifference upon his face."*

Birds

Trained birds that appeared at Ramona were generally cockatoos. **Madame Rose Naynon** appeared with seventy four of them in 1903. **Irma Orbasany's Cockatoos** did pantomime stunts in 1907. *"In one part of the act they man a ship, raising the sails and then lowering them when a storm approaches. They finally escape from the sinking ship in a boat. A clown cockatoo made the hit of the act."* In 1920, **Lucile and Cockie** performed, the latter being referred to as "the human bird" because it possessed a wide range of speech. It told stories, imitated musical instruments and danced.

Animals played a role in the grand vaudeville scheme of things at Ramona Theater, amazing adults and pleasing the children in the audience. Along with the types of acts mentioned, trained seals played ball and rode on horses, kangaroos boxed, baboons put on a play. In the 1920s and later, only occasionally did horses or dogs perform on the stage.

Wild West Shows

In 1911, Ramona Park Theater presented Cheyenne Days which brought to Grand Rapids a taste of the west. The show boasted "wild west thrills" described as "*a cowboy exhibition that includes songs and humor of the plains, daring riding stunts, rope throwing, bucking broncos and the like.*" The notable feature of the show was **Lucille Mulhall**, billed as a skilled equestrienne of the western style of riding who gave a "high school exhibition" with her bronco Red Buck. The term "high school" indicated the highest point of the riding profession with prescribed figures being performed.

Miss Mulhall was well-known by the time she visited Ramona. Theodore Roosevelt, on his way through Oklahoma during the Spanish American War, stopped in at the Mulhall ranch and became fast friends with family members. At age 18, Lucille won a $1,000 steer roping contest, defeating the best known cowboys in the southwest. Her sister Agnes or "Bossie" was also famous for roping and riding, but chose to use her musical talents when performing. It was Lucille who became known as the "Queen of the West," prior to the days of Dale Evans.

Lucille Mulhall

SPECIAL ANNOUNCEMENT
Diamond Dick's Congress of World's Western Champions 40 of Them

MOST ELABORATE OUTDOOR SHOW EVER STAGED AT RAMONA

The Largest Array of Champions ever Assembled in Any Arena, Including

"BEE-HO" GRAY—The Champion fancy and trick roper of the world.

MONTANA EARL—Champion trick rider of the world.

JACK MORRISSY—Stockwhip and Rifle Champ, Australian champion flat saddle rider.

JOHNNY MULLEN—Steer roper and broncho rider. Runner up for first money at Calgary.

LEONARD M'COY—Champion steer bull dogger and fancy roper.

JIM KENNEDY—Champion Roman trick rider and rope spinner.

FLORENCE LADUE—World's champion trick roper. Holder of the gold medal.

ADA SUMMERVILLE—World's champion lady horse trainer.

DOLLIE CLARK—Trick and fancy rider.

MARIE GILBERT—Fancy and trick rider.

FERN KENNEDY—Fancy and trick rider.

IKE LEWIN—Champion cowboy rider of the world.

CHIEF "BAD HOSS," champion Indian rider of the world, and his tribe of Sioux Indians.

BIDLE BILL SELLMAN—A renowned trick and fancy roper and trick rider.

RAY DA COTA—Trick rider and roper.

Russian Cossacks, Cowboys, Cowgirls, Indians, Mexicans.

A SPECIAL FEATURE—The only two wrestling Shetland ponies in the world, an almost human performance.

Wild horses, cow ponies, high school horses, wild steers and wild calves. A real "Wild West" entertainment by a real "Wild West" aggregation that has been doing everything that has been done or attempted in shows of this kind. A good, clean, instructive entertainment of surpassing merit.

Daily at Ramona's New Arena, 2:30 and 8:30 P. M.

RAMONA BOOKS A BIG HORSE SHOW

40 Performers and 60 Horses to be at Park All Summer

Diamond Dick's Wild West Show came to Ramona in 1915. Known also as the Congress of World's Western Champions, the forty performers included twelve world champion rope throwers and riders from various parts of the country. Besides the stars, the cast contained "real Indian" cowboys, cowgirls and a small band of Cossacks. Sixty horses were also a part of the entourage.

This was no small enterprise and it graced the Ramona grounds from late May until the end of July. The arena and a grandstand were constructed north of the Derby Racer. Between 700 and 800 persons could view the show at one time, and on some days as many as three performances were given.

The main attraction of the Diamond Dick Show was **Bee Ho Gray**, world champion fancy and trick roper. He was the drawing card for audiences and performers alike. At the time, he was the only artist to throw three ropes at once, catching three separate objects. During the Ramona engagement, Bee Ho Gray left the show briefly to successfully defend his championship at Cheyenne, Wyoming. Bee Ho Gray came back to Ramona in successive years, with his own show.

Besides performing in the arena outside, Bee Ho Gray and his wife **Ada Sommerville** sometimes appeared evenings on the Ramona Theater stage. She was a well-known horsewoman, and her part of the act was done with her dancing horse, Onion. The troupe provided horses, ponies and instructors so that park visitors could learn to ride. A special track north of the grandstand was build for this purpose.

A bit of excitement was created when a young bull broke loose from his moorings and ran toward the midway. Circle visitors had a first-hand demonstration of roping skills when one of the cast successfully captured the animal before it could do any damage to the park or visitors.

BEE-HO-GRAY CHAMPION TRICK ROPER OF THE WORLD.

Photo postcard showing Bee Ho Gray and his famous three-rope catch.
The image comes from the website, beehogray.com, lovingly maintained by the artist's grand nephew, Clark Gray.

Fenced in arena where the Diamond Dick Wild West Show took place. A grand-stand was constructed here for spectators.

Note the Derby Racer in the background and the back of scenery for the Old Mill ride.

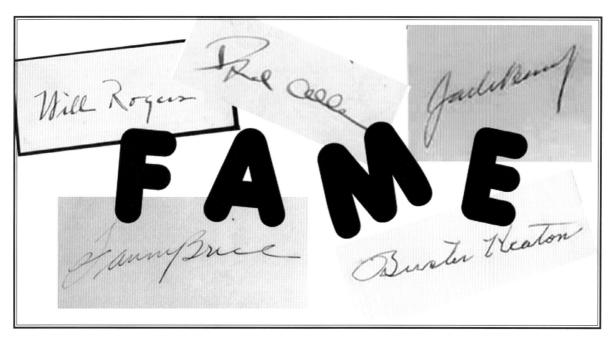

FAME

The Ramona Theater quickly gained national attention because of its setting, its professional managers and its bookings. Dancer Ruth St. Denis told what it meant from a star's point of view to "play" Ramona, when she returned to the area in January, 1918. *"Members of our company are going to enjoy all of the skating that is to be had at Reeds Lake while we are in the city, and we hope to have hours of it Friday and Saturday. Last time we visited Grand Rapids, we played Ramona theater in the summer and went swimming every day. It was the most delightful week of our season, and now we want to see how attractive Reeds lake looks in the wintertime. We shall skate there every morning next week, the exercises will put the girls into fine condition for dancing."*

Miss St. Denis was a pioneer of modern dance, of much renown in her time. Now, perhaps, she is over-shadowed by the fame of one of her pupils, Martha Graham. Other people who performed at Ramona were famous at the time but faded away later. Some of the people became nationally famous beyond the vaudeville stage. This section contains stories of a few of those with recognizable names.

When little **Buster Keaton** appeared at Ramona, he was but 5 years old. His parents at the time of his birth were described as medicine show performers and before long became known as an "eccentric comedy" act. While he was still a toddler, Buster was included in the act by being tossed across the stage by his father. His performance at Ramona in 1902 was announced in the *GR Press* as, *"a grotesque comedy act, replete with eccentric and acrobatic dancing and mirth provoking situations."* He had a natural instinct for comedy and received great attention while still very young. By 1908, a brother and sister were added to the act and they were called The Five Keatons. In that year, Joe Keaton was part of forming an actors' colony in Muskegon and the Keatons built a summer home there. The Keatons returned to Ramona theater in 1911 and again in 1914.

Joe, Myra and "Buster" Keaton are also expected to make a laughing hit. The elder Keaton does some remarkable acrobatic comedy work, in which he is abetted by the infantile "Buster," five years of age, whose antics bring out roars of laughter.

51

CARRIE IS COMING

The year 1902 was also when **Carrie Nation** came to the stage at Ramona. She was not by any means a part of the vaudeville circuit, but appeared on her own. The promotion of August 16 in the *GR Press* stated that, *"The famous joint smasher will be at Ramona with her little hatchet on Monday and Tuesday, appearing immediately after the matinee and evening performances. She will give temperance talks, and exhibit her famous hatchet."*

When interviewed, Mrs. Nation stated, *"Will I do any smashing in Grand Rapids? Yes, but not with my hatchet. I will do it verbally. I am going to talk on Prohibition at Ramona. I don't know just what I shall say at Ramona, I never do before I go on the platform. Like all reforms, we must begin at the bottom and work upward."*

At Ramona, she smashed things right and left through her speech. It was like a campaign speech, the only candidate being prohibition. She blasted the president as a beer-guzzling Dutchman which evoked bursts of laughter from the audience. When Mrs. Nation went behind the scenes in the Ramona theater in the afternoon, a contortionist act was just finishing. The young man reminded her that they had met before when she removed the cigarette from his mouth. He swore that he hadn't had another since then. After her lectures the first day, she sold little stick pins shaped like hatchets. The count of souvenirs sold in the afternoon was between 150 and 200, and she sold all she had in the evening. The proceeds of the sales went to pay for the fines she incurred on her previous visit to Kansas. The evening audience packed the theater beyond standing room.

Carrie and Her Souvenir Hatchet.

Clarence S. Darrow Headliner

The Labor Day celebration at the park in 1916 featured an address by **Clarence Darrow** in the theater. The estimated crowd that thronged Ramona Park on that day was 12,000 people, even though the weather was most unfavorable. Originally, he was to have spoken in the athletic field where many more seats were available, to be followed by a boxing match.

The thrust of Mr. Darrow's speech was to encourage the labor force to *"use their heads. The crying need of labor in the present day is education. The laboring man is poor because he is not educated. The smart man, the educated man, is the man who works with his head and not with his hands, and until you laboring men begin to use your heads, you can look for little encouragement. Labor unions have bettered the condition of the laboring men, but they can do little more until they have pursued another course; they can expect to gain little if one union fights another. They must stand together and help fight each other's battles."*

CLARENCE S. DARROW.

52

From Ramona to Oz

VIOLET MacMILLAN "The Cinderella of Vaudeville"

HOME JUST FOR THE HOLIDAYS

From the New York Dramatic Mirror, Oct. 7, 1914, author L. Frank Baum when asked why the change from writing books to film,

"I'm going to tell you the real reason. My books are rather high-priced because of the colored plates. Many children see them, but a multitude do not. This always has been a thing of regret to me. One night I was passing a suburban theater and saw a crowd of poor children entering the door. Their faces were filled with anticipation and their little voices were eager. The idea came to me—here is the opportunity to solve the problem; to accomplish that which I have been unrestful over. I will put all my books into the film that every child in the whole country may see them. A whole book for a nickel. That is the reason for the Oz Film Company."

Released just one week after the interview, the *"New Wizard of Oz"* came out in movie theaters. The little girl who played Dorothy was Grand Rapids' own, **Violet MacMillan**.

The diminutive little gal was 29 years old when the film was made. By that time she was a veteran of the vaudeville circuit, including time on Broadway. Her nickname, the Cinderella Girl, came from her tiny stature and feet. She was 4 foot 11 inches tall and her foot was the length of a dollar bill, fitting into a child's size 12 shoe.

Violet performed on the Ramona stage in 1901 as an opener for other acts. She returned from time to time as a feature with her singing, dancing and acting. Even though she appeared on Broadway by 1907, and toured the states on the circuit, Grand Rapids was her home. She married a Grand Rapids man, John Hall Folger, and came back to the city to retire from show business in 1922. She became an active part of the Zonta International organization, serving as the local president from 1930-1932.

A book is being written about the life of Violet MacMillan Folger, called, "Violet MacMillan: The Cinderella Girl of Grand Rapids" by her granddaughter, Naomi Billings.

The World of Oz
- The Wizard of OZ
- His Majesty The Scarecrow of OZ
- Patchwork Girl of OZ
- The Magic Cloak of OZ

Will Rogers

AND HIS

Lasso Wonders

According to the book, *"The Papers of **Will Rogers**, From Vaudeville to Broadway,"* when the lanky cowboy performed at Ramona Theater in May 1909, he brought his new bride with him. It states, ***"Whether they had been married one week or six months, the Grand Rapids engagement provided a backdrop for the kind of honeymoon vacation that Rogers had promised Betty in his letters before she rejoined him on the road."*** The advertisement in the *GR Herald* announced *"Will Rogers and his Lasso Wonders."* The accompanying article stated that ***"...he will give his lasso act, offering some unique feats with the lariat. He comes from Oklahoma, where he was a cowboy. He claims to have taught ex-President Roosevelt how to handle the lariat."***

It has long been claimed that while Rogers was at Ramona in 1909, Mr. Louis DeLamarter was the person who convinced him that he should add the comic dialogue to his act. When questioned about the source of the switch in Will Rogers' routine from roping to talking, Mr. Steven Gragert, curator of the Will Rogers Memorial Museum in Claremore, OK, stated that over the years many people have made that claim. One of these was Flo Ziegfeld in the movie *"The Great Ziegfeld."* Will signed up with Ziegfeld in 1915. But, according to newspaper articles describing Rogers' act as he performed around the country, the transition occurred sometime between December 1911 and February 1912.

When he returned in July 1912, the *GR Press* had this to say about his act:

> Will Rogers, the lassooing cowboy, with an act that is far ahead of anything he has hitherto offered in Grand Rapids, keeps the audience alternately applauding and laughing. His comedy is just as naively clever as ever while his roping stunts have taken on a real musical comedy entertaining flavor. His imitations of Fred Stone and George M. Cohan are particularly pleasing.

RAMONA PARK {GRAND RAPIDS
SATURDAY, AUG. 9
SPECIAL FEATURE **JACK DEMPSEY** HIMSELF IN PERSON
SHOWING JUST HOW HE WON THE CHAMPIONSHIP
SELLS FLOTO SUPER CIRCUS

Champion Dempsey Coming Here to Start His Circus Career

Jack "The Giant Killer," "Manassa Mauler" Dempsey appeared at Ramona Park in August, 1919. This was just a few weeks after his "David and Goliath" defeat of the giant Jess Willard on July 4, 1919, earning him the heavyweight title. Dempsey was a good friend of Otto Floto, a fellow Coloradoan, reporter for the Denver Post and partner in ownership of the Sells-Floto Circus. Prior to the big bout, Dempsey promised that he would appear temporarily with the circus should he win the championship. Since Dempsey's mother was ill and in Salt Lake City, he asked for a delay in the performance so he could visit her. Because of that, it happened to be when the circus came to Ramona Park that Jack Dempsey fulfilled his promise.

He received $10,000 for his part in the circus that week. His "act" consisted of a three-round staged reproduction of his winning bout with Willard showing the seven knockdowns and how the bell saved Willard in the first round.

Charles (Chick, Chic) Sale(s), the name was listed several ways in the newspapers, first came to Ramona Theater in 1912. He brought his new wife with him and honeymooned in one of the cottages at Point Paulo. He had return engagements in 1914, 1915 and 1916, later appearing at the Empress in downtown Grand Rapids. His first billing declared that he was a *"comedy protean entertainer"* and he was *"declared to be very funny."* After his first performance he was touted as the biggest surprise thus far in the season. He performed a whole show by himself in his *"Country School Entertainment."* The *GR Press* reporter wrote then that *"Some day we will hear more of him."* He impersonated all seven of the characters in the story, which were taken from real life. When not performing, his favorite place to be was on his farm. He states that while in college, *"All the fellows had special stunts they could do and I just happened to discover almost by accident that I had a talent for impersonation. Those stunts seemed to take so well that I developed a vaudeville act after first having done chautauqua work. Yes, I love the cows and chickens, but I love the footlights and grease paint, too."* In 1916 he was billed as the *"funniest and most artistic of American mimes."* His performance of *"The Rural Sunday School Benefit"* at Ramona in 1916 was its premier, and it was a smashing success from then on.

HARDEEN

THE HANDCUFF KING
In an Exhibition That Has Baffled the Police of Two Continents.

Anyone reading about **Hardeen, "The Handcuff King,"** would think he was just another magician. However, knowing that **Theo Weiss** was the brother of Harry Houdini makes it more interesting to realize that he trod the Ramona boards. Hardeen began his career with his brother in an act called, *"The Brothers Houdini."* They changed their names when they went their separate ways, sometimes appearing in competition with each other.

While at Ramona in August, 1913, it wasn't enough for Hardeen to escape from handcuffs or a regulation army straight-jacket while submerged in a tank of water. Privates from the U.S. infantry challenged him to escape from a regulation "punishment suit." The huge canvas bag with arms, leather bound at the ends, braced and fastened with leather straps and buckles, was first exhibited in Herpolsheimers' window. It was not the first time he performed this particular escape, however.

What was unique to appearing at Ramona Park was the opportunity to execute a stunt in the lake, thereby quelling any suspicions that the theater stage was rigged. Before a crowd estimated to be 10,000 people, he leapt from the roof of the *Major Watson* into 20 feet of water, and resurfaced within 30 seconds. His hands had been chained and locked behind his back. When questioned by youngsters before the performance, he said the trick was easy – he simply held the key to the lock under his tongue and reached up to retrieve it while under water. A young lady questioned how he would do that with his hands behind his back. He shrugged and said he hadn't though of that.

The more famous brother, Houdini, died in 1926, and Hardeen continued to play the vaudeville circuit for many more years. From 1938 to 1941 he was on Broadway, and during the war he performed for the troops. Hardeen was also a founder and charter member of the Magicians' Guild, formed in 1944.

HARDEEN, THE HANDCUFF KING.

Fanny Brice, Snappy Entertainer

The review in the *GR Press* of Miss Brice's performance at Ramona in June, 1914, described her act as *"sophisticated humor,"* going through a variety of tricks and burlesques, coarse but funny. It stated also that Fanny had changed after returning from a tour in England, much lighter *"in pounds and hair,"* but that after *"one line of her first song and one of her inimitable gestures, and there was no mistaking her."*

Fanny Brice reported on her trip abroad in a *GR Press* interview, having spent time in England, intending to rest up and do no work. She speaks frankly of pre-war conditions: *"The things I saw over there are really awful and while I would not want to go so far as to say that I indorse all that the militants are doing, still it would not be fair to say that they have no provocation."* She stayed in that country for eight months so she felt she could speak of the lack of respect that *"the English"* had for women, and that contributed to her understanding of the need for women to have the right to vote.

Even though her trip was for rest, soon after her arrival she was engaged at the London Opera House, her performances becoming a favorite of the locals. She said that London at that time was *"ragtime crazy."* Of the music in existence then (1913) she spoke, *"Honestly, most of the songs they sing are vile beyond words. You may think that I am exaggerating, but I say that I wouldn't even tell you the titles of [what is being] sung in the best theaters."* Her style of music was so readily accepted that *"every bus in London carried my name billing me as The Ragtime Songbird."*

The "Kids" of "Our Gang" were represented at Ramona when three of them performed in 1928. The skit in which they displayed their acting talent was called, *"In and Out of the Movies."* **Johnny Downs,** who played the part "Johnny" in the Our Gang series, continued to act after he became an adult. He performed in many movies and had his own after-school kids' television show, *"The Johnny Downs Show."*

By 1928, **Mary Kornman** became the leading youngster, Mary, in the "Our Gang" comedies, and appeared in more episodes than any other child. Her career didn't end when she grew out of childhood, she appeared in countless movies with such stars as John Wayne, Fred Astaire, and Bing Crosby.

The third member of the troupe was **Scooter Lowry** who was only an occasional actor in the children's series. He was known as the "original tough guy" and played the part in vaudeville acts and movies. Acting was second nature to him since he was born into a theatrical family, and he had already appeared in movies by the time he was at Ramona.

On one of the afternoons, after the matinee performance, these "kids" hosted a public reception on the stage of the theater for the children of Grand Rapids.

While performing at Ramona, when not on the stage, these children played with neighborhood youngsters who didn't realize they were famous.

MARY KORNMAN   "SCOOTER" LOWRY   JOHNNY DOWNS
OF "OUR GANG" COMEDIES AT RAMONA

JACK BENNY
UNIQUE, IRRESISTIBLE IDEAL MASTER OF CEREMONIES

JACK BENNY AT RAMONA

That **Jack Benny** performed at Ramona is a well-publicized fact. At what stage in his career he visited is probably lesser known. The violin, which was part of his identity during his television comedy days, was his ticket into show business, and the means by which he entertained in his early years. After his stint in World War I, during which time he entertained troops with his violin and became friends with Pat O'Brien, he got more comedy spots in the vaudeville circuit. In January of 1927 he married Sadie Marks, who became known as Mary Livingstone. It was also the year he first performed at Ramona. The clipping below, from the *GR Press,* describes his involvement in the Keith-Albee show, and it was repeated word for word when he returned in 1928.

Jack Benny, the unique and irresistible comic, one of vaudeville favorite comedians, will headline the Ramona bill for the first four days, starting today. He is a monologist, an entertainer of rare ability and in addition to all this is recognized as one of the leading moderns in a new line of entertainment, a master of ceremonies, and old English custom now being revived in America's leading amusement places. This extra dash of humor is the savory spice of a vaudeville menu and Mr. Benny's comedy interludes offer a delightful series of wit and humor. For his own specialty he has a full line of laughs, carefully polished and arranged for sure-fire results.

According to the article below from the *GR Press*, July 30, 1927, a gal is performing with Benny whom he called "Marie." She played the same type of character later played by Benny's wife, Mary Livingstone. She decided to change her name when her show business career took off . It is possible that this "Marie" was actually Mary, whom Benny had married some seven months prior.

Benny introduces the various acts, then does a little turn of his own assisted by a clever girl partner, whom he introduces as Marie from Lansing. The two stage a neat comedy turn. Benny is sleek and subtle in his methods. He has a good line of talk, the usual group of Scotch stories, and plenty of "wise cracks." His easy, fluent style and quaint comments on current events occasion much laughter. Marie, who poses as an ambitious amateur, is exceedingly clever and a capital foil for Benny's foolery. The two have style and are genuinely amusing.

RAMONA THEATRE
REED'S LAKE, GRAND RAPIDS
JUNE
16
1930
MONDAY EVE
Established
Price 50c
ADMIT ONE, GOOD DATE ONLY
Management reserves the right to revoke this license by refunding money.

GOOD ONLY
MONDAY EVE
JUNE
16
GLOBE TICKET COMPANY, PHILA.

1 U 3
Sec. Row No.
ORCHESTRA
RAMONA THEATRE
1930

57

"ROCHESTER"

Gordon Wassenaar tells this story about meeting **Eddie "Rochester" Anderson** during the time he was performing at the Ramona Theater.

"On this day, our boat was in the water at the marina operated by Bill Poisson, outside the Lakeside Tavern. When we were preparing the boat to go out for a ride, someone came walking down the bank from the theater toward us. It was Rochester of the Jack Benny Show! He walked up to my dad, introduced himself and stuck out his hand to shake. My dad held back, apologizing that he had gotten his hands dirty on the engine. Rochester said it was okay because his hands had been dirty since the day he was born. He asked if he could have a ride around the lake, so away we went. He enjoyed that."

Rochester, checking out
Ramona's miniature locomotive.

FRED ALLEN & CO.
IN "DISAPPOINTMENTS OF 1928"

When **Fred Allen** appeared at Ramona in 1928, he was accompanied by his wife, **Portland Hoffa**. They were described as *"a popular pair of funsters."* The skit was called, *"Disappointments of 1928"* and the review said, *"it was a bunch of jollity, much of the dialog consists of witty comments on daily doings and dance steps and a hodgepodge of entertaining morsels."*

Allen's stint at Ramona followed on the heels of Jack Benny, which was ironic since the two of them had a long-running mock feud over the radio in later years. Allen was a master at the ad-lib which sometimes resulted in invoking the censor. He died in 1956.

His wife, ten years his junior, was a performer in her own right. In fact, when they were at Ramona, Fred rated a drawing in the paper, his wife, a photograph. She died in 1990.

FRED ALLEN

"This pretty girl with the permanent wave and stylish bob is Miss Portland Hoffa, who will appear with Fred Allen in a skit at Ramona."

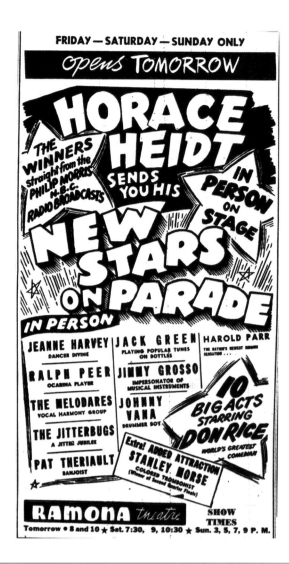
Ramona Theater was the place to go for good vaudeville entertainment in the summer. Grand Rapids area people could see the best performers of the day in pleasant surroundings and in the good company of family and friends.

Over the fifty-three seasons of the existence of The Ramona Theater, a multitude of performers appeared on that stage. The terribly famous and the as-yet unknown or never-to-be-known were brought in to amuse audiences. But, the time came when people were no longer interested in live entertainment and were content to crowd the movie theaters.

'Harmonicats' Coming to Ramona Theater

The 'Harmonicats,' the harmonica trio that made "Peg O' My Heart" famous, will open at the Ramona Theater August 13 for three days.

Five other acts will be presented on the bill, along with the Selma Marlowe Dancing Chorus.

The 'Harmonicats' and the balance of the show are coming to Ramona from the Chicago Theater in Chicago.

On Aug. 20-22 Ramona Theater will present the stars and winners of the Horace Heidt show.

59

A. B. Marcus

THE MARCUS SHOW — QUEEN OF ALL BEAUTY SHOWS

The thoughts of people who still remember Ramona Theater some 60 years later, often turn first to the Marcus Girls. The mystique of the show girls lingers. Of all the varied performers that walked, danced, rode, rolled, or tumbled across the stage in that wonderful old place, these girls took top billing. In a venue where clean entertainment was imperative to the managers of the railroad company, it seems incongruous that show girls performed there for so many years. Mr. Marcus addressed this concern in 1918 in an interview in the Augusta Chronicle. He stated, *"It is good business to run a clean show."* The article goes on to say, *"Marcus believed that women as well as men like to look on their beautiful sisters of the stage in creations that serve to enhance their natural pulchritude. Many of the costumes are startling but never without the bounds of good taste. Mr. Marcus is fully aware of the fact that theatergoers do love to laugh and all of the Marcus shows are arranged with this in view, but never once is the borderland of vulgarity approached."* A. B. Marcus also believed in giving the people in his audiences their money's worth.

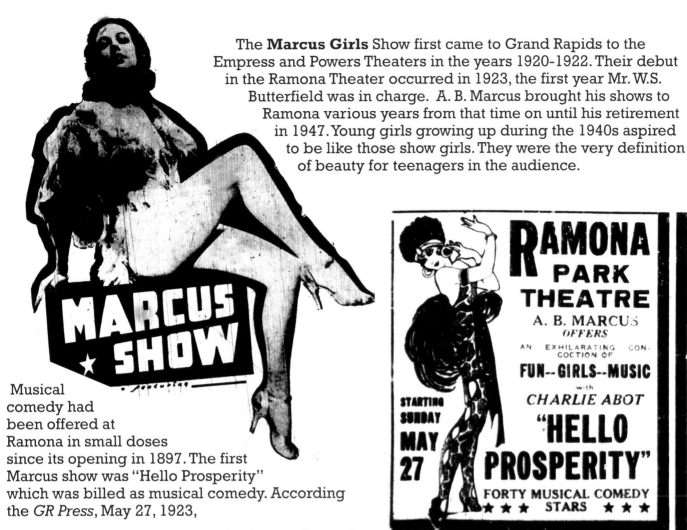

The **Marcus Girls** Show first came to Grand Rapids to the Empress and Powers Theaters in the years 1920-1922. Their debut in the Ramona Theater occurred in 1923, the first year Mr. W.S. Butterfield was in charge. A. B. Marcus brought his shows to Ramona various years from that time on until his retirement in 1947. Young girls growing up during the 1940s aspired to be like those show girls. They were the very definition of beauty for teenagers in the audience.

Musical comedy had been offered at Ramona in small doses since its opening in 1897. The first Marcus show was "Hello Prosperity" which was billed as musical comedy. According the *GR Press*, May 27, 1923,

"The Marcus Show will arrive in the city early Sunday morning and trucks are in readiness to transport the two carloads of scenery and baggage to Ramona playhouse, where the first show will be staged at three o'clock. There are 35 people with the company."

The [Pennsylvania] Reading Eagle theater reviewer stated the following about this same show,

"There was a time when a plot or story was necessary to the success of a musical show. But times have changed. There are 23 scenes in the two acts of the current edition of the Marcus production of "Hello, Prosperity," and not one has any connection with those that have preceded. Speed, jazz music, pretty girls, gorgeous gowns, magnificent scenery, comedy and dancing abound, but not a single inkling of a plot is to be discerned."

Whether this observation was agreed upon by other viewers or not, the Marcus Revues brought in the crowds. In the 1942 the shows drew about 8,000 people per week at 60 cents per person.

Two ads from 1923 shows

61

50
PEOPLE
50

MARCUS SHOW
OF 1930
PRESENTS

LEON MILLER
and THE MARCUS PEACHES
in "RUFFLES"

WEEK BEGINNING JUNE 27, 1931

MRS. BEA MARCUS

Presents

"A NAUGHTY BRIDE"

A Musical Farce Comedy in Two Acts
By F. J. WILLIAMS
Directed by W. F. BOWKER

BUSCH SISTERS *with* MARCUS REVUE
RAMONA.

Farewell Production for Season 1930

A. B. MARCUS

Presents

AU REVOIR

A REVUE IN TWENTY-TWO SCENES

Dances, Ensembles, Tableaus Conceived and Staged by Leon Miller
Music Under Direction of Eula Coudy   Scenes Painted by Miner Reed
Entire Production Under Direction of A. B. Marcus

This story was told by a lady who worked at the Woolworth store on Monroe in downtown Grand Rapids.

"I was a new salesgirl at Woolworths, working on the first floor. One day, the manager stopped by to talk with me and see how I was doing. He was a Dutchman from the old country, a very strict, very solemn, serious gentleman. While we were talking, one of the ladies from the basement approached and asked for assistance with a couple of customers. The manager invited me to accompany him, and we followed the girl to her station.

"There stood a pair of twins. Twins are likely to catch the eye no matter where or who they are, but these two were outstanding. They wore a lot of make up, had the latest in hairdos and their clothes were quite fetching. They certainly looked like show girls. The lady we had followed said she didn't know where to find what these girls were looking for, and asked if one of us could be of assistance.

"One of the twins piped up that they were looking for 'G-strings' and did the store carry them. The manager said, 'Have you tried notions?' The girls attempted to describe the objects but were met with blank stares. In a last-ditch effort, one of the girls lifted up her skirt and pointed to the item. Needless to say, the manager was beside himself with embarrassment. The girls were, of course, Marcus Girls who had come to town to shop before their next performance."

DOLORES TERRY
FEATURED WITH THE MARCUS SHOW
AT RAMONA

About Those Pillars...

Walking down the sidewalk on Lakeside Drive, approaching the corner of Reeds Lake Blvd, a person couldn't help but be curious about the two stone pillars situated on either side of a path trailing into dense woods. There were two more such pillars, apparently situated on the eastern and western lot corners. Such grand monuments must surely signify a grand structure within the forest. The following is the story of this property.

Dr. Alfred M. Webster, secretary of the New Era Life Association, acquired a very young wife during his senior years. According to his neighbors, she apparently had extravagant tastes, and he set out to build her a beautiful home in a choice location on Reeds Lake. The good doctor decided to act as his own architect and contractor, causing him to spend three times the amount that should have been required to build the home. In his position for the association, it was a simple matter to siphon off funds undetected, which he did in order to proceed with the construction. The day of reckoning came when an insurance examiner discovered a discrepancy in his accounts of over $18,000. Rather than face the music, Dr. Webster took his own life, a move that he carefully planned for the evening before the disclosure to the public would occur.

As a result of the death, and because of the stolen funds, the bungalow was released by the widow to the New Era Association. It was difficult to place a value on the home and lot at that point, but it was hoped the sale of it would help to replace some of the lost monies.

Enter the Mills Brothers. Nearly a year after the suicide, the unfinished bungalow was purchased by Mr. H. B. Mills and his brother for $4,000. Their intention was to establish a froggery, at that location. They had conducted a similar enterprise in Milwaukee, raising frogs to sell to restaurants. Whether the frog part of the story was realized or not, the house was finished by the Mills family. By 1911, Emory Mills had joined his father to live in the house with his wife Anna. Anna held down the fort at 512 Lakeside Drive after her husband and father-in-law died. She made a living by renting out rooms in the house.

Another twist in the story happened between 1939 and 1940. For some unknown reason, and by some unknown method, the address of this house was changed to 526. The house had not moved, it was still next door to 514 Lakeside. Anna sold the house in 1941 to the Eli Epstein family.

The story of the house continues through the recollections of the Epstein son, Burt, who lived there until 1950. What appeared in modern times to be a pathway, was actually a driveway, cars entered the property between the two pillars. This driveway made a loop and there was a carriage house within. The house sat to the east of the driveway with steps leading up to a very large porch that ran across the whole front. About 100 feet behind the house was a channel to the lake where their boat was docked.

This "bungalow," as the newspapers called it, had three finished floors. The main floor was where the Epstein family lived. It consisted of a huge living room with squared ceiling beams of dark cherry, formal dining room, master bedroom and a library with a pocket door which became a bedroom for the son. There was also a kitchen, and sun porch that ran the full width of the back of the house, on the lake side. In better weather, that porch with the dining room could accommodate 40 people for a sit-down dinner.

The cherrywood staircase leading up from the foyer went to more bedrooms upstairs, which continued to be rented out by the Epstein family. The basement was outfitted for servants with complete facilities for housekeeping. This area was rented out by the Epsteins also, to the same people every year, **Mr. and Mrs. A. B. Marcus!** Not only did the Marcus couple stay there summers, but some of the girls did as well, usually the ones who had been with the show the longest.

By the mid 1940s, which was during his later years, Mr. Marcus was not well and couldn't drive. Even though his wife was still quite vivacious, she did not have a driver's license. Burt Epstein had received his license at age 14, during the war. So, he was paid by Marcus to drive them around in his 1939 Buick 4-door convertible! As a special privilege, young Mr. Epstein was allowed to take his friends to Grand Haven in the Grand Old Car.

The elder Epsteins stayed in the house after the son left for college. Sometime in the late 1950s, they were approached by a man who wanted to develop the two corner lots bordered by Reeds Lake Blvd. and Lakeside Dr. They made a deal, and the Epsteins were allowed to stay in the house even though they no longer owned the property. The developer never did get the zoning approval for his venture.

After Mr. Epstein died in 1970, Mrs. Epstein moved to Phoenix, and the house went vacant. It stayed empty for years and became a hang-out for vagrants. At one time the house was featured in the *GR Press* as the "Halloween House."

Eventually the house was demolished.

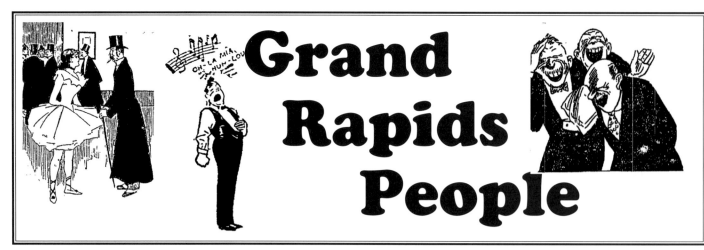

Grand Rapids People

In 1949 the stage of the Ramona Theater was ripped board from board. After 53 seasons, thousands of feet had scratched and polished those boards. Tiny little feet of midgets and children, huge clown feet, even feet of elephants that required the platform to be shored up to hold the weight. Some of the feet belonged to people who became world famous movie and stage stars, and some feet belonged to Grand Rapids people who became housewives or delivery truck drivers. The Ramona Theater was a setting where the people of Grand Rapids could enjoy all kinds of entertainment and where local people could display their talents to bring joy to others.

Opening for 1898

One of the earliest bands to play concerts at the lake was conducted by Frank A. Wurzburg. He started his musical career as a boy with a German band in 1871 and organized his own group in 1881. That band was a principal attraction at the lake for twelve seasons. In 1894 the Grand Rapids Evening Press organized a band made up of their newsboys, initially under the instruction of Prof. Frank T. Cormany. By February, 1897, Frank Wurzburg had taken over the instruction and leadership of the Newsboys' Band and it was escalated into national renown. The band was chosen to play at the dedication of the Ramona Theater in June of that year. In subsequent years the band toured the Midwest including ten days at the world's fair in Buffalo.

Wurzburg's Military Band will render a special program for the week commencing Sunday, Aug. 8.

The afternoon program will consist of selections from the popular operas.   1897

From 1938

During the first thirty some years of performances at the Ramona Theater, vaudeville and musical comedy dominated. Although some of the performers were from Grand Rapids, they played Ramona as members of a national circuit. In the last part of the roaring twenties, local dance groups started to perform their spring recitals on the theater stage. During the forties, besides the A.B. Marcus shows, musicals were put on by traveling troupes which employed local youngsters in the cast and in chorus lines. Local organizations such as the Grand Rapids Municipal Opera and the Civic Light Opera Guild of Grand Rapids used the Ramona stage during the second world war.

In the late 1940s, a form of talent show at Ramona was hosted by local radio celebrities such as Bruce Grant. Members of the audience were given the opportunity to perform. Evie Volmer Miller recalls the time when she and her sister Ann went up on stage to read a comic routine from a script. Winners were chosen by applause.

Dance Studios

From the late 1920s on through the 1940s, local dance studio spring recitals were held on the stage of the Ramona Theater. Two of those were Ollie Wood and Phil Osterhouse. These productions gave the students an opportunity to perform on a stage where famous people had also been.

Below is the program presented
May 25, 1928

OLLIE WOOD'S FOLLIES

MISS OLLIE WOOD

— PROGRAMME —

1. Out of a Hat Box—"A Cute Little Way All Theiir Own"............
   Sung by Pat Walsh anl Carl Holden
   Dancers—June Stiller, Genevieve Fink, Vivian Luce,
   Evelyn Weikert, Eleanor Drieborg, Geraldine Sullivan,
   June Verhow.
2. Dutch Kiddies
   Pantomime—Joan Wills and Rachel Davis.
   Dance—Rita Jane Rademacher.
   Assisted by—Betty Clifford, Barbara Jean White,
   Betty Koster, Peggy Lanier, Phyllis LaBree, Lorrain
   Kortlander, Prudence Joyce Cooper, Betty Jean
   Boorman, Peggy Wilbur, Kathryn Davis, Jean Tuttle,
   Marjorie Carr, Rachel Davis.
3. "Tea for Two".........................Mary Jane Voss and Bobby Gould
4. Acrobatic Dance..Josephine Zomer
5. "Hold Up Rag"....................Sung by Pat Walsh and Carl Holden
   The Pirate Girls—June Stiller, Genevieve Fink, Vivian
   Luce, Evelyn Weikert, Eleanor Drieborg, Geraldine
   Sullivan, June Verhow.
6. Dreams of Toyland
   Mother.............................Miss Florence Caro Lindley
   Song—"Husheen," by Needham.
   Bobby.............................Rita Jane Rademacher
   Betty...............................Betty Clifford
   Baby Peggy Doll..................Bertha Taylor

Ona Munson Doll..........................Phylis LaBree
Buster Brown Doll........................Rachel Davis
Mary Jane Doll...........................Kathryn Davis
Cuddles Doll.....................Prudence Joyce Cooper
French Doll..............................Mary Jane Voss
Irish Laddie.............................Jean Tuttle
Irish Lassie.............................Marjorie Carr
Kewpie Doll..............................Peggy Lanier
Sailor Dolls..................{ Barbara Jean White
                             { Peggy Wilbur
Peter Pan................................Allen Jackson
Tinkle Bell..............................Alean Jackson
Raggedy Anne.............................Charlene Vaughn
Raggedy Andy.............................Ruth Nowacki
Soldier Doll.............................Joan Wills
Triple Tap Dance.................Rita Jane Rademacher
Acrobatic Dance..........................Betty Clifford
Parade of the Wooden Soldiers............Entire Group
7. The Doll Dance.......................Gladys Bolier
8. Gypsy Dance..........................Barbara Dursum
9. In a Flower Garden
   The Rose...............................June Stiller
   Rosebuds—Betty Clifford, Ruth Nowacki, Rita Jane
   Rademacher, Marjorie Bartz, Rachel Davis, Adrienne
   Houle, Kathryn Davis, Virginia Ware, Clarabelle
   Stickney, Mary Jane Voss, Josephine Zomer, Dorothy
   Gavon, Margaret Scheibelhut.

Phil Osterhouse DANCE STUDIO

Close-up of the old Ramona Theater piano

Rehearsal for "A La Carte Revue" ninth annual musical show of Osterhouse Dance May, 1938

Municipal Opera Committee

One day in the late spring of 1943, when Mary Ellen Miklas (Siegel) was planning on a day's outing with friends, her mother steered her to Ramona Park where auditions were being conducted. Mary Ellen was a mere fourteen years old, but a veteran of local dance schools. As a result of honoring her mother's request, she became one of those selected to appear in the summer's productions of the Grand Rapids Musical Opera Committee on the Ramona stage.

While this may sound like a dream come true to many young ladies, it was hard work. Mary

Ellen rode the bus across town to Ramona early in the morning to start rehearsals. Each week a new musical was presented, so while one show was being performed the next one was being rehearsed.

In the chorus lines were students not only from Grand Rapids but Sparta, Belding, Greenville, Lansing and even Jackson. The main characters of the casts included people like Marita Farell and John Gurney of the Metropolitan Opera Company.

Scene from the rehearsal of "Desert Song" on the Ramona Theater stage.
Mary Ellen is third from left.

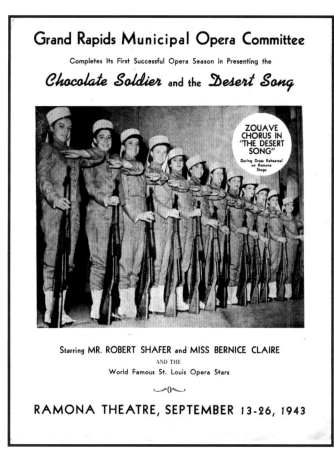

Grand Rapids Municipal Opera Committee

Completes Its First Successful Opera Season in Presenting the

Chocolate Soldier and the *Desert Song*

ZOUAVE CHORUS IN "THE DESERT SONG" During Dress Rehearsal on Ramona Stage

Starring MR. ROBERT SHAFER and MISS BERNICE CLAIRE

AND THE

World Famous St. Louis Opera Stars

RAMONA THEATRE, SEPTEMBER 13-26, 1943

STATEMENT OF
EARNINGS AND DEDUCTIONS FOR EMPLOYEE'S RECORD COVERING PAY PERIOD TO AND INCLUDING DATE SHOWN BELOW.

G. R. MUNICIPAL OPERA

AUG 13 1944

DATE

to *Patricia McPhilieny*

HRS. REGULAR WAGES		
HRS. OVERTIME WAGES		
GROSS WAGES		30 00
F.O.A.B.		
W. TAX	4 60	
BOND		
TOTAL DEDUCTIONS		4 60
NET PAY		25 40

DETACH BEFORE CASHING CHECK

Left, a program cover from a Municipal Opera Committee performance. Above, an actual pay stub.

The hard work paid well for the girls and paid off well for the company. This double page ad in June 1944 shows the sort of promotion that was done. This ad appeared just before the beginning of the opera season in 1944, encouraging people to purchase season tickets.

Civic Light Opera Guild

In 1948, the Grand Rapids Light Opera Guild offered four musicals to Ramona Theater audiences. They advertised, "Large New York Cast."

Deanna Grandstrom and Susie Smith (Bynum), marionettes, in "Marietta"

Civic Light Opera Guild
OF GRAND RAPIDS

Presents

VICTOR HERBERT'S
Naughty Marietta

RAMONA THEATER
EAST GRAND RAPIDS, MICH.

Thursday, Friday, Saturday, Sunday
and Monday Evenings at 8:30

July 1, 2, 3, 4, 5, 1948

Sponsor's Committee
HON. GEORGE W. WELSH
MRS. HENRY J. DOTTERWEICH
MR. RUSSEL W. FORWOOD
MR. FRANK H. GOEBEL
MR. FRANK B. GOODWIN
MRS. C. HUGO KUTSCHE
MR. RALPH F. WINDOES

GUILD OFFICE, 426 HOUSEMAN BLDG., PHONE GL 4-0230

THE GUILD'S STORY

The Civic Light Opera Guild is proud to present this series of operas to the theater-loving public of Grand Rapids and Western Michigan. If it receives sufficient popular support, it will become an annual affair, and our citizens will be justly proud of this civic endeavor. It will provide gay entertainment at a very reasonable price!

AND FOR THE CHILDREN

Each afternoon of the days listed above, we are offering beautiful operettas for the children. Fairy tales — set to music.

July 1 through 5 — "Snow White and the Seven Dwarfs"
July 8 through 11 — "Cinderella"
July 15 through 18 — "Little Red Riding Hood"
July 22 through 25 — "Wizard of Oz"

Send your children out to enjoy them. Or bring them yourself. You will enjoy them too. The price is only 50c for children and 75c for adults. Both including tax. The matinee performances will start at 2:30. Don't miss a single one of them!

Minstrelsy

A representation of entertainment from the Ramona Theater stage would be remiss were it not to include a segment about the contribution of "colored" people. From the birth of the great Ramona until the Roaring Twenties, most often the bill of fare included acts that fell into the category of "minstrelsy" as it was defined in those times. The following section is written in the vernacular of the day.

Terminology

Originally, the term, "minstrel," referred to a performer in medieval Europe who told stories, often hired by royalty or the "upper class." This form of entertainment evolved into the wandering minstrel or troubadour who performed in the streets, sometimes including musical accompaniment. But in the days of vaudeville, the reference to "minstrel" meant blackface entertainment.

According to several modern explanations of the word, "minstrel," it included both the impersonation of "colored" people given by white actors and the performance of "colored" musicians who sang, played the banjo and danced. The Ramona Theater presented both types of entertainment to its audiences. Some of the performers were local and became famous, others were famous at the time they performed or were on the road to fame.

The Grand Rapids newspapers promoted the Ramona Theater programs by announcing the roster with a short description, and, occasionally, reviews of the performances. People who were from Grand Rapids and even Michigan were so acknowledged. An artist from another country or nationality was indicated by the terms Dutchman, Russian, Jap, Yiddish, and so forth. When a person was "colored," they were not referred to as "African" or "black." Instead, the mention of skin color was often obscured in terms such as "dusky" "sepia" "smokey" and "dark." If the performer was an impersonator, the label was "blackface."

As for the form of entertainment known as the "minstrel show" it came into being about the same time as Stephen Foster, who was born in 1826. Much of Mr. Foster's music was appropriate to this genre for its use of the dialect of the south and references to the plight of the slave. The format of the minstrel show developed in the 1840s was a program that included singing and dancing in blackface with the musical accompaniment of violin or fiddle, banjo and tambourine. The semicircle of performers seated on the stage included jokes exchanged between the 'endmen' and Mr. Interlocutor seated in the center.

This famous poster from 1899 shows a theater production of the famous book, Uncle Tom's Cabin. When performed, the play incorporated elements of melodrama and blackface minstrelsy.

Typical Minstrel Show configuration

The Music

Musical numbers presented on the stage during the era of minstrel popularity, the 1890s through the early 1920s, were known as "coon songs." They became a national craze and people clamored to the theaters to hear them played and sung. Near the end of the 1898 season, when the Ramona Theater was just coming into its own, railway manager Johnson set out on a search for the type of music that was most popular in the big, eastern United States theaters. The headline of the article about this search stated,

"MUST DROP WAGNER, Popular Music the Rage in the East—Will Be Tried Here." The article goes on to state, *"In all the resorts in the east people cheer wildly and loudly encore coon ballads, the latest songs being the most popular."*

An essay about popular music written in 1900, stated that the typical 'popular' song would experience a meteoric rise, but then soon fall and die of exhaustion and over-exposure. At the same time, these songs had to *"share the honors with the coon song,*

in the singing comedian's and vaudevillian's repertoire. It became just as indispensable a part of the soubrette's 'property' as the grease paint and blonde wig."

Beginning in the early 1890s, coincident to the rise of minstrel entertainment, was the birth of Ragtime music. It grew out of the "colored" communities in Missouri and New Orleans, popular even before the time of it being published in sheet music for the general public. The key pioneer of the music was **Ernest Hogan**, who performed at the Majestic Theater in Grand Rapids in 1906. It was he who originated the term, "ragtime" derived from the syncopated or "ragged" rhythm, its main characteristic.

Tragedy

The utter tragedy of the minstrel movement in the theater was that it presented "colored" people in dreadful parody, instigating stereotypes accepted as normal by audiences who, in their ignorance, were not able to discern truth from fiction.

The "Blackface" Performers

The first performers listed are in the group of "blackface" or impersonators.
They needed the assistance of burnt cork in order to play the part.

Billed as "America's Greatest Minstrel, Milton G. Barlow performed at Ramona in 1898 and 1901 in the Barlow Brothers' Minstrels. His most notable performance was as Uncle Tom in Uncle Tom's Cabin, and he created the character, "Ole Black Joe"

George Mack was from the duo "Mack and Moran." They also performed as "The Two Black Crows" which became a weekly radio show in the late 1920s.
He purchased a cottage in Point Paulo.

"**Happy Jack Gardner**" joined the Actors' Colony in Muskegon in 1910. At Ramona, he was billed as a blackface comedian, but also sang and played the baritone horn. It is stated in actorscolony. com that he was *"associated with everything from circus to Shakespeare."*

Billy Miller and **Ed Kresko** were known as "The Rag Time Swells," their act consisted of singing, dancing, and repartee.

Waterbury Bros. and Tenney carried around the title, "America's Most Brilliant Musical Trio."

Lew Hawkins, born in Hudson Michigan, wrote his own book of Minstrel Jokes published in 1905 by Ogilvie. He was also known as *"The Chesterfield of Minstrelsy."*

Wilson and Clayton appeared in a Dutch comedy set and also sang popular minstrel songs in German.

Murray K. Hill was a ragtime recording artist, and prominent vaudeville comedian. His specialty was improvisation, with the ability to make something funny out of any unusual happening.

Gene Greene had the nickname, "The Ragtime King," for his vocalizations. As a vaudeville star, he made some of the earliest sound recordings of scat singing in 1911. When he performed in 1917, the *GR Press* reporter said, *"and he keeps the audience in a successive gale of laughter by his stories, chatter, songs and comedy bits. He has personality and a way of 'getting things over' which even adds new luster to old jokes."*

Billy Clark, born in Grand Rapids Michigan in 1875, performed his first black-face in 1893, worked in several nationally known minstrel companies and at one time even formed his own. He was multi-talented, writing his own music and comedy routines and even painting scenery. In fact, he was a scenic artist at the Grand Theater in his home town. His 1907 performance was described as *"a regular rapidfire of quibs, gags, laughers and smilers, and every shot hits."*

The Grand Rapids Boy, RAYMOND TEAL
Blackface Comedian

Raymond Teal was also a Grand Rapids blackface entertainer, who performed nationally in vaudeville for fifteen years before actually coming to Ramona. His tenor voice was praised and his renditions of the songs of the genre were highly popular. He was also a writer of those songs. He was sometimes billed as a comedian and monologuist. When he performed at Ramona, he was chastised for including material that was inappropriate and had to modify his routine.

Al Herman was "The Assassin of Grief and Remorse" and also known as "The Black Laugh."

Creighton Brothers and Belmont appeared in *The Mudtown Minstrels*, *"disguised as three ancient grandsires of the typical 'rube' sort."*

The **Honey Boy Minstrels** were directed by **George Evans**, a Welsh-born entertainer. The local reviewer stated that this group *"gives the best miniature minstrel show in vaudeville."* Among their members was a Dutch yodeler who *"added the touch of the unusual."*

LASKY'S PIANOPHIEND MINSTRELS

Jesse L. Lasky brought his "Phiend Minstrels" to Ramona in 1911. This involvement was early in his career, as later he teamed up with the likes of Cecil B. DeMille and his sister's husband, Samuel Goldwyn. They collaborated on the formation of various companies of players, and later he was part of the founding of Paramount Pictures.

Kaufman Brothers, Phil, Jack and Irving were so good at their impersonations that some reviewers didn't know they were actually white. These men were sons of Russian Jewish immigrants who chose the blackface genre to showcase their talents.

"Blackface" Eddie Ross
and His African Harp

"Blackface" Eddie Ross, from Hillsdale Michigan, called his banjo his "African harp." His skill in playing it was a trademark as well as his banter. While playing at the Empress Theater in Grand Rapids, it was reported that when a mother was asked by her little girl what Eddie had just said, her mother told her, "nothing." The columnist elaborated and wrote, *"Eddie can probably say more and mean less and do it more amusingly than any one else. He has been saying many of the same things for years, but they are just as funny now as ever."* When he returned to the Empress in 1922, he was listed as *"former blackface minstrel,"* having changed his act to ballad singing and dancing as well as comedy.

Shouters

Some of the minstrel performers were called, "coon shouters," which was a particular style of singing. It was described by Frederick Law Olmstead in his 1856 book, *A Journey in the Seaboard Slave States in the Years 1853-1854*, as *"a long, loud musical shout, rising and falling and breaking into falsetto."* Another author, John Niles, described the "shout" as a technique that *"includes the use of voice-breaks, slides and high, rasping, wails."* He further explained that, *"when a clever shouter 'gets hot' he or she can do wonders with most any material."*

Some of the most famous entertainers in this art form were Sophie Tucker, "The Last of the Red Hot Mammas," Fanny Brice, Ethel Waters and Artie Hall. When Fanny Brice came to Ramona, her act had evolved into something different. But **Artie Hall**, appearing there in 1903, was at the height of her popularity in this format. She had previously performed as Topsy in William A. Brady's version of Uncle Tom's Cabin. It was reported in newspapers across the country that Artie Hall died in the San Francisco earthquake in 1906 because she was last seen entering the Orpheum Theater shortly before it collapsed. However, she did not perish, and continued to perform for many more years.

From the sheet music for "Ain't Dat a Shame" by John Queen and Walter Wilson and promoted by Artie Hall

SUNG WITH GREAT SUCCESS BY ARTIE HALL.

Another lady who achieved fame in the shouting business was **Florence Courtney** who performed with her sister Fay. Their act at Ramona was described as, *"comediennes who have flitted back and forth from musical comedy to vaudeville for several seasons. They sing coon songs and Negro melodies."* While Flo's name was perhaps not widely known, her husband, George Jessel, was. The marriage didn't last, but he described her as his first true love.

Children

From the book, *Vaudeville, Old and New* by Frank Cullen, it is stated, *"In turn-of-the-century variety and vaudeville, it was fashionable for white women to hire a group of young, black, singing dancers, between the ages of 6 and 12, to enliven their acts. Eva Tanguay, Nora Bayes, Sophie Tucker, Josephine Gassman and Blossom Seeley all employed 'pickaninnies,' or 'picks' as did many black singers. The youngsters were an inexpensive, novel and lively addition to an act. Although some chroniclers have assumed the term was derived from cotton picking, it more surely seems to have proceeded from the Spanish words for 'small' and 'children' – pequeño and niños."*

Of the aforementioned ladies, Blossom Seeley performed at Ramona, but not in the minstrel genre. **Josephine Gassman** entertained there both in 1899 and 1906 with the tiny ones. She was so successful with this form of entertainment that she took her troupe on an around-the-world tour. Some of these children were launched into their own careers in show business. Grand Rapids born **Mamie Remington** was also very successful performing with the children. When she was in New York in 1902, her performance was described as being one of the best of its kind.

Below, local ad for young performers

Blackface performer at Ramona, posing for the camera in the 1940s.

The Authentic Performers

The following performers from the Ramona Theater ranks were authentic "colored," some of whom achieved a great deal of fame.

The **Hyers Sisters**, Anna and Emma, were born in the mid 1850s and became known as the first "colored" opera singers. Their debut was in the Sacramento Metropolitan Theater in 1867, and by 1871 they were touring the continent. Their comedy company performed at Reeds Lake in the early 1890s. Their step-mother, **May C. Hyers**, sang in the old Jandorf Pavilion in 1896 after the railway company built a stage and added shows to the entertainment on its property. She was the first "colored" female to have her singing voice recorded.

Ten Dark Knights with their kingpin comedian, **Jack Smith** performed at Ramona in 1908. Each of the knights was a good musician, and could sing and dance. They performed in uniforms as a brass band, and provided the scene of a plantation by moonlight, with singing and dancing. Jack Smith provided the comedy and was described as having *"a quaint manner of speech, his ludicrous style of dress, and above all, his 'gum shoe' dancing cause the audience to roar with laughter."*

Fiddler and Shelton were a pair among many such performers during the first part of the 20th century. One was a pianist and singer, the other did comedy routines.

Of **J. H. "Harry" Fiddler** it was said that he could contort his face in all manner of comical expressions. But probably the most interesting thing about this man, who didn't need burnt cork for color, was that he did Chinese impersonations. Besides having the talent for it, Mr. Fiddler had studied the language. His partner, **R. Byron Shelton**, was a ragtime piano pioneer and was called an "eminent trick pianist."

When Miller & Lyles performed at Ramona in 1914, they were described as, *"colored comedians who offer songs and dances and finish with a burlesque boxing bout which is said to be decidedly ludicrous."* However, in 1921, their musical *"Shuffle Along"* premiered on Broadway as the first major successful "colored" musical. It was just the beginning for Aubrey Lyles and Flournoy Miller.

Miller & Lyles
Colored Comedians with a SONG, a DANCE and a Biff or Two.

This modest advertisement for the team of Cooper and Robinson in 1909, gave away nothing of the future importance of the "Robinson" half. The *GR Press* simply described this act, *"Two unusual blackface comedians, will give the skit 'A Friend of Mine,' which is called 'a dramatized laugh.'"* But the fact was, Ramona Theater patrons were being treated to the terpsichory of Mr. **Bill "Bojangles" Robinson** before he struck out on his own.

At the age of five he began to dance to earn money and dropped out of school to follow in the footsteps of the professional. When he was eight, in 1886, he became one of the little darlings in Mamie Remington's troupe in Washington DC. He joined up with George W. Cooper in the early twentieth century, an association that lasted until 1914. Soon after the team broke up, Robinson pioneered the way for solo "colored" acts to appear in white vaudeville venues. Eventually, he went beyond the stage to perform in several movies with Shirley Temple such as, *The Little Colonel* in 1935. In 1943, the film, *Stormy Weather,* was loosely based on his life.

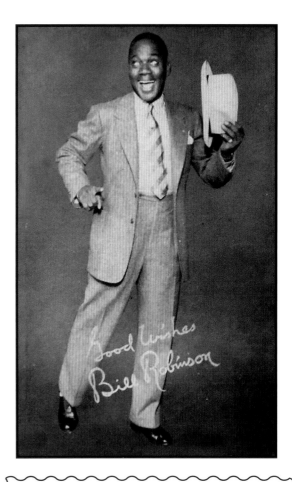

Entertainers in "Minstrel Frolics"

Washboard Dan Denis and the Patent Leather Kid, Pat Denis, in their interpretation of "18th and 19th on Chestnut Street," in the Minstrel Frolics which, under the sponsorship of the American Legion council, will open June 6 in Ramona theater. Mr. and Mrs. Denis, who are Grand Rapids residents, are nationally known as entertainers.

Although **Cab Calloway** did not perform in the theater at Ramona but rather in the dance hall, Ramona Gardens, the following story from 1933 about his performance is proper in this context. *"Cab Calloway has made a fortune though his musical ability. He is an outstanding figure among dance orchestra leaders, commanding a considerable income. During the course of the Thursday night dance we are told that many Grand Rapids Negroes, proud of their racial brother, gathered at the rear of Ramona Gardens. During the intermission they called for 'Cab.' The successful musician didn't turn up his nose at his own people. Instead he took himself to the door and with a genial smile called, 'How to do, folks. Glad to see you. How's everybody?' at the crowd outside. We don't know just how Cab's music rates with the critics of music, but this much seems evident, his success hasn't gone to his head. And that isn't so common as to be beneath notice."*

The "Minstrel Frolics" appeared in the Ramona Theater in 1940. By this time, audience interest in minstrelsy was on the wane.

Another Robinson who performed at Ramona was called, "Sugar Chile." **Frankie Robinson**, child prodigy, was performing his "boogie-woogie" tunes on the piano before he was old enough to go to school. According to the article in the *GR Herald* in 1948,

"Frank 'Sugar Chile' Robinson was sitting patiently in a corner of the audition room of The Michigan Theater in Detroit one day last October when the master of ceremonies of an amateur boogie-woogie contest the theater was holding gave him a weary nod. He was too young for the Detroit contest, but he was not too young to be recognized as a tremendous 'find.' The theater booked him in a featured spot on its regular program and after this sensational debut, he was deluged with offers from various parts of the country.

He is appearing with Van Johnson in MGM's newest musical, 'No Leave, No Love.' He has been playing the piano since he was barely able to walk. He plays a fascinating way all his own—scooting across the piano bench to reach what he calls 'the far-away notes,' whamming with ecstatic glee and singing a low-down chorus now and then in his piping soprano."

"SUGAR CHILE" ROBINSON
With a Broad Grin, He Leaped to Fame

COMING THURSDAY, JULY 4th
ON THE STAGE — IN PERSON
A Happy, Snappy, Sepia Swingsation!
COTTON CLUB REVUE
10 All Star Acts   30 People Mostly Girls   100 Laughs Laughs Laughs
WITH
Melvin Philips Cotton Club Orch.
RAMONA THEATRE
RAMONA PARK

INTERRACIAL GOOD-WILL CONCERT
WORLD'S GREATEST NEGRO CHOIR!
Wings Over Jordan
June 10th, 7:30 P. M.
9:30 P. M.
Tickets available at Grinnell's and Ramona Park or call 8-9105.
Advance Tickets $1.50
Reserved $1.99
Sponsored by True Light Baptist Church
SEE THEM IN PERSON
RAMONA *theatre*

Left, the Cotton Club Revue in 1940.
Above, a concert in 1947.

JITTERBUGS AT RAMONA

One of the acts to be presented by the Cotton Club Revue July 4 at the Ramona theater will be that of Harvey and Ethel, jitterbug artists.

Ramona Theater was torn down in 1949, marking the end of its great entertainment opportunities for Grand Rapids people.

74

The following is from the Grand Rapids Evening Press, an interview with the famous Ernest Hogan in 1906, when he was performing at the Majestic Theater.

The Negro as an Actor

"Some day the negro actor will make for himself a place on the legitimate stage." So declares Ernest Hogan, now at the Majestic, and he speaks with authority as one who knows what his people have done and what they are capable of doing.

"Only a few years ago the negro had little chance on the stage except to fill in backgrounds and do a little singing and dancing," said Mr. Hogan yesterday. "Now the colored actor has established himself in musical comedy. There are five negro theatrical troupes on the road and all are doing well. With such development I look forward to seeing in the near future the negro doing serious dramatic work and the public accepting him. There are now many strong negro characters on the stage. Take Uncle Tom, for instance, or Sassafras Livingston in 'The County Chairman.' Some day negroes will be playing parts like them. I have played Uncle Tom myself.

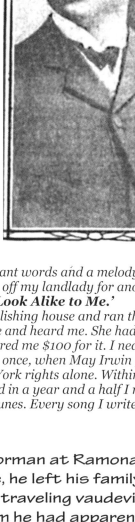

"Why shouldn't the negro do serious work? He has a large element of pathos in his make-up indeed. His whole life is pathetic. He has soul, too, and a great deal of the poetic sense. Why shouldn't he, when properly developed and trained, be able to make people cry and to move their emotions as well as to make them laugh? Pathos is only a step from laughter.

"My next play, now being written by a Boston newspaper man, is along serious lines. It is called 'Emancipation Day' and was suggested by Paul Laurence Dunbar's poem of the same name. I used that poem in vaudeville, putting it in at the end of my act. After making the people laugh for a quarter of an hour I used to be able to turn them to tears with that poem. Of course there are songs and dances in the play--the negro ought always to have a chance to sing and dance --but no chorus."

Mr. Hogan is having an interesting time reminiscing with Manager Orin Stair while here. Years ago when Mr. Stair managed the Grand, Ernest Hogan came here with a play he wrote himself, "Old Tennessee." Mr. Stair financed it and Louis DeLamarter acted as manager. Business was had and Mr. Hogan narrates with great glee how he used to tell stories to the landlords to keep them in good humor.

"After we busted up I went to Chicago and started at my old trade of bricklaying. One night I was outside a negro dance hall where there was a row. The officers were called and they made wholesale arrests. An Irish policeman gathered me in. I had performed for the policemen's benefit a short time before, and when the captain saw me he called the copper down for arresting me. 'I always do me duty,' said the copper. 'All coons look alike to me.'

"The expression hit me like a flash. In an instant words and a melody were running through my head. I went home, staved off my landlady for another day, got to a piano and composed *'All Coons Look Alike to Me.'*

"The next day I went down to Witmark's publishing house and ran the melody over on the piano. May Irwin was there and heard me. She had me play it again. Another actress came up and offered me $100 for it. I nearly fell off the piano stool and was going to accept it at once, when May Irwin gave me the wink. She offered me $100 for the New York rights alone. Within three months I had made $26,000 from that song and in a year and a half I made $41,000. That was the turning point in my fortunes. Every song I write now brings from $2,000 up."

Benjamin D. Jones was a doorman at Ramona Theater. At one point in time, he left his family and became a "wardrober" for traveling vaudeville stage shows, with people whom he had apparently encountered during his employment at Ramona.

Benny's mother, Josephine Jones, and sister, Amanda Mae, worked back stage at the Ramona Theater.

Moving Pictures

When it came to rides, Ramona Park was always on the leading edge. Only the best and newest entertainment devices were good enough, and often the park was ahead of others when it came to novel amusements. It was also true for bookings at the theater, only top quality shows for Ramona. One form of entertainment that fit right into this "best and newest" in shows, was moving pictures.

How it All Began

The art of making pictures move goes back to the early 19th century when the illusion of movement was attained by passing similar photos rapidly before the eyes. Children's toys came along, such as the zoetrope, through which the viewer could see action pictures that were rotated in a drum mechanism. Merging the science of still photography and the moving still picture concept occupied inventors for some time. Thomas Edison was one of these. George Eastman's invention of roll film made it possible by 1891 for Edison to devise his Kinetograph camera. A Kinetoscope viewing box was necessary in order to see moving the pictures, and then, only one individual could see the results at a time. However, in 1895 the device for projecting these pictures for viewing by an audience came along through the genius of Auguste and Louis Lumiere.

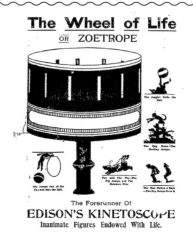

The Wheel of Life
OR ZOETROPE

The Forerunner Of
EDISON'S KINETOSCOPE
Inanimate Figures Endowed With Life.

Just four years after the invention of the projector, in 1899, moving pictures were offered to audiences at the Ramona Theater. During that year, theatergoers saw pictures projected by the bioscope and the kinodrome. They also saw views of the Spanish American War through the "wargraph." Most of the subject matter in these early films was of real life, such as Oom Paul Kruger of Africa, and local views of familiar scenes in Grand Rapids. In July, 1901, people saw, "*an especially attractive feature, as it will present a cyclorama of the Pan-American Exposition. The pictures were taken from the bow of a rapid electric launch, and embraces all the buildings, bridges, tunnels, villages, camps and other features of interest that border the banks of the Grand Canal.*"

Early photo of the inside of the Ramona Theater. The box suspended from the ceiling on the right contained the projector.

In contrast to moving pictures taken from scenes of real life, a revolutionary production by Frenchman George Méliès, played at Ramona in 1900. Cinderella came to Ramona after showing in Chicago vaudeville houses for three months.

In 1903, the year when Ramona changed from just a theater to an amusement park, the name of the movie projection changed to the Ramonagraph. It also had the ability to show still shots from a stereopticon. For the opening of the park in 1906, a separate building housed the motion pictures. It was called the "Motographia," had a facade like a Greek Temple, and was equipped with opera chairs. In 1910, when the Ramona Theater was completely remodeled and expanded, windows were put in the sides and rear, enabling moving pictures to be shown in the afternoons. So the Ramonagraph was moved back to the theater, and the next year the Motographia building was used to house the incubator.

Some of the true-life offerings presented on the Ramonagraph besides weekly news reels from Hearst-Selig and Pathe:

1906 - Olympian Athletic Games at Athens
1906 - The "Pasadena Floral Parade"
1910 - "The Shriners at New Orleans"
1911 - Indianapolis automobile races
1911 - The coronation of King George and
 Queen Mary
1914 - Grand Rapids furniture manufacturers
 in Detroit meeting with Henry Ford
1916 - Arrival of a German submarine
 unloading cargo
1917 - The departure of the Grand Rapids
 Battalion for Grayling
1926 - The Ionia prison and a recent jailbreak

Fiction was brought to Ramona viewers in the likes of:
 - Edward Everett Hale's *"Man Without a Country"*
 - A *"Back to Nature"* movie showing shipwrecked people on the coast of Africa who battle lions, and a lion is actually killed on camera by soldiers.
 - Author O. Henry's short stories, one a week, in 1917.

Ad from 1932

For the year 1932, the theater was turned wholly over to movies. By that time, "talkies" were very big and movies drew greater crowds than live shows. The *GR Press* stated May 28, 1932 for the opening,

"Ramona theater this year will be operated by W. Emmett Goodrich and William U. Murray, who for the last 16 months have successfully managed the Savoy theater downtown. Second run motion pictures will be exhibited at a reduced schedule of admission prices, the policy being to show two features on a bill and change films three times a week. New sound equipment and screen have been installed and the house is now ready for its opening tomorrow. This is the first time feature-length sound pictures have ever been shown in the theater at Ramona. Movies, Girl Crazy and The Greeks Had a Word for Them."

Sundry

The seating capacity of the Ramona Theater made it attractive for other activities for which a large crowd was anticipated. One such event, already mentioned, was the appearance of Mrs. Carrie Nation to expound on the evils of drink. Other speakers came, meetings were held, and ceremonies were conducted in this beautiful location.

Before the first Gerber Baby was chosen, there were contests in Grand Rapids to determine the prettiest babies. The event in 1901 was held in the picnic grove near the Ramona Theater. It was stated in the *GR Press*, ***"Acting on the theory that whatever interests the women, interests everyone, the general Labor Day committee has decided to have a prize baby contest as one of the new features for the Labor Day celebration."*** To be eligible for this baby show entrants had to be the children of a member of some union, and not older than three years. The "prettiest" boy baby and girl baby each received a prize of $5 with the "second best" earning $3. The event attracted 17 infants.

The show was repeated at Reeds Lake the following year, then held at West Michigan Fair, Women's Club House and the Auditorium. For the years 1907 through 1910, the baby contest was held in the Ramona Theater, then reappeared later at other places.

In 1907, ***"The baby show at Ramona proved to be a howling success."*** By contrast to the first such event, three hundred and eighty-nine mothers with babies crowded onto the stage after the regular matinee show, for the judges to begin their work. There were four classes of youngsters by this time. Separate divisions for one, two, and three years old and twins. The first prizes were jewelry or silver cups, second and third place winners received free tickets to concessions in the park for the baby and family.

1907

PICKETS ON GUARD

Great Mass Meeting Is Held In Ramona Pavilion.

Early in the turmoil of the 1911 furniture strike, workers gathered in mass meetings around the city to enroll in the cause, and to hear speeches by the leaders. On April 20, the *GR Press* reports,

"It is probable that the city never before witnessed a mass meeting like that held in Ramona pavilion last night by the furniture workers. The Street Railway company furnished dozens of extra cars and those were packed from early in the evening. They carried a serious and well behaved crowd estimated at more than 4,000 men to the summer resort. The wooden winter covering still was in place and long after the auditorium had been packed to suffocation hundreds of men gathered in the space outside the rear partition. It is estimated 1,000 men were turned away. "

SHIVER AT RAMONA

Twenty-five Hundred Cabinet-makers in Mass Meeting.

Another meeting was held in the Ramona theater on May 3rd, 1911, for the Brotherhood of Carpenters and Joiners. Some 2,500 members participated in the rally, listening to a long program of speeches. This was two weeks after the strike was called. The thrust of the meeting was to instill loyalty in the members to the organization and to the welfare of their wives and children. ***"Hold your position to the end,"*** was the plea of the speakers. By the same token, they were commanded to conduct themselves in the same orderly manner that was exhibited in the first few days.

After the speeches, the Germania Singing Society rendered several selections and a twelve-piece orchestra furnished music.

COMMENCEMENT TO BE HELD AT RAMONA

Five Hundred Eighth Graders In Exercises on June 7.

All the eighth grade students in the Kent County District schools received their diplomas in the same ceremony in 1917. This was the first year for the exercises to be conducted in the Ramona Theater. It was done on a day when *"Michigan's greatest county interscholastic"* meet was held at Ramona Athletic Park. The sports began at 8:30 in the morning so that the eighth graders could be ready for their diplomas at 10:30.

Between 1917 and 1922, there were over 500 pupils taking part each year. During these years, the speakers were college professors, the master of the state grange, and the state superintendent of public instruction.

Twelfth Annual
Eighth Grade Commencement
of the
Public Schools of Kent County
to be held
June 6, 1919, Ramona Theatre Bldg.
Reeds Lake,
Grand Rapids, Michigan

Program

10:15 a. m.

Selection	Rogers' Orchestra
Invocation	Rev. C. W. Merriam
Vocal Selection	Mr. Leon Heyer
Address, "The School and the New Day" Mr. John C. Ketcham, Master State Grange	
Selection	Orchestra
Presentation of Diplomas	A. M. Freeland Commissioner of Schools
"America"	By Class and Audience led by Mr. Leon Heyer
Selection	Orchestra

Class Colors: Light Green and White
Flower: Pink Carnation

Locomotive Boiler Heats the Theater

To assure the opera patrons of a warm, comfortable theatre, the Owen - Ames - Kimball Co. have installed a huge locomotive boiler behind the stage. The ingenuity and community spirit of this well-known Grand Rapids firm got the opera season off to a good start in spite of a cold snap.

In photo are Telman Canfield shoveling coal in the old boiler and R. Dwight Owen of Owen - Ames - Kimball Co.

September, 1943

Ushers

In 1910, the two men responsible for Ramona Park were Benjamin S. Hanchett, president of the railway company, and Louis J. DeLamarter, resort manager. They instigated a program for young boys that would not only benefit the newly remodeled Ramona Theater, but the boys as well. They recognized that these youngsters could be the future leading citizens of the community and were determined to assist in developing some very valuable natural resources. The Ramona Usher Cadets program was thus ushered in.

Based on personal appearance, neatness and politeness, seventeen boys were chosen after personal interviews with Mr. DeLamarter himself. Written consent of the parents was the next step, and then the boys were turned over to Sam DeLong to whip the little band into shape. *"It was the desire to obtain an efficient, well disciplined and mannerly corps of ushers which would be a credit to the new theater and to the attractive white uniforms which at the outset won the hearts of the youngsters."*

Mr. DeLong knew how to achieve order. He was national organizer of Modern Woodmen of America Foresters and led their Grand Rapids drill team. The boys were put on a strict regimen that included constant practice in taking persons to their seats, assembling in military formation, inspections, and even physical exercise as written in the U. S. Army manual. Besides the daily routines, the boys went to Roses Beach three times a week to receive swimming instruction. Also they were treated to drinks at the new soda fountain.

"Patrons of Ramona theater this summer, in the event of an early arrival at the playhouse, must have seen a small band of soldierly looking lads clothes in natty white uniforms marching with the utmost precision to the front entrance and disappearing inside the theater." Each boy was responsible for the care of his own uniform and the one who kept it and his locker in the best condition received a prize.

Usherettes

At the opening of the Ramona Theater in May, 1917, the newspaper announced that girls would be employed as ushers. *"Ramona was the first theater in the city and one of the first in the country to have girl ushers, trying the experiment at a matinee years ago. This year they were dressed in white middy suits with green ties. The reason for the change at this time? The scarcity of boys due to patriotic work caused a return to the old plan."* By September that year, the downtown Grand Rapids theaters were also using girls to usher, and probably for the same reason.

In other parts of the country, Chicago had been using girl ushers for several years before 1914, when an ordinance was drawn up to outlaw the practice – by the Municipal Bureau of Fire Prevention. It stated that, *"Girl ushers are not equal to men in times of emergency such as fires and panic."* However, in February, 1915, the city council voted down the bill countering the charge with, *"Who ever heard of any particular act of heroism on the part of an usher of the masculine sort in time of fire? And who has not heard of the bravery of telephone girls and stenographers in time of calamity?"*

THERE ARE NO BETTER

"There are no better usherettes in the land than those pictured here, who hold forth at the Ramona Theater. And there are no better dressed than this group of girls, who are perfection in everything that pertains to ushering."

Anti-Theater Hat Ordinance

According to the *GR Press*, January 22, 1897, *"Alderman Frank Wurzburg of the Ninth ward is destined to acquire fame at one bound. He wants the council to pass a hat ordinance, forbidding the wearing of high hats by the ladies in the theaters, and he asks the city attorney to prepare a bill to that effect for presentation to the council."* Action was deferred while waiting for sample copies of high hat ordinances to arrive from New York and Chicago. When asked what limit should be put on the size of the hat, Alderman Wurzburg answered, *"They say that there is no harm at all in those cute little opera bonnets, but I would like to bar out those three and four story affairs which shut out all possible view of the stage from behind. There are a few ladies who attend the theaters here who insist upon wearing head gear which resembles hay stacks."*

At the next meeting, January 26, Alderman Wurzburg introduced his resolution to the council and it was met with hearty laughs by men who also uncorked some jokes. However the resolution instructing the committee to prepare the ordinance was adopted unanimously. On February 9, the issue came to a head. The councilmen made sport by proposing amendments having to do with everything from bald pates being covered with skull caps, to forbidding men leaving during a performance to obtain a drink. A vote was taken and the measure was defeated 8 to 7. It was the misfortune of Alderman Wurzburg to have missed that meeting for his vote would have caused a tie that would have been broken by Mayor Stow, who was in favor.

One Relief From the Theater Hat.

—Chicago Tribune.

TPA Delegates to Tour Grand Rapids

Grand Rapids, at the time the seventh largest post of the Travelers Protective Association of America, was the location for the 51st annual national convention. The organization was begun in 1882 and is still functioning to provide a *"blend of benefits for its members, their families and for the community."*

The convention, held June 15 to 19, 1941, had over 600 attendees. On the third day, after a short business session, the crowd went on a sightseeing trip culminating at Ramona Park for a picnic followed by entertainment and dancing in the theater.

A departure from the normal use of the Ramona Theater, the TPA picnic, held on the big round porch .

Promoting Ramona

Local newspapers advertised Ramona Park in every way from small articles or ads to two full-page spreads. They let people know when the park was to open, the latest theater productions, special events and anything else of interest. For many years, Ramona Park was big news.

Some of the ads for the Ramona Theater, seen through the years

Above opening announcement,
the GR Herald from 1903

Above right, GR Herald,
double page from 1919.

Below, even in a real estate ad in 1913

BARGAIN—East Grand Rapids. For sale, seven-room house with lot 47x150 feet, one block from street car and Ramona Park. Fine view. Price $2,200. Citz. 34017.

The Ramona Theater

A place that brought so much joy to so many people for so many years.

POINT PAULO

"*Reeds Lake has a big reputation among the vaudeville players of the country. I heard of it months ago when I was away out in Frisco. That shows how its fame has spread.*" The words of Mr. Frederick J. Mongeon, known to the world of vaudeville as Monsieur Fred Paulo, indicate how far-reaching was the reputation of the setting of the Ramona Theater. He came to the theater to perform while on the Orpheum circuit, just one more stop out of many for the 1907 season. Ah, but this was a stop that changed his life. Fred Paulo felt the tug of the charms of Reeds Lake more strongly than the lure of the grease paint.

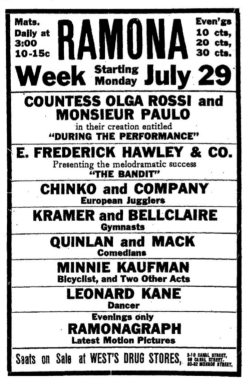

Top left, showbill
July 27, 1907

Above, Mons.
Fred Paulo,
performing

Left, location of
Point Paulo

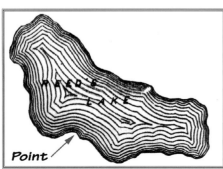

The French opera singer, Fred Paulo, envisioned a resort on Reeds lake that included a hotel featuring French cooking. He had previously run such an establishment in St. Louis. During the week of his engagement at Ramona in 1907, he began the search for property in East Grand Rapids suitable for a resort that would cater to traveling vaudevillians. He was looking for a good investment at the time, unaware of how this decision would later develop.

Fred Paulo continued to perform with the Countess Rossi, finishing out the year 1907 and into 1908 and 1909. Mons. Paulo was the booking agent for several acts including the Bellclaire Brothers who were Maurice Bellclaire, nee Uttal, and Sam Kramer. During this time, back in East Grand Rapids, the wheels of his business venture were turning.

Despite delays and legal difficulties, Mons. Paulo became the owner of 20 acres of property on the south side of Reeds Lake which encompassed the area jutting out to form a point. This choice piece of land was once the original "Miller's Landing," the place where the resort business on Reeds Lake began in the late 1860s. The old farm house was included in the purchase along with upwards of 2,000 feet of lake frontage. In 1909, cottages were built on that shore and offered for rent by M. Paulo. His property became known as "Paulo Point" or "Point Paulo."

The French hotel was a dream, the reality was a little different. Instead of building the hotel, M. Paulo erected cottages on the lake front for expediency in getting the business going. This venture was immediately successful not just for actors but local people also eagerly rented these cottages. And not just performers who were engaged at the theater but those who had at one time seen the lake and wanted to vacation there.

Early 1909 advertisement to rent out the whole farm.

The only two-story cottage. It was named "The Majestic."

By April, 1019, things changed considerably for Fred Paulo. He declared that he was giving up the stage and devoting his time to his resort on Reeds Lake. He was recorded as saying to the *GR Press* reporter,

"Reeds lake is one of the most beautiful spots I know. I am ready to settle down here and stay. I have run back here every chance I got all winter, and now I propose to stay here right along as soon as I get rid of existing vaudeville contracts. I shall continue to manage the act of Bellclaire and Herman, which has been under my direction for years, but I am ready to leave the stage myself to enjoy life at Reeds lake."

By the end of 1910, there were thirteen cottages. People were not only staying in the cabins, but there was also an area for tenting. The cottages were rented furnished or unfurnished from $100 to $125 for the season. Tenting privileges with fifty feet of lake front were $8 per month. A July story in the *GR Press* stated:

"The cottages are not large but plenty large enough. On each, a broad covered veranda faces the lake. There is another porch at the rear of each, which is usually used for a kitchen and dining room. Then there is a living room next to the front veranda and two bedrooms. All the cottages are lighted by electricity and all modern conveniences are offered. The low land just at the foot of the hill has been thoroughly drained so that the walk and drive back of the cottages is always dry. There is a dock for boats and swimming accommodations galore and the cottagers all seem thoroughly pleased with their summer homes. "

View of some of the shore-line cottages, looking west to east.

Fred Paulo's dream of serving French dinners did become a reality. The renovated Miller farmhouse was initially the venue for serving gourmet meals prepared by Paulo himself, a recognized French chef in his own right. The well-to-do of the city soon discovered the luxury of dining at Point Paulo, the richness of the cuisine was catered to the preference of the guest. This house could also accommodate guests who preferred this style of boarding to the more primitive cottage.

But, that was only a temporary arrangement, for in the mind of M. Paulo, the original vision was still vivid. Hence, Chateau Paulo was born in 1912. Perched at the top of the bluff, overlooking the shoreline cottages and the scenery of Reeds Lake, this building was ready for occupancy by the Fourth of July. In order for this to happen, as the construction was only just begun in April, M. Paulo employed large gangs of carpenters, bricklayers, electricians, plumbers, steamfitters and other artisans instead of the normally small squads.

"The chateau is to be my home and I did not intend to have lodgers there, but I have two rooms for that purpose upstairs, upon which I have fixed a price of $20 a week each. Already one of them has been rented to a man and his wife who are coming all the way from St. Louis to occupy it, while I have had inquiries for the other."

The *GR Press* described the new building thus:

The Chateau
1912

"The most impressive feature of the lower floor is the large dining room on the lake side. This is really an inclosed porch. It projects out from the top of the bank in such a way that it is up among the branches of the trees that grow on the side of the steep hill. Through these branches are gained charming views of the lake. The dining room will, it is expected, accommodate seventy-five guests. There M. Paulo will serve his French dinners. The remainder of the lower floor will be given over to reception rooms, parlors, the private suites of M. Paulo and Manager Bellclaire, and the kitchen."

The newly completed "Chateau Paulo" as viewed from the south (top left), from the bottom of the hill showing the pump house (above), and from the lake (left). The cottages named, "Oxford," "Palace" and "Alcazar" are visible. Other names were "Alhambra," "Olympic," "Casino," and "Hippodrome," all famous vaudeville theaters.

86

View of the dining room where dinners were served to as many as seventy five guests at once. The windows were on three sides of the room, all with a view of the lake.

Monsieur Fred Paulo is on the left, Maurice Bellclaire on the right.

Another addition in 1912 was a "Venetian" dock, extending far out into the lake with an 11 X 22 area on the end, covered by a pagoda roof. It was possible for the steamers to pick up and drop off passengers here on their circuits around the lake. As shown in the photo to the right, this dock could accommodate many people at once.

Below, Mr. Bellclaire stands on the dock with a young guest.

Not yet finished with his resort reverie, Paulo built another structure to accommodate guests. The Chalet, or Annex, was ready for occupancy in July, 1915. Not exactly the hotel he envisioned in the beginning, but the Chalet provided even more space for his huge following of vacationers. Referred to as an annex to the Chateau, this building also stood on top of the bluff, but not attached to the Chateau. There were twenty rooms, arranged so that every one had a view of the lake with two or more windows.

Imagine staying in a cottage at Point Paulo where vaudeville stars were coming in at all hours to spend the night after the show. What a lively time it must have been for the "regular" Grand Rapids folk who rented cottages in the midst of this activity. This quote from the *GR Press* in July, 1914 gives an interesting description:

"Every afternoon between 4:30 and 5 o'clock, a water circus, in which some of the best known athletes, acrobats, and gymnasts in the US take part, is staged at Point Paulo on Reeds Lake. George Welch, the eccentric dancer, tries out some of his best steps on the edge of the dock and ends with an amusing fall into the lake. The three Hickey brothers, acrobats, form pyramids with the Abdallahs and the Manchurians, for good fellowship reigns at Point Paulo and the various vaudeville teams mingle in perfect harmony. The whole performance is one the like of which is seldom seen outside of a three-ring circus and even there the water for diving is lacking.

"Billy Abdallah is a specialist in back double somersault dives. He also does a half-pirouette occasionally. Paul Motzeit of the Abdallah team finds his greatest fun in taking a full twister from the roof of the dock house and Patsy Judge, another of the Abdallahs, is an expert at the one and one-half turn forward dive. Another who has particular tricks with which he tries to outdo the others is Maurice Bellclaire, Fred Paulo's assistant."

The top and right photos show the activity described in the paragraphs above.

In the upper view, M. Bellclaire is the gentleman left of center, supporting the "human arch."

In the lower view, M. Paulo is the mustachioed gentleman. Note the pavilion at Manhattan Beach visible on the opposite shore.

Another part of Fred Paulo's dream was to have a farm. This was realized on the same property, which, after all, was a farm long before. He then populated it with all manner of members of the animal world. Occasionally one of the performers, with fond memories of growing up on a farm, would ask to milk the cows, "*for old time's sake.*"

According to a 1911 GR Press interview, *"A census of the livestock taken a few days ago showed the following non-human population of the farm: 150 hens and roosters, 350 chicks, 25 geese, 100 goslings, 15 guinea hens, 6 cows, 6 pigs, 8 white Holland turkeys, 1 American turkey, 1 baby turkey, 175 pigeons of all sorts, 10 Japanese spaniels and 2 King Charles spaniels."*

Paulo and Bellclaire also raised the high-priced and highly prized spaniels to be sold to the "right customers."

HE WRITES PLAYS

Mason Hopper Is a Living Moving Picture Drama Factory.

NOW AT REEDS LAKE

E. Mason Hopper came to Ramona Theater on the vaudeville circuit to perform his newspaper cartooning stunt on stage in 1910. The next year he returned, not to the theater, but to Point Paulo, as a retreat where he could do some writing. About his prior experience at Ramona Theater he said,

"I fell in love with it when I came here to fill my date at Ramona. I stayed over and spent my vacation here then as a guest at Point Paulo. This year when my work took such a turn that I was able to do it where I wanted to, I packed up my pencils and hustled to Reeds Lake. I am going to stay here as long as I can, for a month, anyway."

Not only did the serenity and beauty of the lake draw him back, but he was also an avid fisherman and hunter. At Point Paulo he had it all. So much so that in 1912, he purchased one of the newly platted lots in the resort, on which the Blackstone cottage was nestled. Hopper had a stenographer who went wherever he went, pencil and pad in hand, to take down his inspirations as they hit – under a tree, in a boat, on a walk, wherever. These inspirations were exceedingly well received by the fledgling motion picture industry, and E. Mason Hopper was on his way. His writing was limited to short, comedic scenarios, but his real fame was as a movie director. He directed over 70 silent films before 1935. In those early days at Point Paulo, he also did some filming.

1911 cartoon from the *GR News*, depicting the movie activity of E. Mason Hopper at Point Paulo.

Besides the cottages, the Chateau and the Chalet, Fred Paulo also had a garage built on the property to house *"the machines"* of the guests. It was large enough to accommodate a dozen or so vehicles. But, it was really put to the test when it was temporarily converted to a wild animal cage! The lions of Richard Havemann, which had performed at Ramona in the summer of 1915, and were kept in their own cages for viewing when not on stage, became guests of Point Paulo in the fall that year. *"Seven lusty lions, three beautiful tigers and a bunch of leopards"* visited when the trainer and owner, Havemann, returned in the Fall to enjoy the lake until cold weather set in.

Havemann's Raubtierschule.

89

Artist's conception of the Point Paulo summer resort, drawn during its heyday.
Mr. Bellclaire recalled that they had a total of 45 cottages on those 20 acres,
some of which were rented, some sold. Note on the right side of the picture,
the many-windowed Chalet, or Point Paulo Hotel.

Maurice Bellclaire, business manager for Point Paulo, lived until 1973, far outlasting his illustrious counterpart, Fred Paulo, who died in 1937. He stayed alone in the big house until 1948 when it was sold. That year, a house was built right next door for Mr. Bellclaire where he lived out his life.

Things quieted down before the death of his associate, however. In the 1920s, prohibition made a significant reduction in business, enough so that the resort was simply closed down. The men turned then to their building and real estate development business.

Pleasant memories of the Point Paulo days were told to a reporter in 1948 during an interview with Mr. Bellclaire. He recalled the likes of Will Rogers, Fannie Brice, Evelyn Nesbit, Eddie Cantor, Al Jolson, Olsen and Johnson and Chic Sale, for example, that stayed at the resort. Not all of these performed at Ramona, but they chose to stay at the Reeds Lake resort instead of a downtown hotel near the other theaters. Walter Winchell and Georgie Jessel were two others who visited Point Paulo when they performed as

children with Gus Edwards. Many stories have been told of the stars that stayed there, but these are the ones verified by Maurice Bellclaire himself. Someone who encountered Mr. Bellclaire in later years, recalled seeing him, out in the back yard burning old theater posters because he had no use for them. Oh, the history that was turned to ashes that day!

In Mr. Bellclaire's own words, *"We did a tremendous business and we had great times in those days. Many an act was gotten together, numerous dialogues written and considerable songs composed right here,"* Bellclaire recounted. *"Sometimes they would rehearse on the grounds, or perhaps the rooms would be filled with the music of those gathered around the piano."* Sometimes people who made reservations for dinner at the Chateau were treated to entertainment by the stars who happened to be staying in the cottages. Now and then, Mons. Paulo himself would break into an operatic aria for the enjoyment of all.

Thus, Point Paulo has earned an important spot in the history of the Ramona Theater.

Shall We Dance?

Dancing with the stars, in the early days of Reeds Lake resorts, meant dancing under the starry sky, or dancing until the stars disappeared. People were happy to wile away the hours pursuing terpsichorean delights. Back then, all it took was a fiddle with possibly another musical instrument, and a surface suitable to be trod by rapidly moving feet. In the later years, "dancing with the stars" meant with the best bands in the nation providing the music.

In the early days, people went out to the lake for the boating and picnicking, but also for dancing. Most of those early resorts had pavilions that were fitted out for dances. Sometimes dancing was done outdoors on the lawn. Mr. Hobart Miller even held dances in his home. At the height of the summer season he often entertained as many as 20 to 30 couples.

In 1875, shortly after the street railway had made its way to Reeds Lake, the Sons of Industry held a picnic attended by over 1000 people, and dancing at Judd's Grove until nearly daylight was the way they ended the festivities. Various public conveyances ran all night long to take people back to the city. On another occasion, one announcement of a 'social dancing party' at Brown's landing stated that *"cars on the street railway will leave the lake at 12 o'clock or sooner if the ball breaks up."*

Not only did people dance on lawns and in pavilions but also on the water. Crook's Barge was built for the purpose of holding dances out on the lake. Later, the steamers *Major Watson*, *Hazel A.* and *Ramona* also 'cleared the decks' for evening dancing as the lighted vessels cruised under the stars.

Over the years, visitors to the lake danced wherever the music beckoned. Some of the resorts around in the late 1800s and early 1900s that had provisions for dancing, were The Lake View House, Alger Park, Leland Park, Schoenfeldt's Grove, Ross' Pavilion, the boat clubs, and even Manhattan Beach.

The railroad pavilion which was built in 1882 and its 1893 replacement were used for dances as well as picnics and for the occasional theater performance, but in the grand Ramona Theater built in 1897, dancing was only done by performers on the stage. In 1912, the construction of a huge building strictly for dancing brought sophistication and much attention to Ramona Park. The opening of the Ramona Dance Academy right in Ramona Park was an event that changed the dance scene at Reeds Lake.

HUGE DANCING HALL BUILT AT RAMONA

New Academy Has Larger Floor Than Saugatuck's Big Pavilion.

As was typical of the way this resort was managed, only the best was good enough for the new building. The dance pavilion at Saugatuck, constructed in 1909, was built to out-do the one that was in use in South Haven since 1904, and the new Ramona dance hall had to be better yet. The building was approximately 100 x 200 with a dance floor 60 x 80, and was billed as *"the largest dancing floor in Michigan."* It was said to accommodate 400 couples dancing at the same time.

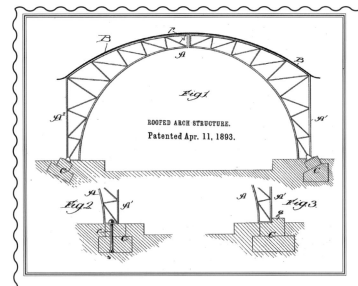

The construction of the Ramona building was essentially the same as for the pavilion in Saugatuck, with the steel arch vaulted roof. It was the most distinguishing feature of this building, and made it immediately recognizable wherever it appeared in photographs taken at the park. The type of construction was relatively new having been patented in 1893. The Ramona Dance Academy roof was composed of 9 great steel arches rising up thirty-six feet from the floor. They were hinged and bolted together in four sections for easy assembly. Thus, there was no need for supporting pillars which would interfere with activities inside. People might describe this building as a "Quonset hut," but for one difficulty. In 1912, the building style hadn't been invented yet – it was used during the first world war.

From the US Patent Office, patent number 495,222, included three possible methods of anchoring the sides.

When a picture of the structure appeared in the newspaper, the caption was, "New Dancing Building at Ramona is a Whale."

The arches were not only used for roof support, but for striking lighting effects. Originally the arches were studded with more than 500 electric lamps which contained forty-watt tungsten bulbs. Between the rows of white bulbs were alternating pink and green, and combinations of colors could be cut out or left on. These lights had theatrical dimmers making possible a variety of lighting effects from moonlight dim to blazing glory.

The dance floor was a marvel as well. A company from Chicago put the finish on the maple wood using four grades of sanding paper and automobile sanding machines. Afterward it was smoothed with felt and wax. In 1955, when the building was taken down, the *GR Press* interviewed Mr. John Knecht, a retired motor coach executive who had helped supervise the construction of this building. In his words, ***"The dance floor was built on furring strips over a sub floor, which gave it an unusual springiness and resiliency that was popular with dancers. Two inches of seaweed was packed between the floors as a water barrier."***

There was no foundation under this building, but the condition of the floor was still good enough to be reused after the building was moved in 1955.

Left, detail of the roofing boards and lights on the steel arches.

Dancing Pavilion, Reed's Lake, Grand Rapids, Mich.

P-67237

The Ramona Dancing Academy officially opened
June 13, 1912.

As was in keeping with the philosophy of the railroad to maintain a resort that was free from the vulgar element and safe for families, the new dance hall was advertised as a high class establishment. On June 11, 1912, prior to its opening, the *GR Press* announced,

"Ramona Dancing academy will be conducted along the highest club lines. All the standard dances will be used, but a strict ban will be placed on freak dances of the turkey trot and grizzly bear order. These will not be tolerated. Assisting in the management will be a corps of uniformed attendants. The uniforms will be of white."

Resort manager Louis J. DeLamarter also declared that even though Sunday could be a huge day for receipts, under no circumstances was there to be any dancing on Sundays, and the place would be closed up tight. For the gentlemen, coats and ties were required attire.

The new facility, stated to be without a competitor in the Grand Rapids area, was immediately a grand success. Since the policy of catering only to legitimate amusement seekers, barring objectionable persons and behavior, it was a venue where children could go as well. Just two weeks after its opening, the Ramona dance hall inaugurated Saturday afternoon dancing for children.

Tonight is Instruction Night at Ramona Dancing Casino

LEARN THE NEW DANCES.   ADMISSION 25c

This includes instruction and entire evening of dancing.

While the title "Academy" was part of the name for the first few years of its existence, the Ramona dance hall was not primarily an institution of instruction. The managers in the early years were members of the Frank Harris Peake family from Chicago who were popular in that town for their instruction and management talents. In 1915, instruction was offered *"in the simple forms of the new dances."* In that year, music was provided to accommodate modern dance steps, but the public seemed to demand the waltz and two-step rather than the tango and hesitation. However, the tango devotee was invited to indulge at special times. In 1926, Phil Osterhouse was named floor manager and offered, *"Free Instruction in Fancy Dance Steps by Expert Dancing Master."*

93

In 1925, the opening of the Ramona dance pavilion was a "Mardi Gras Night" event. At this time, the hall was still being referred to as a "casino."

Ramona Gardens

Originally, the pavilion was called the Ramona Dance Academy, becoming the Ramona Dance Pavilion, then Ramona Dancing Casino. The latter term had no relationship to a gambling establishment, which the name might have implied. Shortly after the building was opened for the 1925 season, the announcement (right) was made to change the name to Ramona Gardens. It was known as Ramona Gardens up until the time the building was removed from the park grounds in 1955.

A complete change of policy is in force at both the Ramona theater and Ramona gardens, formerly known as the Casino, for the summer season. L. J. DeLamarter has resumed personal supervision of the entertainment to be offered at the theater, in which he will be assisted by Danny Boon, who also will have complete charge of the dancing arrangements in the gardens.

Elaborate rearrangement of the interior of the dancing pavilion, coupled with installation of thousands of dollars worth of decorations, has changed the appearance from that of a hall to a garden.

GR. Press, June 27, 1925

Postcard showing the outside decor.

This postcard shows the front entrance around 1937. Notice the sign telling that beer is sold within.

In 1934, the interior of the pavilion was again renovated, this time with novel lighting and decorative effects. The theme was "Old World," and booths were constructed around the dance floor representing different nations. Each booth was covered with a colorful canopy. The north side booths were fitted up with tables and chairs for dancers seeking refreshment. On the opposite side were benches for dancers to perch upon to rest. The seating could accommodate nearly 300 people. Special lighting effects were installed for the floor and booths.

The caption of the picture, right, from the *GR Press*, read,

"Like a trip to the old world is a visit to the newly-decorated Ramona Gardens. Under the artistic eye of Louis J. DeLamarter, the place has been transformed into a beautifully quaint recreational center, where good food may be enjoyed and cooling drinks quaffed in an environment designed especially to please the fancy of all nationalities."

Glimpse of Beautiful Ramona Gardens

There were six entrances to the building, two each on the north, east and south sides with a total of nine ticket offices. It was a good thing because not only was there an admission charge, but originally patrons paid for each dance as well. This policy lasted until Alex Demar stepped in as manager in 1935 and instituted the single-ticket admission plan.

Left, main entrance
as it looked in 1936.

Below, highly decorated
arches for a special event
in 1937.

The Dances

This piece about the Old Residents' Picnic from the "GR Eagle" June, 1882, mentions some of the old time enthusiasm for dancing. The name of the dance, "pigeon wing," begs to be described. For the most part, the dance step imitated birds doing their courting rituals. The dancer strutted like a bird, scraping the feet and flapping the bent arms like wings. It has also been described as a bird trying to fly. Variations even employed slapping the back of the calf of one leg with the opposite foot. Originally it was just shaking one leg in the air. The Can-Can dance was an aberration of this move. It tickles the mind to imagine a sophisticated and respected elder in a group cutting a "pigeon wing."

Dancing? Of course. How can the "Old Residents" have a reunion and stir up the remembrance of the pleasures of the early days without awakening the desire to "double-shuffle," go "down the outside," or "right and left?" No use. The muscles brace up and the nerves quiver again. When somebody touched a measure of "Old Zip Coon" on that fiddle, a white-haired pioneer of three-score and ten and upward sprang upon his toes, cut a pigeon-wing and broke out with "Hoorah! where's my girl? I must dance!" Coffinberry with his clarionet and Porter with his fiddle.

Over the years, dance music changed and the style of dancing changed. In the example above, there was simply a "clarionet" and a fiddle to accompany the dancers. After the Ramona dance hall opened, bands and orchestras were hired to entertain the crowds and provide music for dancing.

Through the late teens, the twenties and thirties, music was swift, syncopated, and innovative, so the style of dance changed from the favorite waltz, two-step and foxtrot of the earlier years.

Latest Dance Crazes
"*Teens*" - cakewalk, tanglefoot, shimmie, toddle

"*Twenties*" - stumbling, charleston, black bottom, stomps, varsity drag

"*Thirties*" - hot cha, boop-a-doop, tango (suave rhythm), continental, truckin', big apple, Lambeth Walk

How to Dance the Tango Fox Trot Like Valentino

You Can Learn Fascinating New Steps by Following These Complete and Simple Directions.

By ARTHUR MURRAY
Director of the National Institute of Social Dancing

Ballroom dancing lessons were one way to learn the latest dances. These tango-fox trot instructions came from the *GR Herald* in 1923.

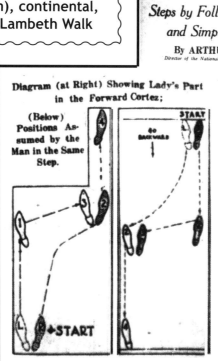

Diagram (at Right) Showing Lady's Part in the Forward Cortez;

(Below) Positions Assumed by the Man in the Same Step.

Dance Music

When Ramona Park is mentioned in publications, famous people who played the theater are always listed with great pride. Ramona Gardens had its share of illustrious performers who came for one-night stands, working this small-town venue into their busy schedules. When the dance academy first opened, the music was furnished by local groups engaged for the whole season.

The band or orchestra performed on a very large stage occupying the western end of the building and surrounded by a shell. At either side of the orchestra stage were "retiring rooms" for men and women. In 1934, the orchestra shell was given a new background, a scene from Old Heidelberg. Large mirrors flanked the stage.

The management of the academy, for the first 13 years, was Mr. and Mrs. Frank Harris Peake, who previously had thirty years of experience in dance instruction in Chicago, and their son Chandler. In 1925, Danny Boon assumed charge of the dancing arrangements. Then Philip Osterhouse stepped in for a couple of years and returned in 1934. The years in between were filled once again by Danny Boon. Then in 1935, Mr. Alex Demar assumed management of Ramona Gardens and he went all out in securing nationally known orchestras and dance bands. Toward the end of 1941, the building was thrown over to roller skating, and only occasionally did a band come to play for a dance after that.

This section contains some of the better-known musicians who appeared at Ramona, along with the information about them that was printed in the local newspapers.

Local Band Leaders Who Made it Big

Jack Crawford

Pictured at Ramona Gardens, Theodore Pease, Jack Crawford and Russell R. Cook

There were some local fellows who made it into the big leagues of dance music during the golden era of swing and jazz and big bands. **Jack Foster Crawford** attended the Chicago Conservatory of music and then formed his own band by 1920. He earned the nickname of *"The Clown Prince of Jazz"* from his own performances that included singing, comic storytelling and costumes. He weighed nearly 300 pounds and dubbed himself

"America's overstuffed orchestra leader." His music was described as snappy, and *"lilting comedy syncopation."* He became a favorite in the Midwest by the mid-1930s, and toured coast to coast. He played the Gardens when he was just a local orchestra in the early 1920s, and after he became very famous, in 1938 and 1939. In 1942, after losing several musicians to the war, he formed a four-piece cocktail lounge group.

Frank Winegar

Ramona Gardens

Frank Winegar was born in Grand Rapids and at age 16, formed his first band with Jack Crawford. He enrolled in the University of Pennsylvania majoring in architecture. There he organized a band which in 1923 won a contest that sent the group to Europe. He appeared at Ramona Gardens with his band, The Pennsylvanians, in 1925 for a four week engagement. In 1927 he was doing recordings for the Victor label. He did actually practice architecture in Grand Rapids, but kept going back to his music which included writing songs. When he was leading a large orchestra in New York, it featured Judy Canova and a young Charlie Barnet.

By the time Frank Winegar appeared at the Gardens in 1937, his lead singer received the attention in the *GR Press*:

"Betty Jane Blair, song stylist with Frank Winegar's orchestra, playing at Ramona Gardens Saturday and next Thursday evening, started her singing while in high school. Her first professional engagement was with Henry Biagini's orchestra and later she was featured with Morrey Brennan's orchestra at the Greystone Ballroom, Detroit.

"She visited Grand Rapids, singing with Ted Weems' orchestra as guest star, and Winegar signed her for his band. With Betty Jane as vocalist and Lew Douglas' popular arrangements, Winegar's orchestra ranks as one of the best of Michigan's dance bands. Billed as the orchestra that features 'Music That Charms.'"

Betty Jean Blair eventually went to Hollywood and changed her name to **Betty Hutton**.

BETTY JANE BLAIR.

Lew Douglas

Lew Douglas played at Ramona in 1935 and again 1938. In 1935, his band was engaged for the whole season with other guest orchestras added from time to time. Stated in *GR Press* in 1938,

"Lew Douglas and his orchestra are well-known through the state, as well as by local dancers who have enjoyed the Douglas brand of entertainment for more than seven years in Grand Rapids. Douglas, a Grand Rapids man, is known for his unusual arrangements of popular songs for his own 10-piece orchestra and other famous bands such as Ted Weems. When Weems played his engagement at the Gardens, he contracted with Douglas for several new arrangements."

Some of the singers who recorded with Lew Douglas were Joni James, Cathy Carr, Valjean Johns performing the "Theme from Ben Casey," and The Four Jacks .

"All-Girl" Bands

Cleo Balcom

When **Cleo Balcom** and her "Eleven Musical Aces" came to Ramona Gardens in 1931, the introduction in the *GR Herald* said,

"The city is now host to a real girl dance band that is proving girls can provide good dance tunes. When this band arrived at the park a week ago, there were some misgivings among the hundreds who dance there each night. Many of them felt that a girl band might be OK for a stage attraction, but that when it came to pumping a big pavilion full of music, it was a man's job. The band was proved unusually popular and is remaining over for another week. The band plays fine dance music and has plenty of volume with which to fill the big hall."

Agnes Ayres

When **Agnes Ayres** played at Ramona in 1935, it was during a short span of time when she was touring with dance bands instead of acting. One year later she was back in Hollywood, unable to withstand the demands of one-night stands.

Her greatest fame was not because of her music, but her acting. She was known for her role playing Lady Diana Mayo opposite Rudolph Valentino in *"The Sheik"* and *"The Son of the Sheik."* That was the height of her career and going on the vaudeville circuit afterward was just a way of earning money.

View of the orchestra stage at Ramona Gardens in 1938.
Pictured is Constance Duin's "All Girl Band," billed as,
"8 Beauteous Darlings Playing and Singing"

Colored Bands

McKinney's Cotton Pickers

McKinney's Cotton Pickers *"One of the finest Negro dance bands in the United States, comes to Ramona Gardens tomorrow evening for one engagement. This band is widely known to radio listeners and is now working its way back to New York from an engagement in Hollywood."* This was the announcement in the *GR Herald* 'heralding' the arrival of the famous band in 1931.

This jazz band was founded in Detroit in 1926 by drummer William McKinney, and was transformed into a full-fledged big band by Don Redman. They disbanded in 1934 due to the depression.

Cab Calloway

The renowned **Cab Calloway**, master of energetic scat singing, brought his famous ensemble to The Gardens in 1933 to provide the best in dance music for visitors. The story in the *GR Herald* about this great man included these words,

"Cab 'Cabell' Calloway, whose given name was shortened to 'Cab' by his schoolmates in Baltimore, where he was graduated from Douglass high school in 1927, studied law for two semesters at the Crane college in Chicago, but deserted the course when he discovered that it was interfering with his work as entertainer in clubs and theaters.

"Today Cab, who will be featured with his famous orchestra at Ramona Gardens has no regrets about his interrupted higher education. His income for one week from his distinctive music and inimitable style of singing is far in excess of the sum he might expect annually as a struggling young lawyer.

"'I just followed the career which interested me most and did the things for which I seemed to have the most talent, as well as inclination,' he says. 'I don't regret the time I spent in school and college, because an education is a valuable asset in any field of work. But I'm not fretting about the law course that I didn't complete either.'

"Cab is at the height of his fame and it is possible that Ramona Gardens has never seen a crowd as large as it is destined to have tonight. It is to be a gala event that no one will want to miss."

Duke Ellington

When **Duke Ellington** performed at Ramona in 1931, the *GR Herald* has this to say:

"Duke Ellington and his famous orchestra, whose playing at the Cotton Club in Harlem, won him the title of 'The Hottest Band on Earth,' will be featured at Ramona gardens on Tuesday, Sept. 1. They are presented to Grand Rapids' dancers by the West Michigan Charter of Hotel Greeters.

"Duke and his boys have an instinctive feeling for Jazz rhythms and broken time and they have the reputation of doing the most inconceivable things to the most trivial of melodies. They can play 'sweet' and discreet jazz in the manner of Mr. Whiteman; then turn about and twist their music into weird and primitive strains, with the barbaric rhythm of the jungle. The distinctive Ellington brand of music is familiar to almost every radio owner. His unique arrangements have created a definite new style in dance melody, and his musicians are masters of syncopation and hot jazz. A brief review of Mr. Ellington's sensational rise from an obscure Harlem cafe to his present role of the 'colored king of rhythm,' lists engagements in the foremost night clubs, cafes, theaters, and ballrooms in the country."

Jimmy Raschel

The fourteen piece band of **Jimmy Raschel Sr.**, with Lazy Bones Bacon, performed at Ramona in 1935. The article in the *GR Press* stated,

"Ramona Gardens, the spacious dance pavilion which was elaborately redecorated and remodeled last season, will open for the summer season under the management of Alex Demar. A preliminary gala opening will be held Saturday, May 18, when Jimmy Raschel's Negro band of 14 pieces, featuring Lazy Bones Bacon, will provide the dance music."

Jimmy Raschel Jr. followed in his father's footsteps. Growing up in the town of Niles, Michigan, Jimmy Raschel Jr. was influenced by great musicians that existed in his father's world. As a fairly famous big band leader, the senior Raschel associated with Count Basie, and Dinah Washington among others.

Groups of National Renown

Emil Velazco

Emil Velazco came to Ramona Gardens in 1935 bringing his famous musical instrument. The *GR Press* tells about this group,

"One of the novelties in the way of dance music is Emil Velazco and his portable pipe organ, which is the center of his dance orchestra organization. This unusual orchestra will come to Ramona Gardens Monday night to play a program of dance music. The orchestra at present is playing at the Graystone ballroom in Detroit, one of the most popular dance places in that city.

"Starting as organist in a Chicago theater 17 years ago, Velazco made his first big success in Buffalo, where his salary jumped to $400 a week. Later he taught organ in New York. He plays the only portable pipe organ of its kind in a dance orchestra."

Ted Weems

Sometimes people who were members of famous dance bands and orchestras became more famous than the band. Some might suggest this was the case with **Ted Weems**. Among big band aficionados Weems was a big name, but the fame of his singer Perry Como was legendary. The article from the *GR Herald* in 1938 describes the contribution of this band leader.

"The 'master of novelty tunes,' Ted Weems, direct from a successful engagement at the Trianon ballroom in Chicago and station WGN, brings his orchestra to Ramona Gardens next Thursday evening for an open and informal dance program. Included in his orchestra of 14 outstanding musicians are many featured entertainers such as Perry Como.

"Weems was the first maestro to introduce whistling to dancing America, the dance music innovation that became so popular with the fans the country over. Ted Weems is the recipient of an honor that has never before come to a dance maestro. He is the only orchestra leader to be listed in the 'Biographies of Great Men,' issued by the Congressional Library of the United States. This recognition, doubtlessly, grew out of the contribution Weems has made to the advancement of American dance music.

"This attraction comes under the management of Alex Demar as the first big feature of the summer dance season at Ramona Gardens."

Shep Fields

"Shep Fields and his 'rippling rhythm' orchestra comes to Ramona Gardens Friday for an evening's engagement, direct from the Empire room of Chicago's Palmer house. He will present his musical innovations for Grand Rapids dance fans under the management of Alex Demar. Fields and his orchestra were featured in 'The big Broadcast of 1938.'" This was the report in the *GR Herald*.

Among the people who played in his band at one time were Ken "Festus" Curtis, and Sid Caesar who was a sax player.

Jack Teagarden

Tommy Dorsey claimed his trombone style was heavily influenced by musician, **Jack Teagarden**, who brought his orchestra to Ramona in 1939. According to the *GR Herald*,

"Jack Teagarden, one of America's foremost trombonists, will bring his orchestra to Ramona gardens for one night's dancing engagement next Saturday. Teagarden, who just concluded a successful engagement at the Blackhawk restaurant in Chicago, brings such stars as Charlie Spivak, trumpet player, and Linda Keene, songstress. Teagarden was picked by Paul Whiteman, with whom he formerly played as the trombonist on the All-American swing band."

Charlie Barnet

Charlie Barnet was born with a silver spoon in his mouth, but chose the life of the road. Leaving Yale in his freshman year with a new band, off he went. He was in good company with singer Harry VonZell, clarinet player Artie Shaw and the vocal backing of the Modernaires. Others who were affiliated with Charlie later were Lena Horne and Doc Severinson.

In 1940 when the Barnet orchestra played for Ramona Gardens patrons, the *GR Herald* announced:

"Charlie Barnet and his orchestra of 18 players will come to Ramona Gardens next Saturday night to play for the farewell party of the season, under management of Alex Demar.

"Barnet aroused interest last year with his appearances at the Famous Door, New York City, and later in Paramount theater in that city. Engagements at Playland, Rye, and Meadowbrook NJ, have followed. Featured vocalists with the orchestra when it plays here will be Harriet Clark and the Barnet trio."

102

Jackie Coogan

Most people think of **Jackie Coogan** as a child movie star of Charlie Chaplin fame, or toward the end of his career as Uncle Fester in TV's 'The Addams Family.' But, when he came to Ramona in 1937 it was in the capacity of an orchestra leader. He brought with him a pair of well-known lady performers as well. The *GR Press* told its readers that,

"Jackie Coogan will make his first personal appearance in Grand Rapids on Labor day night at Ramona Gardens, where he will present his orchestra and a group of Hollywood stars, appearing in the "Hollywood Hit Parade" under the management of Alex Demar.

"Jackie directs his own Hollywood Swing band, which plays for the dancing, and is featured in the 45 minute floor show. Lila Lee, for several years a screen star, will appear in the floor show. She has a featured role this season in Republic's 'Two Wise Maids.' Princess Luana, dancer, a native of Honolulu, will be seen in native dances. She recently was featured with Bing Crosby in 'Waikiki Wedding'."

The *GR Herald* added some information: *"Coogan needs no introduction to any public. He began his screen career at the age of 4 when he appeared with Charlie Chaplin in 'the Kid.' Now at 21 he has a fortune estimated at more than $2,000,000. He still retains his winning smile and personality, but, of course, has matured. His talents have improved and his knowledge of acting broadened. Coogan and his orchestra will play for dancing and will take part in a 45-minute floor show. "*

PRINCESS LUANA

Eddie Duchin

Surprisingly, **Eddy Duchin** was a pharmacist before turning to his greater love, music. He played the piano as a hobby, but he turned that into success as the leader of a band which became a favorite of New York society. He applied the styles of Bach and Beethoven to "jazz up" band music scores, and that brought him attention. It was unusual for a pianist to lead a band in the early 1930s. His style was sometimes described as "sweet" music rather than jazz since it was rooted in classical music.

By 1938, when he appeared at Ramona, he was praised thus in the *GR Herald*:

"According to theatrical records, the first step to success is to appear with Eddy Duchin, who brings his orchestra to Ramona Gardens Saturday night through arrangement with the Music Corporation of America.

"Eddy Duchin's first recording was made with the now famous Frances Langford. Eddy's first theatrical tour introduced Dorothy Lamour who is no mystery to radio and screen fans. Kenny Baker, the wonder boy, won a contest Eddy promoted. Velos and Yolando were Eddy's first dance team. Nat Brandywine was Eddy's first pianist. All of the above personalities are now at the top of the heap with Eddy."

For all his success, the story of Eddy Duchin's life ended in tragedy. He served in the Navy in World War II, and after the war was not able to regain his former prominence. He died at age 41 of leukemia in 1951, and a movie was made of his life in 1956, appropriately named, **"The Eddy Duchin Story."**

Artie Shaw

It was before the war, it was after the worst of the depression, it was the best swing band in the country that performed in The Gardens when **Artie Shaw** appeared. Early in his career he performed with many groups, one of which exposed him to classical music which he incorporated this into his own arrangements. The *GR Herald* offered:

"Artie Shaw, 'King of the Clarinet' and his orchestra are coming to Ramona Park for a one night's engagement, Monday, August 7. Shaw's band was recently voted the 'best swing band' in the country in the annual poll taken by 'Down Beat,' swing's trade paper, beating out Benny Goodman's band which had reigned unchallenged for two years.

"While Shaw enjoys the reputation of being a swingster in the fullest sense of the word, his orchestra has achieved a reputation for fine harmonies, delicate musical shadings, and intricate arrangements, yet Shaw's men employ just the bare printed outline of a melody and improvise each number.

"Shaw will bring his cast of entertainers, that have appeared on stage, screen, and radio, including Helen Forrest and Tony Pastor."

Art Jarrett

Singer and actor **Art Jarrett** brought his band to Ramona in 1941. He played the banjo, guitar and trombone as well. The *GR Herald* told his story,

"The Final dance attraction of the season at Ramona Gardens will be Art Jarrett, the handsome leader with his new orchestra, composed of members of the late Hal Kemp's outstanding band. They will play here Tuesday night, according to Alex Demar, manager. As a soloist, Art first distinguished himself with Ted Weems and Isham Jones and then co-starred in the movies with Joan Crawford, Carole Lombard, Ann Sothern and Sonja Henie, where his combination of good looks and a good voice carried him far. Art, who started his band leading career at the Blackhawk restaurant in Chicago, recently finished an engagement there that lasted over three months. Versatile Art is an all-around athlete, among his other accomplishments, and the holder of two tennis championships, for which he keeps in training every day."

Harry James

In 1947, **Harry James** provided a very special evening in Ramona's ballroom, a departure from the normal skating routine. The *GR Herald* simply said,

"Harry James, direct from Hollywood, where he has been making motion pictures and playing in Hollywood night clubs, will appear with his band in Ramona Gardens Saturday evening, June 7. This appearance will be one of the few engagements that James will make this season. Buddy DiVito and Pat Flaherty, singing stars, will be heard with the band."

Bob Crosby

In 1940, when **Bob Crosby** played at Ramona Gardens, the *GR Herald* told this story:

"Bob Crosby and his Dixieland Dispensers will appear in Ramona Gardens June 14 under the auspices of Alex Demar, manager of the Gardens. Bing's younger brother, Bob, climbed to the top rung of the orchestra ladder without undue pressure being exerted on his behalf by his family's powerful connections. Today his band is rated tops in that style of jazz music.

"'Metronome,' one of the leading trade magazines of the popular music industry, read by dance band followers, recently published the results of its annual all-star band poll. For the third year in a row, the Bob Crosby orchestra demonstrated they are to jazz what the Yankees are to baseball.

"Besides capturing the most first places—Eddie Miller, sax; Jess Stacy, piano, and Bob Haggart, bass—the band had Irving Fazola, who rated just behind Goodman and Shaw on clarinet; Ray Bauduc, nosed out for second in the drums division; Billy Butterfield surpassed by only two trumpeters, and Nappy LaMare, fourth among guitarists. The same predominance of individual performers from the Crosby band featured the rival 'Downbeat' poll. "

BOB CROSBY

Glenn Miller

Also in 1940 Gardens-goers were treated to the music of **Glenn Miller**. By this time his fame was legendary. Just four and a half years after his appearance at Ramona, Glenn Miller's status changed to "missing in action" when his plane was lost traveling from the U.K. to Paris. He was on tour performing for American troops.

The *GR Press* reported on his visit to Grand Rapids,

"Glenn Miller and his 17-piece swing orchestra will play a dance program at Ramona Gardens Monday night, it is announced by Alex Demar, manager of the dance place. Miller has been known to the dance music world a dozen years, playing with Benny Goodman, Tommy Dorsey, Gene Krupa, Bix Beiderbecke, Ben Pollack and Red Nichols. He played a swing trombone before swing came into the musical language. As an arranger for the Dorsey brothers, Glen Gray and Goodman, he helped launch the type of dance music in lilting tempos which are predominant today. When the Dorsey brothers organized their orchestra, they went to Miller, seeking his aid in getting together the right men and starting their arrangements in the books."

105

Tony Pastor

From the *GR Herald*, July 13, 1941

"Tony Pastor and his orchestra will come to Ramona Gardens for a single engagement next Wednesday night, under the management of Alex Demar. Before organizing his own band, Pastor was in the organizations of Smith Ballew, Joe Venuti, Vincent Lopez and Artie Shaw. He is a saxophonist and a composer of note."

This notice followed the story of the Pastor engagement:

"Following the Pastor engagement, Ramona Gardens will discontinue weekly dancing, substituting roller skating."

Woody Herman

The June *GR Herald* in 1941 stated,

"Woody Herman's band, national collegiate poll choice as the number one dance band of 1940, will play a one-night dance engagement next Friday at Ramona Gardens, Alex Demar, garden manager, announced. Herman's band features a rhythmic, melodic style many critics feel to be far in advance of 'swing.' Herman, although only 25 years old, is a veteran of orchestra circuits and has played in most of the nation's leading dance spots.

"An all-star musical revue will be featured with the band, starring Muriel Lane, blues singer; Frankie Carlson, one of the country's leading drummers; Trumpeter Steady Nelson, Cappy Lewis and Neal Reid and the woodchoppers, Herman's six-piece 'band within a band.' The Four Chips also will appear."

Lawrence Welk

When **Lawrence Welk** was invited to appear at Ramona Gardens in 1948, it was the beginning of a new plan put forth by Fred J. Barr. Roller skating had commandeered the Gardens building late in 1941 and dominated it since that point. The new plan was to have dancing with name bands every Thursday, Friday and Saturday night for the remainder of the season. One of those bands was to be Glenn Miller's orchestra led by Tex Beneke.

Note in the ad on the left that he was to be playing his famous "Champagne Music."

Tommy Dorsey

The legendary **Dorsey** brothers, Tommy and Jimmy, at one time performed together. By the time the younger **Tommy** came to Ramona in 1938, he was on his own. And by that time, he was extremely well known, famous not only as a band leader, but as a musician in his own right, noted for his smooth-toned trombone sounds.

The next year after his engagement at Ramona, his band started to turn more toward the jazz sound. In 1940, he "appropriated" singer Frank Sinatra from Harry James, and made some eighty recordings with the crooner during the next two years.

The *GR Herald* had this to say about Tommy Dorsey:

"Tommy Dorsey, 'The Sentimental Gentleman of Swing,' completely recovered from his recent illness while in Hollywood, brings his well-known radio orchestra to Ramona Gardens Thursday night, under the auspices of Alex Demar, manager of the Gardens.

"Featured with Dorsey's band are radio stars including Edythe Wright, songstress; Jack Leonard 'romantic baritone'; Allen Storr, tenor and the Three Esquires, singing trio.

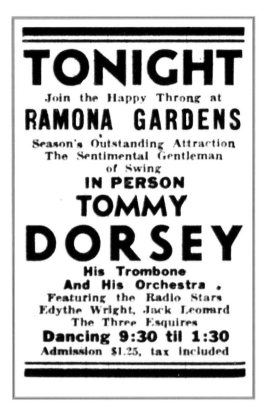

"Dorsey, acclaimed as America's ace trombonist, has one of the country's outstanding swing bands and is billed as the 'Sultan of Swing.' His appearance here will be the first since he left Hollywood. The Garden's management is planning to enlarge the dance floor for the occasion."

Jimmy Dorsey

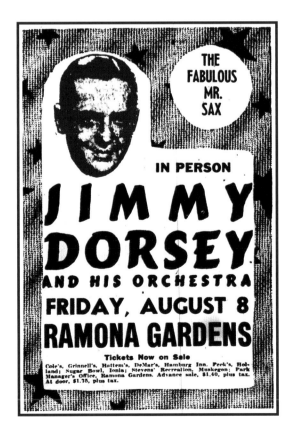

Nearly a whole decade after brother Tommy appeared in the Gardens, **Jimmy Dorsey** brought his talent and his orchestra to the Ramona venue. By this time, skating was the major activity in the pavilion, but Fred Barr occasionally brought in high-profile music for dancing.

The year was 1947 and the *GR Herald* announced the coming of this great performer and his music:

"Jimmy Dorsey, whose 'contrasting music' comes to Ramona Gardens Friday, August 8, is regarded as one of the world's greatest saxophonists. The E-flat alto saxophone is his preferred instrument. With it he can play notes both above and below the ranges of the horn, and play them with purity and mellowness of tone.

"His own theme, 'Contrasts,' is one of his saxophone specialties, adapted from his composition 'Oodles of Noodles,' and displays Jimmy's virtuosity. His dexterity on the clarinet is proved by the fact that he is believed to be the only one able to play double stops and triple tongues."

JIMMY DORSEY

107

Shall We Skate?

Moving about on roller skates is like having miniature roller coaster cars attached to the feet. No special tracks are needed and ice is not required, just a flat surface. Once the effect of gravity is conquered, there is freedom to glide around at will. With practice, the gliding can be turned into maneuvers. It can be done in concert with another person, moving in harmony to music. Roller skating was a great source of amusement throughout the history of resorts at Reeds Lake. It ranged from simple fun to out-and-out competitive sport. The facilities changed through the years as did the skates themselves.

Early references to roller skating rinks in Grand Rapids city appear as early as the 1870s. The mention of a floor for skating at Reeds Lake is found in the *GR Evening Leader*, in 1884, two years after the Railroad Pavilion was built:

"Near the pavilion a platform 60 x 90 feet in area will be erected for a skating rink and dancing bower. This will probably be under the management of Prof. Payne. Arrangements will be made to have a band within easy call to play for parties during the summer."

The skating craze in the big city of Grand Rapids waned a bit by the early 1890s, for in 1893, Finn's Hall on Plainfield was leased for the purpose of inaugurating a skating facility to revive the "old craze."

Grand Opening Roller Skating Rink
The Palace rink, Lockerby hall, under the management of Eddie Smith, the well known and popular fancy skater, will be open to the public Saturday evening, Oct. 6. Mr. Smith has just returned from a successful theatrical tour through the East and will give one of his un-excelled exhibitions of fancy and acrobatic skating. Good music in attendance. (1894)

Formerly known as Lockerby Hall, *The Auditorium* became its new name in January, 1898. The next year, W. S. Daniels, sporting goods dealer and entrepreneur, opened a roller rink in the building. This was done on a rather grand scale with all manner of events to lure customers.

In 1897, this humorous account appeared in the *GR Evening Press*:

"All sorts of uses are made of the corridors of the city hall and it keeps the janitors busy in the attempt to maintain order there, but the most novel scheme for putting to use the tile floors was adopted by two lads last night. When Nightwatchman Fortier entered the building he found the boys having a very pleasant and not particularly quiet time in utilizing the tile floor for a skating rink. Roller skates worked excellently on the hard floor and the boys felt quite insulted when the watchman tried to stop their sport. They were quite defiant until taken to police headquarters, where they were convinced that they had not chosen the proper time nor place for skating. After receiving a lecture they were released."

How It All Began

The first roller skating experience is credited to an unknown Dutchman, who was used to traveling by ice skates on the canals, and who experimented with summertime skates. Nailing wooden spools to strips of wood on the bottom of his wooden shoes, he was able to move about on a non-frozen surface. These shoes were called "skeelers," a term now used in the Netherlands for in-line skates.

In the early years of the 16th century, attempts were made to create rolling skates by attaching wheels to the bottom of boots or shoes, in a straight line, to emulate the blade of an ice skate. In 1760, the first recorded roller skates were invented by Belgian John Joseph Merlin. He was a musician, builder of fine instruments, inventor and all-around mechanical genius. His design used a row of small

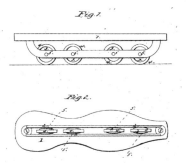

metal wheels attached to a boot. Choosing to introduce his new invention to an elite crowd at a masquerade ball, he made a grand entrance by gliding into the hall while playing the violin. Though he was an accomplished musician, he was not adept at skating, and finding himself unable to stop, he crashed head-long into an expensive mirror. At least this antic put his invention into the history books.

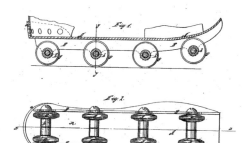

The first patent on roller skates was held by Monsieur Petitbled, in 1819, for a version of in-line skate having three wheels made of wood, metal or ivory. His marketing claim was that a person wearing this invention could do all the maneuvers performed on ice skates. The claim proved false as did his hopes for success, since the skater could not actually steer. In the words of Charles Dickens in 1876, in the 16th volume of **"All the Year Round,"** the skates were **"fitted with ivory or wooden rollers—two, three, or four in number—arranged on a single line: and, if of uniform size, effectually preventing any curves being described by them."**

Many attempts were made at creating a good "parlor skate," but success was achieved in 1863. As Mr. Dickens stated: .**"..at last the genius of Mr. James Leonard Plimpton, not without study and long experiment, hit upon the 'rocking' skate. The great feature of the Plimpton skate is, that it does not require forcing round a curve by sheer strength, but can be guided by the lateral rocking of the foot."**

Plimpton's skates had a pair of side-by-side wheels under the ball of the foot and one pair under the heel. The four wheels were mounted on rubber springs. This arrangement has carried

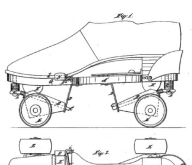

over into the modern four-wheeled roller skates, which allowed for turns and the ability to skate backwards. It is interesting that the introduction of in-line skates in the later years of the 20th century was thought to be such an innovation. The invention of pin ball-bearing wheels in 1884 made rolling easier and skates lighter.

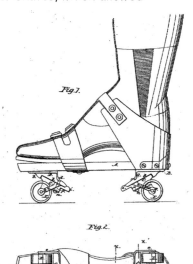

Plimpton also established roller skating halls in New York City by 1865. According to the **Kansas City Star** in an article on the history of skating in 1885, the halls **"were attended by staid and orderly people, including ministers, deacons and church members, and on one occasion the good folks astonished their friends by skating a waltz figure during Lent. They did not awake to the enormity of the offense until some of the newspapers began to write them up."** The article also stated that there was a very extensive roller skating craze in America in 1872, and in 1885 the craze was the third of its kind.

With roller skating activity once again becoming popular in the area, it was logical for the new amusement park, Ramona, to build an indoor skating rink. It was indoor because it had a roof, but open air, for summer use only, and it was billed as the largest facility of its kind in the country. This was the 1904 season. The Princess Roller Rink, operated by Detroiters George W. Leihy and son, offered the latest patented ball bearing skates for the use of its customers. It operated in the summer and the Auditorium rink was open in the winter.

TONIGHT GRAND OPENING!
Princess Roller Rink
Finest Open Air Rink in the World.
Ramona Park, - Reed's Lake
Four sessions daily, afternoon and evening.
Ball-bearing Skates.   Chammer's Military Band.
Admission, 10c.   Use of Skates, 10c.

For the pleasure of skaters in the new facility, instructors were in attendance and live bands played at every session. People started to form skating clubs and parties. The next year, a series of roller races were held at the Princess. On the last night, cash prizes were awarded to the winners who skated the fastest rounds.

In 1906, the Leihys moved to Saginaw to pursue Roller Polo interests and Austin McFadden stepped in to manage the Princess. Then it became known as, "Roll-Away Roller Rink."

Roll-Away Roller Rink
(REED'S LAKE)
Skating every afternoon and evening.
LADIES FREE.

Big competition came along in 1910, when The Coliseum was built in downtown Grand Rapids. The opening drew nearly 1,000 skaters and spectators. Its manager was the enterprising George Zindel who instituted many innovations for the pleasure of the participants. One of the reasons for choosing the location of Commerce and Oakes streets was to rejuvenate the neighborhood. It drew skaters during the cold months while the Ramona facility was populated in the warmer seasons.

Alice Teddy The Roller Skating Bear **Coliseum**
Every Afternoon and Evening for One Week---Feb. 5 to Feb. 12
Admission, Balcony 10c   Don't Miss This Most Wonderful Act.

In 1907, the skating building was called the "Ramona Roller Rink," a name it held until being torn down in 1912. Special affairs were masquerade parties, skating carnivals and a Hard Times Party as well as various races and contests. Performers who did tricks and exhibitions also brought people into the rink. These ads are from the *GR Press* in 1907.

Grand Masquerade
SKIDOO
CARNIVAL
At Ramona Roller Rink
Tuesday, July 23
Prizes   Prizes   Prizes
Richardson Ball-Bearing Skates
GET YOUR COSTUMES READY

EXTRA ATTRACTION!
RAMONA ROLLER RINK
GUS NELSON
In Sensational and Daring Roller Skating Feats, Leap the Gap, etc.
Saturday Afternoon, Aug. 10

ALICE TEDDY
The Roller Skating Bear at
COLISEUM
This Week

Don't miss seeing this wonderful act every afternoon and evening all this week. Will wrestle and race a man or lady every evening.

Alice Teddy, the Roller Skating Bear, one of the special performers at The Coliseum. She also wrestled and took on all comers.

Competition

Roller skating was not only for romancing couples, society ladies' skating parties or family outings. The male of the species found ways to utilize the roller skate for serious competitions. One of these contests was called, Roller Polo.

Like ice hockey, this game was developed from lawn or field hockey. It was popularized soon after the Plimpton skate was introduced. A team consisted of five players, designated thus: one goal-tend, one half-back, one center and two rushers. A rubber-covered ball, similar to a cricket ball, was used and it was propelled with heavy, long sticks. Goal posts rose at either end of a rectangular rink, and stood about three feet high with a net stretched between each pair. This game could be played any time of year.

FOR ROLLER RACES

First of a Series Will Begin at Ramona Next Week.

(1905)

Speed skating contests were also held locally. Winners competed in mile-long races. At the rink at Ramona, this meant sixteen laps. One of the winners clocked the mile in 3 min. and 10 sec. in 1905, for example. The following narrative was printed in the *GR Evening Press* that year:

"Starting next Sunday night and continuing for six nights skating races will take place nightly and on Saturday, the seventh night, the six winners will compete in a final race for cash prizes. The leading roller skaters of the state are expected to take part, and Manager Leihy announces that he intends to back the winner against any skater in the country, and that the fastest skaters in the US will be here to contest during the summer months."

Through the years, skate designs improved, and local merchants carried the latest and greatest models.

Roller Skating

One of the most fascinating and popular forms of recreation for boys and girls.

We are showing a splendid assortment for both sidewalk and rink use.

Sidewalk Skates, wood rolls, per pair...35c
Sidewalk Skates, cast iron, per pair....50c
Sidewalk Skates, pressed steel, pair...$1.25
Sidewalk Skates, pressed steel, pair...$1.50
Rink Skates, ball bearing, pair, $2.50 to $6
Extra rolls, per set of 8, 25c, 50c and up.

W. B. JARVIS CO.

The Sporting Goods Store
28 CANAL STREET

1909

Our Big Toy Dept.

ON the Fourth Floor has many interesting features for the healthy out-of-doors child which all parents should consider.

Genuine Ball Bearing Roller Skates.

$1.19   Other styles at 48c and $1.

1915

Roller Skates

Roller Bearing, best made

$1.90

1922

111

Ramona Gardens

The Ramona Roller Rink, built in 1904, was removed in 1912 for the construction of the Dancing Academy building. The story of that construction and enterprise is told elsewhere. The new facility was built for the express purpose of dancing, consequently roller skating enthusiasts had to go elsewhere to enjoy the sport.

By August of 1941, the dancing pavilion, known by then as Ramona Gardens, was turned into a roller skating rink. Mr. Henry Nieboer was responsible for this conversion, adding a second hardwood floor designed for skating. He continued to operate the amusement through its life at Ramona Park and beyond.

Ramona Gardens Skating Rink, opened originally as Ramona Dancing Academy in 1912, became known as the Dancing Casino and then officially Ramona Gardens in 1925.

RAMONA GARDENS ROLLER SKATER

Published by The Grand Rapids Roller Skate Club

May 1/1942 - four years

Grand Rapids, Mich.
April 14th, 1942.

Grand Rapids Motor Coach Co.,
GRand Rapids, Mich.
(Attention Mr. Glerum)

I would like to make the following offer:
For the rental of Ramona Gardens I will pay $4,500 per year, plus the cost of a new floor and give the Railway Company title to the gas heaters now at Ramona Gardens.

In return, I will expect to receive a four year lease for Ramona Gardens, and the privilege to pay for the new floor at the rate of $500.00 down, balance to be paid in equal monthly installments through out the life of the lease.

Very truly yours,

Henry Nieboer.

For your information we have today executed a lease covering the Ramona Dance Gardens with Henry Nieboer, for a four-year period, May 1, 1942 to April 30, 1946.

Rental price $4,500. per year, payable weekly in advance, or $86.22 on May 1, 1942, and $86.54 on each Friday of each week thereafter during the term of this lease.

Nieboer also agreed to deliver to us a bill of sale covering the gas heating equipment he originally installed in the building, such property to be the property of the Company. Such bill of sale is attached hereto for your records.

The Company is to install a new floor in such building at a cost of $4,200. The Company will pay the original cost but Nieboer in his lease has agreed to reimburse us for such expenditure, paying $500. on the signing of the lease; $50. on the first of each month from June 1, 1942 to April 1,1943; and thereafter $87.50 on the on the first day of each month from May 1, 1943 to April 1, 1946; Nieboer has the privilege of payment in as large a amount as he desires if he wishes to bunch the advance payments.

These two letters from April, 1942, give the details of the agreement between Henry Nieboer and the Railway Company in making the conversion to a skating rink.

Something of a local celebrity, Russell Thrall played theater organ in accompaniment to silent films as a very young man. He would stun audiences with his mastery during intermissions. He also played in roller skating rinks and on radio. Mention is made of his playing at Ramona as early as August of 1941. He also played on occasion after the building was moved to Plymouth Ave.

THE TEEN-AGE SKATERS OF GRAND RAPIDS
Present

RAMONA ROLLER REVUE

JUNE 3-4-5 — 8:30 p.m.

AT

RAMONA GARDENS ROLLER RINK

SEE— *The Beauty and Grace with Which the Skaters Perform*
The Gorgeous Costumes

THE FIRST SKATING SHOW EVER TO BE GIVEN IN GRAND RAPIDS WITH ALL-LOCAL TALENT — PROCEEDS TO GO TO CHARITY

TICKETS NOW ON SALE AT
GRINNELL'S
RIORDAN'S DRUG STORE
RAMONA GARDENS ROLLER RINK

ADMISSION
$.90 TAX INCL.

The "Ramona Roller Revue," held in June, 1947, was sponsored by the Mary Free Bed Guild which received 25% of the revenue from the show. The cast of 50, with the exception of five professional members, were all amateur skaters. The teenagers made their own costumes and scenery to hold down expenses. This photo from the "GR Press" was taken at dress rehearsal.

The ultimate skate.
Ad from 1947

Every day of the week was designated for either certain groups, certain events or certain kinds of skating. The schedule below was provided by Al and Marty Staal who worked at Ramona Gardens during its later years at Reeds Lake, and for a while after the building was moved. They were "Floor Guards" in the rink. The gal who became Marty's wife was the "Bell Ringer" at that time.

"We customarily skated backwards the entire time, wearing a whistle, which we would blow if someone fell or was skating recklessly and had to be escorted off the floor. During the evening there would always be a time for couples only or trios only or for the more skilled skaters to perform dances on skates to exhibit special forms of skating. However, most of the evening was devoted to 'All Skate,' which was a circular counter-clockwise movement. During the 'All Skate,' individuals could still perform special dance moves and twirls in the inner circle of the skate floor as long as they didn't infringe upon the circular flow of the larger body of skaters."

There was a room where the skates were neatly stored by size and were doled out to customers who paid the rental fee. Workers in this room kept the skates functioning in good order. The wooden wheels on the skates had to be sanded for re-shaping; wheel bearing surfaces would get worn and needed to be replaced. Otherwise, the skates might make a sudden stop on their own.

The Skate Week, 1950s

- <u>Monday</u> – No white people skated on Monday. The group had their own music and rhythms which they preferred for skating. Many of them had the habit of not lacing up the skates, which then fit very loosely while they skated.

- <u>Tuesday and Wednesday</u> – Businesses and other groups reserved the building for the exclusive use of their parties. The Bissell Company was one example. The Gardens was closed to members of the public these two days.

- <u>Thursday</u> – Almost exclusively adults and older teens, who dressed up for the occasion. These "better" skaters didn't have to be concerned about anyone cramping their style.

- <u>Friday</u> – Family night, more casual. Moms, dads and lots of youngsters.

- <u>Saturday Afternoon</u> – Regular skating but with times set aside for races. The Floor Guards set up markers that defined courses for racing.

- <u>Saturday Evening</u> – A blend of all ages

- <u>Sunday Afternoon</u> – Geared toward dancing. Practice sessions were held after regular hours for anyone interested in honing their skills. Competitions, dancing, some instruction offered.

- <u>Thursday, Friday, Saturday</u> – had the "special skates," like couples, ladies choice, etc. There were also the Grand March, and music for three dance steps: the 14-step, collegiate and the waltz.

Jack Thomasma & Pete VanEnk participating in tomfoolery as seen in the 1949 "Memoir" of GR Christian High School.

Pretty participant poses.

Thursday Night Skating

At Ramona Gardens, Thursday night was the time to skate for the city's "best" skaters. By the time they arrived for the evening's festivities, the skatemaster would have shooed away the younger and less sophisticated crowd to make way for the real skating crowd. These were largely teenagers with the exception of a few intrepid adults. They came to hear their music played by a real band which only played on that night of the week. It was directed by a drummer who taught at Knapp Music.

Skaters could make requests by shouting titles of favorite songs as they glided past the band. Good skating music was "Five Foot Two" and "Lady from 29 Palms," but if the band played clinkers like "Shoo Fly Pie," everyone sat down because the rhythm just wasn't right.

The floor of the skating area was treated with resin for better traction of the wooden wheels on the skates. This allowed for more skilled performance on the boards but avid skaters would occasionally have to replace worn down wheels. Not only the wheels wore down during the course of the event, but the resin was loosened and became airborne. It would cling to the skaters' clothing and the young gals who arrived as brunettes would leave as blondes.

The skatemaster was the key to the success of the evening. Besides riding herd on any rowdies, he would keep the horde from skating too fast – or too slow, and shoo away those who were not skilled enough to participate. He was also in charge of the "dingers." These were special activities which were announced by a large illuminated sign sitting near the bandstand, the ding of a bell signaling a change of events. Such specialties as Ladies Only, Ladies Choice, Trios, All Skate, Waltzes

and the grand finale, The Grand March. Any skater who didn't behave according to the sign was ushered off the floor.

Two young men of Dutch extraction, accomplished skaters who regularly attended the Thursday night events, during an attack of mischief decided to test the competence of the skatemaster. They disguised themselves in the attire of immigrant Dutch farm boys, replete with mis-matched plaids with generally unkempt appearance and drove to the Gardens in a Hudson. Once on the floor they skated like rank beginners, achieving a level of proficiency only bordering on the favorable side of ineptitude, and this caught the watchful eye of the skatemaster. When the bell announced the first "dinger," they went into action. Continuing to skate together during a "Ladies Choice" event, the two fellows were rapidly confronted and notified that they must sit on the sidelines. The skaters answered only in Dutch and successfully convinced the skatemaster that they couldn't understand what was going on. This behavior continued through the evening, culminating in a grand performance during the final Grand March when they succeeded in causing grand traffic jams. As they left the building, they completed their evening of merriment by bidding farewell to the proprietor ... in perfect English.

By Don Bratt, participant and skate owner.

The more serious skaters owned their skates, complete with lockable carrying case

Advertisement from the mid
to late 1940s

Ramona Gardens was known as a
"good place to pick up chicks." Some
couples, who met while skating at
Ramona, married each other.

Two couples during the
Grand March

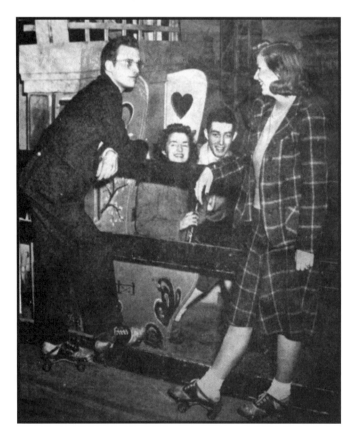

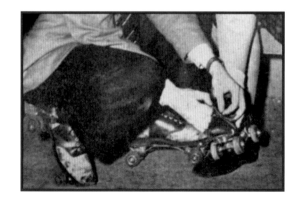

Skaters pause to chat with a couple
who are enjoying soda-pop in a booth.

Skate installation assistance.

On The Move

When Ramona Park was literally torn down throughout the year of 1955, one building was not destroyed. Ramona Gardens roller rink, was preserved. Manager Henry Nieboer had purchased the building the previous year, and had it moved to his farm on Plymouth Avenue at the corner of Oak Industrial. He engaged the services of Robinson Cartage Company which trucked the building in sections, averaging 17 x 30 feet. The nine steel, 32-foot radius roof arches were detached from the building and moved separately. The hardwood floor, which was installed by Nieboer in the early 1940s as a skating surface, was cut into quarters in order to be moved.

After the disassembling was started in April, 1955, skaters were allowed into the building for about three weeks while the stucco was removed from the outside walls. By mid-June, sixty feet of the 100 x 200 foot pavilion had been moved. The rebuilding was completed in December, 1955, including the installation of corrugated iron sheathing on the outside. It was reopened for skating soon after.

The contractor in charge of the move, Adrian Versluys, said that it was remarkable that the building was in such good condition, having been built in 1912. He stated in the *GR Press*, December 10, 1955: ***"So well preserved was the building, despite it having had no foundation but the ground at the park, that we were able to use the old sub-flooring and supporting timbers to put new ends in the structure."*** The article also states that the moving project cost $40,000 which included a new parking lot on the premises.

As the building looked in December, 1955, having just been reassembled in its new location on the north-east corner of Plymouth Rd. and Oak Industrial Blvd.

Nieboer's

After the building arrived at its new location at 632 Plymouth NE in 1955, it was used for another 19 years. This was amazing for a structure which was built in 1912 and wholly moved from one site to another. Henry Nieboer continued to operate Nieboer's Roller Rink through 1960.

Organ accompaniment at Nieboer's was initially provided by Russell Thrall. There was a young man who loved to hear the organ music at Nieboer's and would go to the rink just to hear Mr. Thrall play. One night when Mr. Thrall didn't show up due to illness, the young man, John Vander Meer, piped up and said he could play the organ. He was hired on the spot and continued for some years after that.

Announcement
December 14, 1955

Skate-O-Rama

In May of 1961, there were amateur skating competitions held at this facility. Skater Doug Taylor tells of entering the contest in 1961:

"The winter of 1960/1961, I would take the bus from the 4-mile and Coit area out to Michigan and Plymouth to go skating to practice for competition just about every night. I won the Silver Medal (second place) for Free Style skating, but I did enter Speed skating and I believe I finished 4th in it."

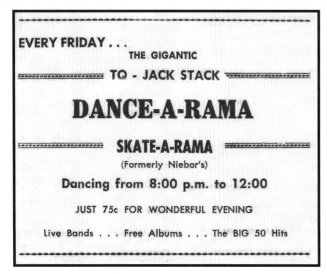

According to local historian Kim Rush,

"At that time, 1961, it became the Skate-O-Rama. During February and March of 1963 WLAV disc jockeys Tom Quain and Jack Stack held dances at the Skate-O-Rama.

"On March 1, 1963, Dion performed for a concert sponsored by Quain and Stack at Skate-O-Rama. Local musician Tom Madden arranged to have local vocalists Lin Nowicki and Mary Rudolph assist Dion with background vocals."

3,500 in Riot At Roller Rink

Mr. Rush continues, *"In 1965, this building was still being used for concerts and dances. An Impressions show was canceled because the band's vehicle reportedly broke down in route to the performance. A large dance orchestra was hired as a substitution, and they played for 45 minutes. Reportedly, at that point, the individual attending the ticket booth began refunding money to disappointed ticket holders (2.00 of the total 2.50 ticket price) and 'disappeared' after handing back $50.00 worth of refunds. A riot ensued, and parts of the building were ransacked by angry people in attendance."*

The Place

This same building, 632 Plymouth NE, was listed as "vacant" in the Grand Rapids 1966 city directory. It came alive again in 1967 when the venue was dubbed, **"The Place."** Kim Rush says,

"Concerts and dances that were held during that time are legendary to people who were Grand Rapids teenagers in the late 1960s. Many local performers and some national acts played there. In 1967 and 1968, the owners of The Place were Tom Regis and Syl Dick. Also, during the 60s, Grand Rapids basketball star and artist Delton Heard ran an establishment called the Psychedelic Shack at this same building.*

In the year 1970, there are references to this venue as being called both, **"The Psychedelic Shack"** and **"Lothlorien."**

The "Funkadelic", To Appear Here In Concert, May 31 st

Sunday, May 31st, Delton Heard will be presenting the fabulous FUNKADELICS & THE PARLIMENTS in concert from 8:00 til 1:00 A.M. The concert will be held at the "Psychedelic Shack," formerly known as "the Place," Plymouth Rd. and Industrial Drive.

This sensational recording artists have recently released a new album called "FUNKADELIC" This album includes several hits: I bet you, What is Soul? I got a thing, You got a thing, everybodys got a thing, and Gold old music.

The album is produced by George Clinton "A PARLIA-FUNKADELICMENT THANG." The FUNKADELIC Label is put out by Westbound Records and Distributed nationally by Janus Record Corp., New York., N.Y.

Mr. Heard is asking all 17 years old and under, to please observe the curfew law. Donation is $2.50 at the door. **1970**

THE PLACE
"Michigan's Largest Teen Dance Spot"
Presents
BiG Tuesday, July
—SPECTACULAR—
"SCOTT MORGAN AND THE RATIONALS"
National Recording Artists
DIRECT FROM THE ROOSTER TAIL IN DETROIT
Admission $1.75
On Plymouth, N. E. - Just N. of Michigan

✷ CITY CHAMPIONSHIP ✷

··· THE PLACE ···

BATTLE of the BANDS

Support *your* "Band"

1. The JADES
2. The SOUL BENDERS
3. The STEEL BLUES
4. PETER & THE PROPHETS
5. INTRUDERS

SATURDAY MARCH 25, 1967

produced by
The Grand Rapids Junior Chamber of Commerce

$1.25   **7:30 P.M.**

Local Bands That Performed at The Place:

Band X
Soulbenders
Phlegethon
Steel Blues
Peter and the Prophets
Intruders
Fugitives
Root Beer Stand Band
Don and the Wanderers (Belding)

Nationally Known Bands:

SRC
Pleasure Seekers (with Suzi Quatro, TV's Leather Tuscadero of "Happy Days")
American Breed
Scott Morgan and the Rationals
The Music Explosion
The Rainmakers
The Bossmen

The Final Years

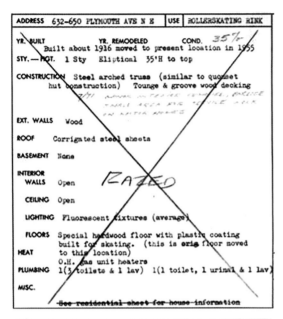

"*During the year 1970, the building was used as a dance and concert hall named Lothlorien. Local rock band Phlegethon played in a support role for Alice Cooper and rock band Maxx on September 5th. The Lothlorien did not admit people under the age of 17, which was in disparity to the audience for The Place.*"

Kim Rush

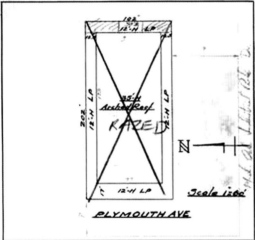

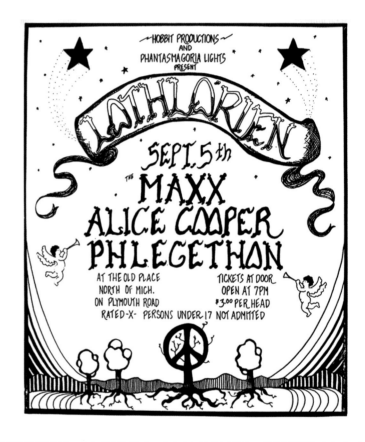

The building and property description, above, and the outside view, right, came from the 632 Plymouth card in the demolition files of the GR City Archives.

The razing of the grand lady occurred in 1974

Amusements

Ramona Park had the very latest and best in attractions for pleasure-seekers who came from near and far.

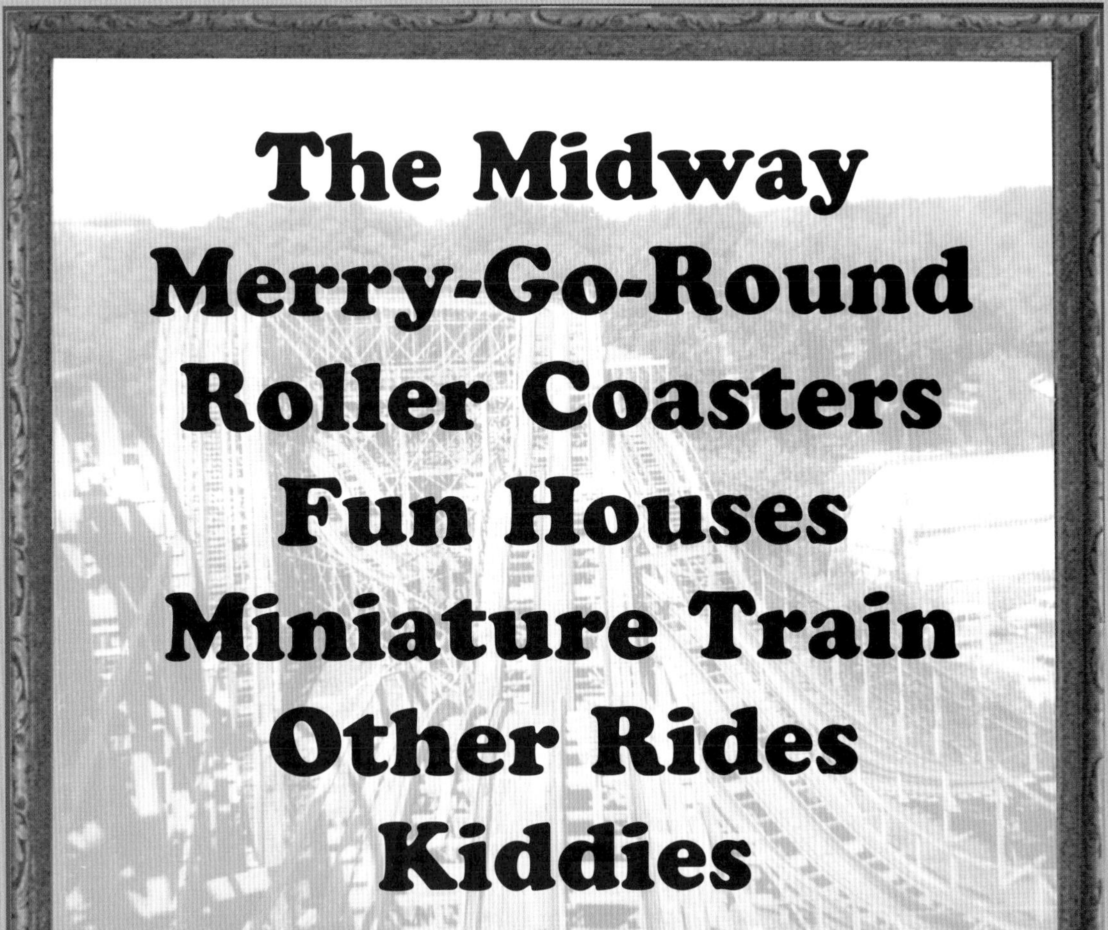

The Midway
Merry-Go-Round
Roller Coasters
Fun Houses
Miniature Train
Other Rides
Kiddies

As the big rides and amusements began to populate Ramona Park, small attractions began to appear as well. Games, refreshment booths, exhibits and curiosities were situated around the perimeter of the park property. Each year the composition of this area changed as enterprises came and went. The constitution of the walkway itself was altered from dusty avenues to cinders to paved or bricked pathways. In 1906 the park sought a designation other than just the word "midway" and the area became known as the "Circle." It didn't cost anything for people to stroll along the Ramona Circle, and many an hour was spent doing just that.

"CIRCLE" IS NAMED

Chosen for the Midway at Ramona

"Circle" Offers

Roller Toboggan, Olde Mill, Laughing Gallery, Circle Swing Roller Rink, Carrousel, Box Ball Alleys, etc.

This photo from mid-May, 1950, shows the midway during "spruce-up,"
just before the official opening of the park.

Games

Ring Toss

There were many varieties of ring-toss type games on the midway. One of the early such games on the Ramona Circle was the "**cane rack**." Colorful canes standing in a rack had handles pointing upward. The player tossed rings and if successful in "ringing" a handle, won that particular cane. For variety carnations were added so a swain could take the prize to his sweetheart. This was apparently a popular booth because it lasted a couple of decades.

A similar game, which operated at the same time as the cane rack was called the "**knife rack**." As one may imagine, the targets were knives fixed in a rack, and the lucky winner would tote home the knife that snagged the ring. Also found at Ramona were **doll racks** which offered baby dolls or kewpie dolls to the marksmen.

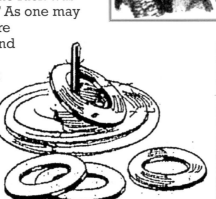

In the "Ring the Duck" game four live ducks and three decoys are exposed floating about in a tank and rubber rings are thrown at them after the principle followed in the familar cane rack game. Every time a player succeeds in getting one of the rubber rings around the neck of a duck, live or artificial, a prize is awarded. The ducks are artful dodgers and this adds to the excitement. The rings are soft so as not to hurt the ducks.

In 1910, the game described above in the *GR Press*, used real ducks. In the later years of the park, there was a pond with "artificial" ducks. The ticket-holder would merely grab one of the floating quackers and receive the prize indicated on the bottom of it.

More Fun Than Last Year
"On the Circle"

— Including —

Aerial Scenic Railway
Roller Toboggan
Circle Swing
Roller Skating
Laughing Gallery
Merry-Go-Round
Olde Mill
Box Ball Alleys
World's Fair Launches
Steamboats
Rowboats
Cane Racks
Knife Racks
Japanese Ball Game
Japanese Fish Pond
Miniature Railway
Postal Photo Gallery
Beautiful Picnic Grove
Swings, Teeters, Etc.
Cage of Monkeys
Teddy Bears
Fish Exibit

Ad for the opening of Ramona in 1907

Japanese Ball Rolling

Rolling ball games were another type seen on Ramona Circle. An early one was called the **Japanese Ball Game**. The game appealed to women because the prizes were pieces of imported Japanese hand-painted china. Winning was accomplished by accumulating a score from rolling billiard-sized balls into holes that had points assigned. The skilled ball-roller might acquire a complete set of china. A cumulative score kept throughout the season could win special prizes at the end of the summer.

Ladies out for a stroll on a very early Ramona midway. Before them is the brick walkway. Behind them, the Japanese Ball Game pagoda is just visible. The game had its own building, it was so well attended.

Visit the Japanese Rolling Ball Game

MOST FASCINATING GAME ON THE CIRCLE. YOU CAN FURNISH YOUR HOME WITH THE CHOICEST OF IMPORTED JAPANESE CHINA.

DON'T FAIL TO VISIT THIS BOOTH

View of the midway in 1912 showing the Japanese Rolling Balls and next door, The "Electric" Fish Pond.

124

Skee-Ball

A game similar to the Japanese Ball Rolling game was **Skee-Ball**. This appeared at Ramona in 1926 and continued through the life of the park. Several "alleys" were set up in a building dedicated to this game. The building was relocated to different places around the park. In the 1940s, a miniature version of the game was offered as well.

The game first appeared in amusement places around the country in 1909. The name "skee" came from the bump in the alley which was placed in front of the target area to cause the ball to jump, much as a skier going over a mogul.

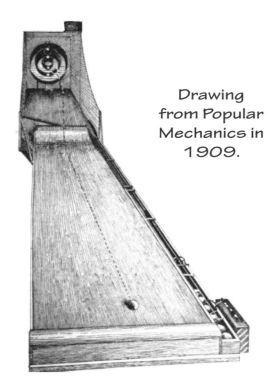

Drawing from Popular Mechanics in 1909.

"'Skee-ball' was a test of skill in which the player rolled a ball about as big as a croquet ball down an alley about eight feet long where it would hit a ramp and zoom up into the air, dropping into a series of ringed (concentric) zones. The big outer ring counted "1 point", next small ring inside that circle counted 3, the next one was worth 6, and then there was a small center ring only twice the diameter of the ball that was worth 10. A dime got you three balls to roll. An accumulated score then allowed you to pick any of the prizes that were within the point category of your total score. Everyone got something - a stick of gum for 1-3 points, etc. up to large kewpie dolls for a really high score. I stumbled on a system of rolling the balls against the side wall at a certain spot and made the ten-ring quite often. With much fanfare the man would award me the biggest, brightest doll on the shelves; I would proudly walk away telling everyone I won it at the 'Skee-ball' place; and would then sneak around back and return it to the proprietor! I got lots of free dimes so I could play some more."

Ham Berry

View of the Skee-Ball building back of the miniature train. Behind it, other buildings in the midway are visible as well as a glimpse of the lake.

The notice on the right is from Billboard Magazine in 1950

Baseballs

Throwing rather than rolling balls at targets also provided many test-your-skill opportunities. Hitting a target with a ball rewarded the thrower with a prize in some games. In other games, success in causing the ball to hit the target resulted in an action that was its own reward. For example, in the dunking version, the target was attached to a mechanism which caused a person to be plopped into a tank of water when the ball found its mark. There was even the "**Bathing Girl Baseball Game**" where a direct hit on the bullseye opened a door through which a bathing beauty appeared, slid down an incline, and presented the ball-flinger with a box of candy.

In the mid 1920s, the targets in the **Walking Charlie** game were man-sized dummies which moved about in front of the shootist. Mounted on trolleys, these roving targets strolled along but then suddenly disappeared into doorways just to bob out again. The hurler had to separate the hat from the dummy to win the prize.

In the 1950s, the targets were simply three milk bottles stacked one-on-two on stands, and the prize-winner was the person who knocked all three off the stand. Not as easy as it may sound because the bottles were weighted.

George L. DeWit won this little guy for his daughter, Linda, by knocking down *"tall, fabric dolls, with a fuzzy sort of trim around the edges."*

Darts

Another missile which was hurled at targets was the dart. Those targets consisted of under-inflated balloons arrayed on the back wall of the booth. Upon successfully skewering and bursting three of the balloons, the dart thrower could claim the prize indicated on a paper underneath. In the years following the end of the second world war, after certain commodities once again became available, the selection of prizes changed. Since nylon stockings were much sought after at this time, pairs of them were offered as prizes in the Dart Booth to the top winners.

One young man, [Don] who regularly attended Ramona Park with a limited amount of funds, on one occasion impulsively decided to spend his last available dime on this game of skill. At home he owned an elaborate dart wheel, given to him by his father to keep him out of trouble. This fellow had become accomplished in the art of dart-throwing, even inventing varieties of games to put his skills to the test. Thus it was no contest for him to break the required three balloons with the first three darts. His reward was a pair of nylons. Upon arriving home, he displayed this prize to his mother, and she reacted with alarm as to how her son might have acquired such an item.

Being satisfied with his explanation, the mother gladly accepted this gift and wore the stockings to church the next Sunday. Since nylon stockings had been so rare during the war, few ladies owned them, so hers were readily noticed by the other ladies. This mother proudly explained how her skilled son had won them at Ramona Park. During the next week, his mother's friends duly supplied this young man with funds to get to the park and play the game, providing in return that he bring them nylons. With no effort at all, he performed flawlessly at the dart booth, and walked away with stockings for his mother's lady friends. However, the following week when he appeared at the booth with his fistful of dimes, the proprietor recognizing him, limited him to only one game. After that he had to return to paying his own way to the park.

By dart-thrower Don Bratt

Fish Pond

In 1903, a fish pond was advertised along with the shooting gallery. The promotion said, *"offers inducements to those who prefer angling to shooting."* Over the years, the game known as the fish pond changed in style, but was basically the same game. Catch a fish and win a prize. The particular fish that was snagged designated a particular prize. One version of this popular game was the Electric Fishing Pond, appearing in 1912. *"This is bound to puzzle the crowds whether they are anglers or not. There is a pond of blue water in which the fishermen angle with ordinary poles, lines, and hooks. Presently they 'get a bite' of the regular piscatorial kind. They pull up the line and a metal fish is found caught in the hooks. This fishing is mysterious but realistic. Electrical magnetism has something to do with it."*

Whether the angler's pole waggled a hook or magnet on the end of its line, the wielder would always win something. In the later years of the park, at least, the wooden, floating fish whizzed past the player in a trough of swiftly moving water. Sooner or later, one of those targets would connect with the line and the game was over, the prize was won. At that time, the booth was located toward the west end of Fun House Row.

Dick Ryan tells of working in the booth, where he took in the fares and oversaw the operation: *"I remember one particularly busy day, holiday or something, when the manager said to remove the one fish that had 'choice' written on the bottom. A person could choose any prize with that one. Prizes were stuffed animals and little plastic animals."*

Penny Arcade

Another way to extract precious pennies from the fists of park-goers, was the penny arcade machines. Over time, these instruments produced a variety of prizes. In 1903, the announcement of the park opening stated this:

"In the pavilion, north of the auditorium, is the Penny Picture gallery. Forty penny-in-the-slot picture machines are stationed here. They offer the usual slot-machine views. The company operating these has other picture machines, as well as punching and magnetic machines scattered through the pavilion. There are fifty-five machines in all."

Machines that took a photo of the customer hadn't been invented yet, these pictures would have been of "interesting" subjects, which were made visible through viewers upon receipt of the coin. A variation of this was the short moving picture. Another "reward" to the former owner of pennies was the sound of a gramophone, which in 1905 was quite a novelty.

In 1931, when the Mystic Chutes burned down, the McElwee brothers lost 70 penny arcade machines in the fire. This was an indication of the popularity of this type of amusement. In the 1950s, there was still a "penny" arcade building. It was known as "Nickeltown" and was located on the western end of the park.

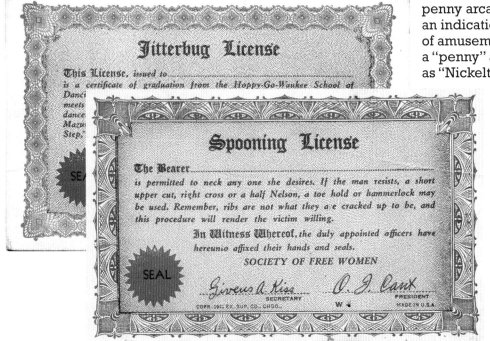

Examples of "trophies" acquired from one of the penny machines.

High Striker

The first year that the hammer machine or high striker was mentioned at Ramona was 1914. The player swung a giant mall down upon a target and the reward was to see lights appearing on a tower as the striker made its climb toward the bell at the top. Striking and ringing the bell was a sign of real strength, and, as in the shooting gallery, won bragging rights for the hammer swinger. This device apparently stayed in the park, in one form or another, until the end. Once in a while, a "ninety-seven-pound-weakling" would come along who knew the secret of hitting the target on just the right spot where the mechanical advantage would send the striker swiftly to the top, to the amazement of all on-lookers.

Part of midway crew in the early 1950s.

Miniature Golf

Miniaturized golf entered the amusement scene around 1929 atop Lookout Mountain in Chattanooga TN. The game enchanted adults as well as children and by 1930 had become a thing of national tournaments. That was also the year that the game made its appearance at Ramona. The son of the proprietor, Jack Sousley, described it as a *"carpeted putting course,"* and the newspaper reported it to be modeled after the Tom Thumb course in Miami FL.

Aerial view of the miniature golf course, photographed in 1930. The cars at the bottom are parked along Wealthy street.

128

F.A. Wurzburg directed the construction of the 1930 course, and, as always, it was promised to be the best in the middle west. Nighttime illumination extended its attractiveness. It also boasted opportunities for the golfer to improve *"skill in hopping over obstacles and solving puzzling situations."*

This is the last hole on the 1930 course. The cars on the left are on Lakeside Ave. Also visible are the former Phoenix Club building, left, and Ramona Athletic Park, right.

Ad from 1930

In the late 1940s, the park had a different miniature golf area. Park employee Jim Chrysler recalls that his great uncle, Freeman Chrysler, operated the concession.

The photo shows a group of neighbors assisting in the re-railing of the miniature train in the late 1940s. It also shows the booth for the "carpet golf" and the location of the game relative to the entrance from the bus landing area on the southeast corner of the park.

Gambling?

Besides the try-your-skill games on the midway, from time to time there were the try-your-luck type. Those who took away prizes did so out of pure chance. There was a rickety line dividing these games from gambling. One of them was the **candy wheel**, a specific game of the paddle-wheel type. The wheel, not so different from roulette, had a pointer that indicated the winning number when the wheel stopped spinning. Players purchased markers inscribed with a number and the holder of a winning number won a box of candy. This appealed especially to youngsters and women to the consternation of the vigilant eyes of the moralists in town.

An incident was instigated in a meeting of the Grand Rapids Ministers' Conference in 1918. A special committee investigated the candy wheel at Ramona, managed by George B. Zindel, and chose to step-up efforts to have the wheel abolished. The smooth-talking manager convinced the group to allow him to finish out the current year. It was a consensus that since they had been guilty of neglecting the matter for several years, another year wouldn't matter, so nothing more was done. In fact, the candy wheel was up and running again in 1919, in its own building.

Apparently it was acceptable to use the paddle wheel game to raise money for good causes, however. In 1921, a benefit was held in Ramona Gardens which earned over $1,500 for the Blind Relief War Fund for allied soldiers and sailors living in the Evergreen Hospital near Baltimore. *"Various articles were raffled by the paddle wheel method, including baskets of groceries, cigarettes, cigars, hams, chickens, balloons and flowers."*

By October, 1921, another wave of enthusiasm reared up for abolishing gaming devices in the city and environs. The *GR Press* article on the subject stated,

"Sweeping charges that certain sections of the amusement park at Reeds lake have become only a 'cheap midway' where paddle wheels and other 'gaming devices' flourish and that the abundance of gaming booths at the West Michigan State fair

this year was 'a disgrace' were made this week by Prosecuting Attorney Cornelius Hoffius and city Manager Fred H. Locke. Officials indicated all such devices may be barred from the county and city next year.

"'Paddle wheels as conducted at Reeds lake and the fair this year undoubtedly were gambling devices,' asserted Hoffius. 'At the time we abated the Lakeside Gardens at Reeds lake as a public nuisance, I talked with the officers of East Grand Rapids and advised them to rid themselves once and for all of gambling. I suggested that they issue licenses with the provision that the instant proprietors of concessions put in paddle wheels their licenses would be revoked.

"'They seemed to favor the idea but did nothing about it. Now for the sake of a few dollars in fees to the village they are permitting conditions which are a disgrace. I have been out there and seen the conditions and decided to let them breathe their own dust. Certain sections of the resort have become nothing but a cheap midway. The conditions at the West Michigan State Fair were a disgrace. The time is coming when decent citizens will rise up against such conditions as these.'

"The situation is the more complicated because many of our prominent citizens smile at the situation and even take part in such gaming. Churches, societies and other organizations conduct raffles and paddle wheels."

Weight and Age Guessing

Pay money and the expert guesses your weight or age. At Coney Island this "game" was fixed. The patron would magically weigh in on the park scales whatever weight was guessed. Not only were the scales phony, the operator was skillful at picking the pockets of the unsuspecting person being weighed in.

But at Ramona, it was done differently. According

to Dick Ryan, when he "worked" the game, he wasn't trained in the art of estimation although he only manned the station for one day. The chant was, *"guess your weight within 5 pounds, age within 3 years."* The manager told him it didn't matter if he was right or not, the prizes cost less than the fee. It was to the distinct advantage of the operator to guess very low on the weight or age of a lady!

Shooting Gallery

Throwing objects at targets was one thing, but the more serious sort of competition was shooting guns or rifles at targets. In peacetime, used as a tool for obtaining food, the rifle was also an instrument of entertainment in target shooting. Early shooting galleries were set up in various places around town, including Reeds Lake. In May 1890, pre-Ramona Park days, there were three licensed shooting galleries in Grand Rapids, and the number grew as the summer wore on. Licenses were issued to proprietors at $3 per month. The price for shooting was "3 shots for a nickel," and on a good day, the owner would realize $8 to $10. On holidays, the take was several times that amount.

A rather frightening description of an early range appeared in the *GR Evening Leader*, May 28, 1890,

"The shooting stalls are generally constructed of canvas, a tent being made for this particular business. The tents are lined with board inside as a protection against accidents and for the benefit of the marksmen of unsteady and uncertain aim. The targets are of all conceivable shapes and patterns, but the whitewashed round targets with a bull's eye through the center, backed up with a piece of old mill saw or sheet iron to furnish the ringing sound, are the most popular. Sometimes figures of pretty women and brave men, actors and actresses, statesmen and prize-fighters adorn the target boards.

"At the Reed's lake resorts, the shooting galleries are blossoming out in abundance, but here they are generally patronized by a class of older citizens—men who are out for pleasure and who make wagers upon their shots. The ladies patronize the summer resort shooting tents frequently, but the large majority of customers are the boys from 10 to 20 years of age."

WANTED—Man of experience to run shooting gallery at Ramona Park, Reed's lake, for this week. Inquire John Merryweather. 19

Shooting just for the pleasure of hearing the ringing sound when the bullseye was hit, and the bragging rights that went with it, kept people coming back.

The *GR Press* reported this in 1914:

"There is a shooting gallery, for example. The time-honored clay pipe, the whitewashed birdie, the elusive iron rabbit and the scores of other metal victims silhouetted against the sheet iron ought to anger any red-blooded citizen to a point where he had to get a gun and shoot them. It makes no difference if the charge in the rifle is no more severe than a good blast of air, it is enough to snap the stem of one of the arrogant clay pipes.

This *GR Press* article from 1917, before the U.S. entered the war, puts a different spin on the game.

"The only feature at the park which so far has shown America's spirit of preparedness is the shooting gallery which is conducted by George Brown and Arthur Drain. 'America and especially Grand Rapids is learning to shoot,' Mr. Drain says. 'Last year more than 75,000 cartridges were shot at the targets in my gallery. This year, even though the attendance at the park has been somewhat smaller, we are way ahead of last year's business. Young men who have never handled a rifle before are now coming here and learning to shoot. I expect that we will use almost double the number of cartridges this year.'"

The popularity of the rifle range, or shooting gallery at Ramona continued in some form through to the end of the park. In the mid 1940s, Jim Chrysler managed a miniature skeet-shooting booth. *"We used 4 or 5, 22 calibre rifles (pump action) which used 22 short birdshot cartridges. I had a little spring loaded clay pigeon ejector that used about 4 inch clay pigeons. There were high white walls on the three sides to keep the pellets from causing harm to others."*

At the shooting gallery in 1947, during the Twins' Day event. Note the malted shop and a corner of the carousel behind the girls.

Rifle Range buildings in 1912, left, and 1954, right

Pokerino

The building with the name, "Pokerino," appears in various photos, located in the string of buildings culminating with the Fun House on the north side of the park. It is the recollection of former employees that this building housed machines, almost like a penny arcade. The game was not unlike the skee-ball type where rolling balls landed in targets. In this case, the targets were playing cards, and the better the resulting poker hand, the more grand the prize.

Below, a collection of buttons, consolation prizes acquired by NOT winning at the games.

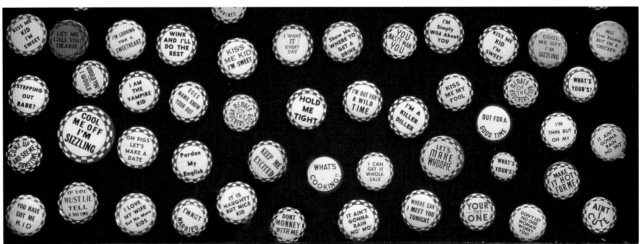

Photographs

Souvenirs of a day at Ramona that didn't require skill or luck, were personal images made on the spot. For the opening of the Ramona Theater in 1900, a new little steam merry-go-round was introduced along with a booth that made tintypes. Since that form of photographic procedure had been around since the 1850s, and since by 1900 paper photos were being produced, this was almost a novelty. But it was an inexpensive way to get an image with less processing.

The cover of this souvenir tintype said, *"As we were at Reed's Lake 1905"*

Very early photo of the tintype booth on the Ramona Midway.

During the first decade of the 1900s, postcards were immensely popular. Companies promoted their purchase, and collector clubs were springing up all over the globe. The Kodak company bought the rights to market photo paper with a pre-printed postcard back. Between 1906 and 1910, Kodak offered the service of processing and printing postcards for a fee. Such a service was also offered at Ramona by various vendors.

The ad to the right appeared June 26, 1909. In August the same season, this notice appeared in the *GR Press*:

"Roy Beck and his wife, Minnie, obtained one of the concessions at Ramona and began a penny photograph business. It is alleged on the part of the wife, the business did not pay and the husband went away, setting up for himself at Manhattan. Left to herself, Mrs. Beck says she put the business on a paying basis and during the Fourth of July celebration cleaned up a fine sum of money."

133

Ramona Photo Gallery.

No one ever goes to a resort park, especially with their friends, that they do not get their picture taken to remember the day. Post cards are the latest craze and the most sensible for a small, low priced photo. The Shootrite Fotografers have realized the demand and have set up their stand at the Ramona Post Card Gallery, near the "Teddy Bears."

They are using some brand new ideas, such as making a fleshy person thin, a short person tall, a tall person taller, playing cards with oneself, the mysterious second person, the long and short of it, etc.

The Shootrite Fotografers retain the ever popular moon and automobile, have added several now backgrounds painted to order and expect to put in more new ideas as space permits. They urge all to have their picture taken the "Krazy Way."

Story from 1913

Example of a "Shootrite Fotograf." At the time of this image, the big steamer "Ramona" was not around. This is merely a scene by which a visit to the park was to be remembered

MOVING PICTURE PHOTOGRAPHS.

The Latest Fad.

After several years' experimenting there has been a camera perfected for making moving picture photographs of yourself or friends. Although it has been on the market only a very short time it has met with immediate favor. These moving picture photos must be seen to be appreciated and they can be seen and made for you by Royal T. Gillett, proprietor Royal Photo Co., at Ramona park.

Mr. Gillett has secured the exclusive rights for Grand Rapids and vicinity and will operate this camera at his summer branch gallery at the lake. He wishes to extend a cordial invitation to all his friends and customers to call and see these wonderful pictures. A regular photographing business, so to speak, will be carried on at the above mentioned branch. Regular quick postal cards, while you wait. Picnics and groups will be given special attention, also copying and enlarging, amateur finishing, photos made for lockets and watches and several other novelties. Good work, reasonable prices and satisfaction our motto.—Adv.

Exhibits

In the early years of the midway, traveling exhibits were brought in by park manager Louis J. DeLamarter as a part of his endeavor to provide new and different delights for visitors every year. Sometimes special buildings were built to house the exhibits, and subsequently were reused for different exhibits. While these amusements attracted people to the park, many were also educational in content.

An exhibit that truly amazed people started out as a hobby for a young man who couldn't participate in vigorous activities. Fred A. Kempf, from the little town of Capac, constructed a miniature city which was worthy of display in venues of major importance. Scale models of the buildings, vehicles and humans in this city came from his imagination or real places seen in books or were copied from those he had seen while traveling. The scale of the city was one-eighth inch to a foot. His humans were about three quarters of an inch high.

Mr. Kempf invented ways to mechanize a little train, autos, trucks, boats, a draw bridge, a dredge in the harbor and even an operating mine using electrical relays. Vaudeville shows were visible in the tiny theater and men were building a tiny steel skyscraper. Even experts in the field of electronics and mechanics were amazed by his genius. This work was done in his home whenever he could muster a few spare hours from chores and schoolwork.

This exhibit came to Ramona three times, while it was on a circuit that covered other major cities around the country. Eventually he joined the Herbert A. Kline Shows and then the Kennedy Circus, and traveled with his wife and young daughter. In November 1915, their circus train was involved in a collision with a passenger train, and Fred and his wife perished in the flames. They had managed to move their daughter out of a window and she was saved, but the magnificent miniature city was not. After that, Fred's brothers, Bruce and Irving, built another miniature city, taking 7 years to complete. It toured the country successfully for a number of years and now resides back in Capac, Michigan, in the Kempf Museum.

Akin to the Model City was a working model of the Panama Canal. Mr. Fred Kempf started his model of the building of the canal in the winter of 1907 and had it ready for display by the time the park opened in May the following year. This was during the time when the real canal was still being built, and the display depicted the construction process, complete with little steam shovels, dredges, locomotives, and dump cars. To do this, he had a work room on South Division in Grand Rapids, and used drawings, pictures, maps and literature in order to make it realistic. After a few weeks, this display was replaced by a return engagement of Kempf's miniature city.

Then in 1913, one year before work on the actual canal was finished, a different model of the Canal was exhibited, this time showing the completed project. It was built on a scale of two miles to the foot. It was first displayed downtown in the old Corl-Knott store on Division before being brought out to the park.

KEMPF'S WONDERFUL MINIATURE CITY

Admission 10c

A MODEL CITY CONSTRUCTED BY FRED S. KEMPF

THE PANAMA CANAL

One of the greatest engineering feats of history in miniature, showing the Gatun dam, the Culebra cut, the locks, miniature railway, the wireless stations, lighthouses and harbors. It's a working model, operated by electricity and of vast educational value.

Wooden Shoe Shop
Unique, Interesting.—A Bit of Holland.

Appropriate to the Grand Rapids area was the wooden shoe factory and store which was set up in the circle in 1912. The Old Holland Shop, run by Gerrit W. VerNooy, was billed as the sole survivor of the industry in the city. Spectators could watch all the steps in the operation of creating the wooden footwear and then purchase the resulting products. This was an entertainment that was educational and historic to boot.

Prior to this, in 1906, an envoy from the Netherlands was sent to Western Michigan by Queen Wilhelmina. Minister VanSwinderen visited Mr. VerNooy's wooden shoe factory in his home and reported back to the queen about the craftsman. She requested a pair of shoes which Mr. VerNooy made and shipped to her. While Mr. VerNooy had his shop at Ramona, he received a request for another pair of shoes for Queen Wilhelmina, which he made and put on display. His compliments to the queen were engraved on the shoes in Dutch, ***"To the queen of Holland, from a former subject now manufacturing wooden shoes in America."***

Two years later, in June, 1914, Gerrit VerNooy died from a heart attack brought on by a heat wave in the city. His son William carried on the traditional craft for a while after his death.

Winnebago Indian Village at Ramona

Another traveling exhibit that provided an educational opportunity for park-goers was the "Winnebago Indian Village" that was set up at Ramona in July, 1908. At that time, it was said that only about 1,200 members of the tribe still existed in the states of Wisconsin and Nebraska.

THE INDIAN VILLAGE

Genuine Ottawa Indians showing the process of making baskets, birch novelties, leather goods, etc., in the same primitive manner popular in the days of the early pioneers.

TONIGHT
Christening of Four Weeks' Old Papoose in Indian Village

Besides having the opportunity to view the habitat of the early tribe members, something very special happened while the exhibit was at Ramona. There was an infant born mid-June that was christened at the park. The ceremony followed tribal traditions, complete with a feast of stewed fowl which was killed by the chief according to ancient rites.

A similar exhibit was brought to the Circle in 1913, this time the inhabitants of the display village were of the Ottawa tribe. Illustrating their traditions and customs, these descendants of former inhabitants of Western Michigan served to educate visitors in the lore of their people. The tribe was still present when the merchants had their annual outing and banquet in June, and they joined in the merriment as the visitors trooped by.

The midway at Ramona was not without its curiosities and oddities:
people who performed odd feats, or appealed to the public
by virtue of the curious billing they received.

THE STRANGEST GIRL ALIVE !!!!!

EMMA

MIDWAY BOASTS TWO REAL NOVELTIES

Every year Ramona patrons are treated to something new and novel in the way of high-grade attractions.

This year is no exception to the rule, for the Midway, with its bright lights and thousand amusment palaces, now boats two wonders.

Emma, the fat girl, and Mabel, the strange girl, are the rather peculiar names under which the wonders travel. Emma, although only 22 years old, weighs more than a quarter of a ton. What makes Mabel the strangest girl in the world can only be guessed after a visit to her palatial home on the Midway. Hurry! Hurry! Hurry!

NEXT FREE ACT STARTS AT

Above, some people will do anything for an audience!

Pictured at left is a pair of twins - flanking a set of Siamese twins who were visiting Ramona for one of their "Twins' Days" events.

137

The Season's Sensation Is
The Baby Incubator
A BOON TO THE CITY AND A NOVELTY TO SPECTATORS.

Three units from the 1909 exhibit.

The thought of tiny, helpless babes on display for public viewing at an amusement park is at first repugnant. It happened at Ramona Park in 1909, 1911 and 1912. The story behind the baby incubator show explains how the management of the park could even consider including the display.

Most often, the premature birth of a human spelled certain death, depending on its age and birth weight. The popular thought was that the infant should be in the care of the mother for the best chance at life. An underdeveloped baby also had underdeveloped lungs, immune systems and digestive tracts. No amount of love and caring could overcome such terrible odds in most cases. Even so, people were not receptive to the idea of placing a pitifully weak youngster in a glass cavity to spend its first days and weeks of life. It seemed inhumane and cold. On the other hand, this invention was saving lives.

One of the early developers of the baby incubator, Dr. Martin Couney of Germany, was also the force behind the business of promoting the invention through exhibitions. His first such endeavor in the United States was the Trans-Mississippi Exposition in Omaha, Nebraska in 1898. Since the acceptance of this invention was so strongly opposed, his idea was to demonstrate first-hand the success that was possible through its use. Exhibitions and amusement parks were places where people gathered in great quantities. Such people were eager to see new things and witnessing the success of the infant incubator was an educational experience as well.

Ramona Park was chosen as a site for the incubator show in 1909, encouraged by park manager, Louis DeLamarter. The "show" came to Grand Rapids directly from Electric Park in Detroit having been in Chicago, Cleveland and the Toronto Exposition. The hospitals in Grand Rapids had no facilities for meeting the needs of premature infants. The costly equipment required the approval of boards and the public in general before such expenditures could be made. Also, people had to be specially trained in order to manage such a unit. Ramona Park served as a catalyst, in this respect, by providing opportunity for the incubators to be viewed by the public, and hospital personnel. In 1913, St. Mary's Maternity Hospital installed its first incubator, financed by one of the guilds. Perhaps that was a direct result of the Ramona Park exhibit.

As incongruous as it may seem, the first exhibit at Ramona was set up in the building previously known as the Laughing Gallery. It was closely situated between the roller coaster and the shoot-the-chutes amusements. The building was outfitted with special air filtration and heating plants. The germless, dustless, 85 to 90 degree air was circulated by small fans though the incubator cavity, while it was in use. The area was divided into different rooms, which were used for various tasks associated with infant care, and which provided for stages in the development of the tiny child.

The head nurse, traveling with the exhibit for the past 6 years, had studied with Dr. Couney for 15 years prior and had practical training in Chicago. Besides overseeing the care of the infants in the exhibit, she worked with local physicians and nurses. With the babes needing 24 hour care, it was necessary to provide quarters for the staff as well. These dedicated people also helped convince viewers that the exhibit was not cold and inhuman because of the loving care that they exhibited.

Ad from 1912, when the exhibit occupied a different building

138

The Nursery -- the ordered sanctum of the kindly women and their charges. Photograph taken through the glass partition dividing the nursery from the exhibition room.

On the left, photo taken in 1912 of the building which then housed the baby incubators.

The map below shows the location of this building in 1911, and 1912, next to the Chinese Restaurant

For the first appearance, 1909, three infants came with the exhibit from Detroit, the head nurse convincing the authorities that they still needed care. All three were orphans and were later adopted. While at Ramona, the baby incubator exhibit did save the lives of some local infants, which, had the facility not been there, would likely have perished. Not all infants brought to the incubators lived. Several were under 2 pounds in birth weight, and as yet, no infants that small had lived.

The parents of the premature babies were not charged for service rendered. While not fully self-supporting, most of the expenses were covered by the fees paid by people entering the exhibit. It was, in fact, a proposition by which all parties gained. The acceptance of the incubator as a viable tool in maintaining human life, the education of the public as to the need for such equipment, the increase in visitors to the park who came to see the exhibit, and most of all, the saving of little Grand Rapids lives were the benefits of the baby incubator show.

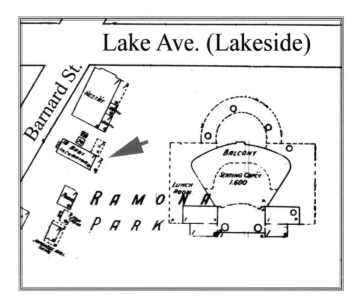

Animals

When Mr. Orin Stair first became manager of the Ramona Theater, before the days of the amusement park, he envisioned adding "*some attraction in the animal line*," perhaps a cage of monkeys stationed in the grove near the pavilion. This became a reality in 1906 when a colony of monkeys was purchased by the new manager, Mr. Louis J. DeLamarter. Throughout the years of Ramona Park, various critters were lodged in habitats on the Circle for the viewing pleasure of children visiting the park, and free to the observer.

Monkeys

Eleven monkeys, purchased by Manager DeLamarter, were installed in their new home at Ramona in mid-May, 1906. They arrived packed in boxes, shipped from New York, apparently not very well taken care of during their passage. But they seemed to thrive in their East Grand Rapids environment, and provided much amusement that summer.

Actually, a little too much amusement was felt when early in June, two of the little rascals escaped. Jocklets, the largest and oldest monkey of the lot, along with a small companion, made a successful dash for liberty when the cage was opened by Mr. Dennis McCarthy, also manager of the Motographia vaudette. The small fellow was captured easily but not so with the more experienced simian. He sought refuge in the Roll-Away Rink, causing panic among the skaters until he ducked into a side store room. Unfortunately for Mr. McCarthy, this room was used for storing paint. Sir Jocklets happened to be quite the marksman and when the keeper entered the room, he was bombarded with opened cans and pails of paint. The monk was captured only when he ran out of ammunition, and both man and monkey emerged from the fracas wearing different colors than when they entered.

Over the years, other monkey escapes provided amusement for the neighbors, but the inconvenience was small compared to the entertainment value of the monkey cages at Ramona.

Ramona's Own
MONKEY TOWN
A 3-RING CIRCUS OF SIMIAN STARS
THE FINEST AND LARGEST COLLECTION
OF MONKEYS IN THE UNITED STATES
HIGH DIVERS AND TIGHT ROPE
WALKERS · BIKE AND PONY
RIDERS · MIDGET APES
TRICK PONY · TALKING DOG
3 POUND TOY MANCHESTER

In 1945, Ramona's Monkeytown was advertised downtown in early May when the monkey, Jimmy, performed on the streets with his trainer.

In 1945, a complete monkey circus was booked for the whole season, and they performed twice a day, doing such tricks as walking the high wire and riding bikes and ponies. The entourage included a mother with a new baby, christened Lili Marlene, and Joppo, a 20-year-old blind monkey, who traveled with the show but didn't perform.

A birthday party was held in the park for the one-year-old Lili, complete with a three-foot-high cake baked especially for her. Startled at first by the excitement of the party, the baby had a crying tantrum in its mother's arms. With that episode over and done, Lili finally sampled a nice big hunk of the cake and was once again happy. The mother was not happy about all the hullabaloo, however, and wouldn't turn loose of the babe until she was relegated back to her cage. Little Lili was born in Belleview Michigan.

The party included a banana-eating race between the 18-year-old monkey, Sally, and 10 year-old Terry Barr, son of manager Fred Barr. Terry finished his three bananas first but the contest was determined to be a draw since the monkey had also eaten the peelings.

Bear Cubs

A steady fixture at Ramona from 1907 until the end was the bear cub exhibit. The original cage was circular with a cement floor and a tree in the center, but the location and construction of the cage changed over the years. The cage was populated each summer with cubs imported from "Portage Wild Animal Company" in Portage La Prairie in Manitoba, Canada, to which they were returned at the end of the season. Most often two young bruins would arrive, but occasionally there were as many as four to entertain the young park-goers.

Newsboys looking on while the caretaker feeds the bears.

On the left, not to be outdone by monkeyshines, on one occasion in 1922, the bear population escaped its confines when the cage door was not properly secured. The slower of the two fugitives was nabbed right away, but his sister succeeded in climbing a nearby-tree. Rather than match his shinny skills to those of the bear, the caretaker, Ed Myers, camped in a comfortable chair beneath the tree and waited for her to descend, which she did after several hours.

Left, animal cage on the midway in 1912. Right, a sad reminder of those venerable, by-gone days. The cage which provided summer habitat for so many animals loved by young visitors, sits empty in the winter of 1955, never to be filled again.

Ostriches

In 1906, a very unusual animal exhibit came to Ramona Park. Billed as a **"South African Ostrich Farm"** but coming from Jacksonville Florida, these big birds were likely the first live ostriches ever seen by most park visitors. There were ten full grown birds, placed on view in a special fenced-in area at the northwestern end of the park. Two of the flock were trotting birds which regularly raced against each other. Spectators were treated to a lecture by the handler, a 20-year veteran of the trade, who told of the nurture and habits of the creatures. He also demonstrated how the bird was easily subdued by a hood placed over the eyes.

The arrival of the exhibit in town evoked the following description from the *GR Press,* August 7, 1906:

"For a time this morning it looked as though a section of the Ringling Brothers' circus train had broken loose on Monroe street. Flat cars bearing mysterious looking crates, with long necks and hooded heads protruding from holes in the top, were hauled along by a street railway motor. The aggregation attracted considerable attention and caused much comment. It developed that it was not part of the circus, but instead was the South African ostrich farm which will exhibit at Ramona for two weeks beginning tonight.

"The birds arrived from Milwaukee via lake boat and the Grand Trunk

this morning and the crates containing them were hauled to the lake on street railway flat cars. The birds were hooded because they are more easily handled when their eyes are covered."

As a benefit of this exhibit being in the park, besides the educational value to visitors, the proprietors offered an

SOUTH AFRICAN OSTRICH FARM
Ostrich Egg Supper Tonight. Free to All Who Attend.
See the Trotting Ostriches and the Running Ostriches.

ostrich egg supper from the "proceeds" of the two regularly laying birds. It was said that just one egg weighed between four and five pounds and would serve several people. The bill of fare was ostrich egg omelet, scrambled ostrich eggs, and ostrich eggs in various forms known to professional chefs.

The visit of the traveling ostrich farm ended on a rather awkward note. A local printing company sued the manager of the exhibit for an unpaid bill, and as collateral, two of the ostriches were "confiscated." While the wheels of justice turned round, the birds were taken to The Island for care and safe-keeping. The problem encountered by the constable designated as their guardian, was finding food for them. Luckily for man and bird, the waiting period was cut short when the claim was satisfied in Justice Court, and the lien on the birds was lifted.

Sundry

An exhibit which was more or less educational was the Silkworm Colony, which shared the Miniature City building. Visitors could watch the active little fellows in all stages of their life-cycle, hatching, eating and spinning. The harvesting of silk threads from the cocoons was also demonstrated.

Visitors to the circle in 1907 could view a display of all the varieties of fish living in Michigan waters. The Michigan State Fish Commission supplied the fish while the Grand Rapids Railway Company furnished the building and maintenance of the display. This presentation was free to the public. Exhibits like this were previously a feature of the state fair in Pontiac until a lack of funds cut them off. Ramona provided the venue for the exhibit to continue. Superintendent Dwight Lydell of the Mill Creek Hatchery assisted in this endeavor.

In 1913, Circle-strollers had a week of free animal shows. Buckley's Animals, coming from their stint in Chicago to perform at Ramona Theater, arrived a week early. While this was a surprise to Manager DeLamarter, he quickly arose to the occasion and had cages built immediately. This allowed everyone visiting the park to view the four skating rhesus monkeys, two roller skating bears, a big eighty-pound baboon and nearly a score of dogs. Also present, and thus far untamable was the tiniest bear, a Japanese sun bear, weighing only 15 pounds. This menagerie was joined later in the week by a baby tiger, only a few months old. What was an error in scheduling by Mr. Buckley was serendipity to the children of the area.

SEES SNAKES, BUT HE FINDS THEY ARE REAL

Ramona Watchman Has Fine Time When He Finds Zoo In Strange Place.

If the night watchman at Ramona Park had not been a person of perfectly good and regular habits, he certainly would have sent for the doctor Monday night or sought the refuge of a hospital.

This was the night of the big rain and the cold wind. Because of the weather, which was in an especially ugly mood, the watchman was told he might have the use of the switch-house and keep out of the cold and rain. when he turned the key and threw open the door, he heard strange and ominous sounds, but thinking these resulted from the storm, he switched on the light. Paralyzed with horror, he saw the place swarming with snakes, alligators, ring-tailed monkeys, a young grizzly bear, foxes and rabbits.

He did not stop to count them, but bolted out into the night and didn't stop running until he collided with a day-time employee of the park, who explained the Ramona Park zoo had been temporarily housed in the switchhouse.

Then the watchman made friends with the animals and fed warm milk to the bear cubs who had had a long journey from Portage La Prairie in Canada.

GR Press, May 25, 1917

ONE MUSKRAT CAUSE OF PANIC AT RAMONA

When Lights Go Out Crowd Is Terrified as Furry Fellow Seeks Safe Place.

ANIMAL MEN CAPTURE IT

When a storm knocked out the lights, and wind ravaged the animal show, an enormous black muskrat was uncaged. In the eerie light, its appearance was monster-like, and sent the crowds scurrying.

Refreshments

As soon as people began to travel to Reeds Lake on pleasure excursions, their recreation included eating. Packing picnic repasts was part of the process. When the resort business began at the lake with rental boats, providing food for patrons followed. Every resort that emerged offered refreshments of some type, from beverages to full meals.

The first railroad pavilion, built for the convenience of picnickers, offered refreshments and picnic supplies at first and then branched out into full dinners. Up until the time the theater building was erected, the managers of the railroad pavilion were all caterers. The Ramona Theater offered refreshments for theatergoers, but its primary business was stage productions.

In 1885, the railroad company allowed George Griggs to build a popcorn stand on its property. He had once been a successful land-owner and speculator, but was down on his luck. After that time, many private food and beverage enterprises were operated on the railroad grounds.

Below, the Ramona popcorn stand in 1909, when it was situated between the merry-go-round building and the theater pavilion.

EARLY 1900 WANT ADS

WANTED-- Six boys about 18 years for peanut stand; two young ladies for cashier. 1900

WANTED-- Two men for popcorn stand; candy makers preferred. 1901

FOR SALE-- Cheap popcorn fritter machine, with instructions for making same; just the thing for any resort. 1903

WANTED-- Bright young lady with some business experience to help in popcorn stand at lake. 1905

WANTED-- Extra Sunday help at Reed's Lake popcorn stand. 1906

WANTED-- One experienced soda dispenser, two extras for Saturdays and Sundays extra help at popcorn stand. 1908

In the gay nineties, East Grand Rapids patrolmen frequently scouted around looking for illegal liquor traffic and gambling devices, particularly on Sundays. An article, published in the *GR Herald* in 1893, telling about the extent of the efforts of the local constabulary, says:

"James Doherty, deputy marshal of the village of East Grand Rapids, and deputy sheriff under McQueen, took two men with him yesterday and visited the lemonade and ice cream stands, soda fountains, photograph galleries, boat houses, cigar stands, etc, and patronized them, even having their pictures taken, for the purpose of obtaining evidence upon which to base an application for warrants."

This article affords a glimpse of the kinds of businesses that plied their trades of a Sunday in those days.

Restaurants

The railroad pavilions always offered food to visitors, from light lunch-fare to full-blown meals, but through the years, various restaurants within the park also served meals to customers. In 1905, Mr. George L. Sing opened a "Chinese American Restaurant" in the pavilion. This was moved out in 1908 to its own building in the park, across "Lake" street from the Lakeside Club. It came to be called the "Ramona Chop Suey Restaurant" in 1919.

"Mom" and "Pop" Jones maintained a *"dining room to care for the hungry crowds who come to them annually"* starting around 1920.

Another regular that was established in the park was Mrs. Nickerson whose lunch stand was located in the southern tower of the Derby Racer. This was "fast food," available for people on the run, anxious to get to their next park destination.

Shortly after opening in 1914, the north tower of the Derby Racer, selling "cones, peanuts, buttered popcorn" to visitors.

Decades later, the Derby Racer lunch stand, in the south tower.

In later years, restaurant space was leased to a proprietor under a contract agreement. For example, the 1935 contract with Alex Demar stated: *"The party of the second part is hereby granted the privilege of operating the concession, so-called, for the sale of Peanuts, Popcorn, Ice Cream, soft Drinks and Crackerjack for the summer season of 1935, in certain buildings or stands owned by the first party and located upon its grounds at Reeds Lake, described as follows:*

"Main Fountain Stand, Main Stand, Dock Stand, New Stand, Hires Stand Point Stand"

- The building was to be maintained at his expense and kept up to the standards of the park
- No merchandise was to be sold that did not agree with the rules of the park or was in competition with other vendors
- The rental was to be paid by the second party during such term at the sum of $750.00
- Lessee was responsible for any accidents or other liabilities, and for taxes and license fees owed the city of East Grand Rapids.

In these two photos, taken about 25 years apart, the girls are enjoying popcorn on their boat rides.

Left, seated on *The Hazel A*; right, on *The Ramona*.

Right, the "Ramona Lunch Counter" occupied various places on the grounds and was managed by various concessionaires.

Left, sandwich stand located "in the loop" and across from Ramona Athletic Park, the entrance to which is just visible on the left side of the photo.

String of eateries on The Circle in 1912: Lowney's, noted confectionery; steaks, chops and sandwiches; The Creole Cafe; spaghetti and chili con carne. The Lakeside Club is just visible to the right, located directly across the street.

Ice Cream

From the earliest days at the railroad pavilions on Reeds Lake, ice cream was offered to customers. While it seems hard to imagine, it was most often made right on the grounds. The railroad company maintained its own private ice house on the property, so ice was available for making the treat as well as to put in cold drinks and for food refrigeration. The ice would have been a product of the very lake on which the resort was perched.

In 1892, the youngsters from the Children's Home were treated to a picnic at Reeds Lake. Upon returning from their cruise on the *"Belknap,"* according to the *GR Herald* reporter in attendance,

"Mr. Swetland treated them to ice cream, and as many of them had never eaten it before, it was very amusing to watch them. A dimple-faced youngster crammed a whole spoonful of the delicacy into his mouth and the unexpected change in the temperature of his tongue made the tears start. He thought the stuff burned him and he had to take a big drink of ice water to cool his mouth. One little bright-eyed girl, declared that she could eat all the ice cream on the tables and more too. Three handsome little boys devoured the cream with an avidity most astonishing."

For the opening of the Reeds Lake Resort in 1901, it was announced in the *GR Press*:

"The public will be pleased to learn that Mr. Merryweather has charge of the refreshment features in the pavilion and on the grounds. He has added many valuable improvements, has six fountains in the main building and a seating capacity of 360 people. He will serve everything the best that can be made and at popular prices. All ice cream, candies, etc, are made right at the pavilion, every facility being provided. His popcorn, peanut and crackerjack booth will be a feature again this season. Polite and competent help will be employed and every one will be given personal attention."

Not big ice cream cones, but an early 1920s treat, cotton candy

Mr. Tony Bott worked in the park 1953 and 1954, at the cotton candy machine and making candy apples. To make the cotton candy, he would pour the sugar mix into the machine and turn it on. This stand was located between the penny pitch game and the fun house. One day when business was very slow, and he was getting tired of hearing the laugh machine from the fun house, he went to the penny pitch to "practice." He was approached by "Old Bob" who was on his rounds patrolling the park in search of empty pop bottles. Bob asked him about his new assistant. Tony went to investigate and found a raccoon eating the cotton candy.

The Ramona Theater Pavilion Ice Cream Parlor in 1908,
decorated like a pagoda for Japanese Fete.

In 1947, seventeen-year-old Ken Ellis leased the concession which had
become defunct. He had to clean out the room and outfit it. He did the
painting himself and bought used equipment. One July 4th he took in
$740 selling ice cream and soft drinks.

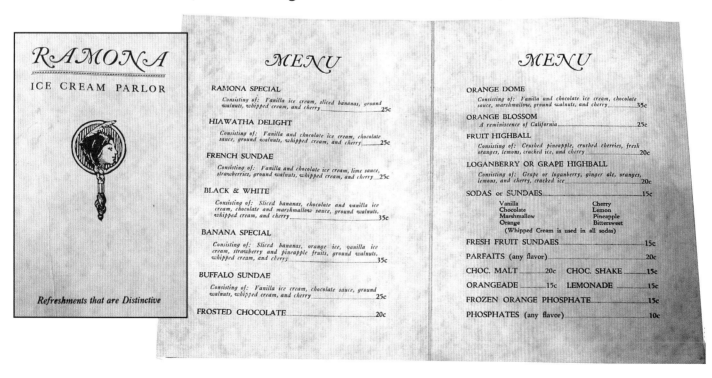

RAMONA
ICE CREAM PARLOR

Refreshments that are Distinctive

MENU

RAMONA SPECIAL
Consisting of: Vanilla ice cream, sliced bananas, ground
walnuts, whipped cream, and cherry_____25c

HIAWATHA DELIGHT
Consisting of: Vanilla and chocolate ice cream, chocolate
sauce, ground walnuts, whipped cream, and cherry_____25c

FRENCH SUNDAE
Consisting of: Vanilla and chocolate ice cream, lime sauce,
strawberries, ground walnuts, whipped cream, and cherry___25c

BLACK & WHITE
Consisting of: Sliced bananas, chocolate and vanilla ice
cream, chocolate and marshmallow sauce, ground walnuts,
whipped cream, and cherry_____35c

BANANA SPECIAL
Consisting of: Sliced bananas, orange ice, vanilla ice
cream, strawberry and pineapple fruits, ground walnuts,
whipped cream, and cherry_____35c

BUFFALO SUNDAE
Consisting of: Vanilla ice cream, chocolate sauce, ground
walnuts, whipped cream, and cherry_____25c

FROSTED CHOCOLATE_____20c

MENU

ORANGE DOME
Consisting of: Vanilla and chocolate ice cream, chocolate
sauce, marshmallow, ground walnuts, and cherry_____35c

ORANGE BLOSSOM
A reminiscence of California_____25c

FRUIT HIGHBALL
Consisting of: Crushed pineapple, crushed cherries, fresh
oranges, lemons, cracked ice, and cherry_____20c

LOGANBERRY OR GRAPE HIGHBALL
Consisting of: Grape or loganberry, ginger ale, oranges,
lemons, and cherry, cracked ice_____20c

SODAS or SUNDAES_____15c

Vanilla	Cherry
Chocolate	Lemon
Marshmallow	Pineapple
Orange	Bittersweet

(Whipped Cream is used in all sodas)

FRESH FRUIT SUNDAES_____15c

PARFAITS (any flavor)_____20c

CHOC. MALT_____20c **CHOC. SHAKE**_____15c

ORANGEADE_____15c **LEMONADE**_____15c

FROZEN ORANGE PHOSPHATE_____15c

PHOSPHATES (any flavor)_____10c

Beverages

Everywhere around the lake resorts offered cooling drinks to summertime guests, probably chilled with ice right from Reeds Lake. The railroad company always maintained that it would not allow alcoholic beverages to be sold on its premises. It was stated thus in the *GR Press* in 1912:

Can Quench Thirst.

The resort is notably free from the ribaldry of drink. Well policed and with the resort proprietors as solicitous of the safe keeping of the park's reputation in this respect as the street railway company itself, there is never a moment when unescorted women are not as safe and free from approach there as on the main thoroughfare.

Early 1900s drink token.

In keeping with the railway directive, a new beverage was introduced to the park in 1917, a sort of "imitation beer." As stated in the *GR Press*:

"The new refreshment establishment will feature 'Bevo,' the famous soft drink which has replaced beer in hundreds of 'dry' communities."

In the 1940s and 1950s, Nehi was the favored soda at Ramona.

Nehi Days

In the early 1950s there was a soda pop company in GR named Nehi. I specifically remember the grape and orange flavors. Every year, on a Saturday, at Ramona they had a 'Nehi Day' and all the pop and hotdogs were free. Pop wasn't that plentiful back then and kids would drink as much pop and eat as many hot dogs as they could hold. The park was packed and it was a great time. It was really that simple and what little Dutch kid wouldn't go for free anything?

Bob VanDongen

Park Favorites

Wintertime view of the stand that sold the most talked-about food at Ramona Park: The French Fries

FRENCH FRIES

French fries at Ramona Park are as popular a memory to former park visitors as the Derby Racer. In the 1940s, fries were more of a novelty, and those at Ramona were just plain better than anywhere else. Perhaps it was the excitement of being in the park, walking among the crowds holding a greasy but fragrant paper cone full of goodness, and being a part of the scene. Some people had their very first taste of French fries at Ramona. Others bought them because they just couldn't resist, even though they thought the 45 cents was too much. The aroma of the freshly cooked delicacy permeated the park, and became a part of "the Ramona Park experience" for so many people.

The stand was under the operation of the Williams brothers, sons of the park manager, Don Williams. Mr. Ray Seidel, who lived in the Seidel Boat Works house across Lakeside from the park, remembers the first time the stand was opened. People were lined up two and three deep, just waiting for them.

In the recollection of Mr. Dick Ryan, who worked at the stand for a short time, *"A tumbler took most of the skin off the potatoes, I had to remove the eyes with a knife. Cutting potatoes into fries was done by a big machine with a lever."*

PRONTO PUPS

In 1947 I was 17 years old when my mother opened a food stand at Ramona Park. My father had recently died of cancer so my brother and I helped my mother. After she signed the contract for the stand, the manager told her she could not sell hot dogs or hamburgers, only sandwiches. She didn't think this would sell, so my brother, Cecil, remembered eating in California what today is called "Pronto Pups" or "Corn Dogs." My brother experimented with a batter that would adhere to a hot dog and we made sticks and deep fried them.

At first no one tried them until my two brothers and some friends acted like customers and stood in front of the stand and ate our "Frankfurters on a Stick." It was such a good advertisement that we soon had a lot of sticks on the ground left over from real customers who had purchased and eaten our hot dogs.

We lived on Sheldon Street so I took the Cherry bus in the morning to clean up the stand for the day and to make coffee for the carnival workers and stars. My brother took my mother to Ramona Park in the afternoon and she stayed until closing time.

Our stand was located next to the manger's office and on one side was a pond with artificial ducks. We only had the stand one season as my mother didn't like the next contract.

Ernest San Miguel

151

Miscellaneous Midway Moments

Crowds of people waiting in line for the Derby Racer, the miniature train making its way around its circuit and midway attractions in the background.

Midway view a couple of decades later. The theater building just visible through the trees to the right, an airplane ride on the left. The fellow nearest the camera is a member of the security force.

View of deserted midway in 1912. Ticket booth, bear cage, fire-hose house and theater porch and stairway.
Note the bricked walkway, lower right.

Crowded midway scene from mid to late 1920s. Visible are the Walking Charlie booth and Ramona Photo building.
Also note the style of architecture.

Another 1920s view showing the Aeroplane Swing, double train tracks, a waiting queue and possibly the train station.

This photo of the midway also shows Kiddie Land seen in its place in the lap of the Fun House clown, the line of concession stands to the left of the clown, the Ramona Park manager's office, left, and the Ferris wheel, extreme left.

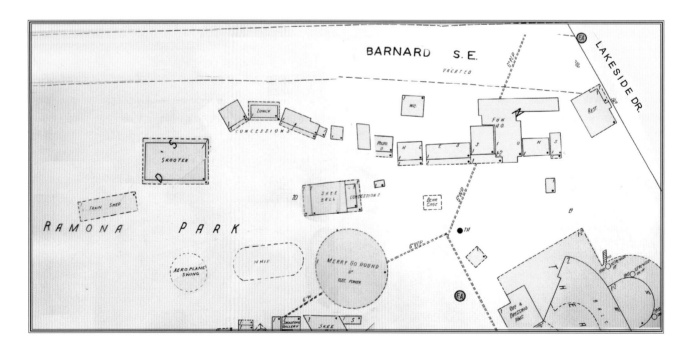

Sanborn Fire Insurance map of the midway area,
near the end of the life of the park.

Those Were the Days

What fun I had! A day at Ramona in the early 1940s was a day of smiles, giggles and laughter that as far as I was concerned, couldn't be found anywhere else in the City of Grand Rapids. I was about ten years old and had two big brothers, Harold and Jerry, to look after me. Sometimes kids in our neighborhood rode their bikes, but our day to the park began with a ride on the city bus. I probably went to Ramona only a few times. On one occasion, I remember that my Father gave me $2.00 and I felt rich. We stayed for hours!

We called the midway "Barker's Walkway" from the game proprietors who shouted to get our attention. Harold could throw balls at wooden bottles, shoot basketballs into hoops, or fire guns at targets and try out many other competitions. The walkway didn't interest me except for the Duck Pond, which was nothing more than yellow plastic ducks happily floating in a long, narrow container across the front of the Concession Stand. Each duck had a number on the bottom. All I had to do was pay the money, pick up a duck and win a prize. I remember getting a tiny little glass mug and I was especially pleased to take it home to my Mother; she used it for toothpicks.

Jerry's favorite was the electric scooters—bumper cars that are still popular today. It was fun to see kids jarring one another, but I only watched. Both my brothers and I loved the Derby Racer. We would wait in line with expectancy knowing it would be a thrill and we would get butterflies in our stomachs. After the ride, we would pay the fee and get in line again. I don't remember riding the miniature train at Ramona, but years later Walt and I rode on it with grandchildren around the outside of the Burley Park flea market near Howard City. The train is currently being refurbished.

At Ramona, there were many different kinds of foods and drinks at concession stands, but as a little girl I learned early on that in the big pavilion there was a man who dipped up ice cream cones for only a nickel, and that was always the choice I made. What a treat on a hot summer day!

The Merry-Go-Round was always one of my favorites at Ramona, not only for the ride, but also for the music. But, if I had to decide from all the enjoyable choices at Ramona, I think my very favorite was the Fun House. It had a jolly clown painted outside inviting me in. I could stay as long as I liked and return to play and laugh at will, which I always did. While my best friend, Dee, rode the Derby Racer once and vowed she would never do it again—my foibles were the two slides on the left part of the Fun House. Side by side, the two slides began at the top of the upper floor, with a divider of some sort in the middle. One slide was conventional and the other had sweeping curvy humps in it. Kids were given a gurney bag to sit on and when they reached the bottom, they could turn to the right, climb two flights of stairs and slide down again.

One look at the slides from below was all I needed; I remember saying, "I'm going to stay here," I believe I feared the height of the slides and preferred to play on the turntable. The turntable was a large, flat wooden disc, nearly the size of the room. It was fastened and moved slowly. The floor of this large room was constructed much higher in the back of the room and slanted to the bottom in the front. I could get on the turntable for a ride, but the disc was positioned so that as I came down from the higher part of the room I began to slide off. It was total fun to see how long I could stay on—then be gently thrown off at the bottom of the room. This was another occasion to laugh, and then get onboard again.

Other places in the Fun House included slanted-floor hallways, where a ghost appeared or a different place where a puff of air would come from below and startle me. Upstairs in the building were the mirrors. As we posed in front of each mirror, we laughed at ourselves and everyone else and it was all in jest. I could look wide as a barn or skinny as a rail. Each of the many mirrors brought a howl or jeer from myself or someone else.

Though I was young I was kept aware of the war; our "Weekly Readers" at school carried articles and, in fact, as kids we were involved in the war effort. Even so, the special days at Ramona were wonderful. In late afternoon, Dad picked us up in the Model A Ford after his day at work. I arrived home penniless and worn-out but with a happy heart and mind, filled with music of the merry-go-round, shrieks from the derby racer and laughs in the fun house—enough memories to last me a lifetime—and they did!

Shirley May DeBoer

Somehow it all worked in spite of the dangers that went unnoticed.

It was just a magical place of fun.

Whirligig Menageries

What is it that causes the human to want to go round in circles? And not just to move in a circuitous route, but to move up and down at the same time? What is this overwhelming yearning to be spun into a state of dizziness? This desire led to the popular amusement park ride, the merry-go-round. At Reeds Lake, the availability of this sort of ride spanned the years from 1883 to the last summer of Ramona Park in 1954. The various contraptions were of different sizes and means of propulsion, but the appeal was the same.

How It All Began

Whether the 20th century merry-go-rounds evolved from ancient maypole rituals or training exercises during Turkish fledgling knight combat preparation, it was during the second half of the 19th century that the merry-go-round, carousel, whirligig, roundabout, etc, came into its own as a much sought-after amusement for children and adults alike.

The term "carousel" or French "carrousel" was the name of a tournament where horsemen executed revolutions, derived from Italian "carosello." The "flying horses" was a version of the ride in which the wooden animals were attached above by chains or poles, not supported from the platform below, and would fly outward from the force of spinning. Either type of carousel was first powered by the riders themselves or a person or animal that trod the grounds in circles.

One of those credited with bringing the invention to America was Gustav Dentzel. In the early 1800s, his grandfather, Michael, toured Germany with his grand machines. Just after the American Civil War, Gustav began production in Philadelphia. His carousel business has been continued by successive generations. Sources differ as to the actual time and inventor of the steam-powered merry-go-round, but its advent spurred on the burgeoning popularity of the device world-wide.

The street railway company built its first pavilion at the lake in 1882, and the next year a newspaper story about a Sunday School picnic mentioned that the teachers and officers of the group enjoyed the merry-go-round "*with as much abandon as the small folks*."

By 1893 at least one more carousel had appeared because the amusement was referred to in the plural. The newsboys, at their first picnic in 1894 at the lake, made a mad dash for the merry-go-rounds. These must have been playground equipment, self propelled by the most ambitious of the passengers. An interesting reference to the method of propulsion occurred in 1895 in an article about the entertainment at Reeds Lake as viewed for the first time by an "innocent" visitor. He stated,

"That merry-go-round with its strange up and down movement is a queer contrivance, too, and I don't see how people can enjoy riding in it when they know that the poor man who pulls it around is working so hard. I shouldn't think it would be pleasant anyway, to whirl round and round that way. It would make me dizzy, I know."

The playground devices are described in greater detail by the *GR Press*, when a new play area was opened in 1909:

"The merry-go-rounds or carousels are prominent. There are two of these, one a 'crowd affair' that will accommodate sixteen children at a time. This is propelled by the youngsters themselves and works on the principle of the 'Irish mail cars.' Each youngster has an individual seat and when all are pulling merrily the carousel spins around at a lively, yet safe pace. The merry-go-round is covered by a canopy that adds to its gala appearance. A smaller merry-go-round has a capacity of four persons. It works on the same principle as the larger machine and also has a canopy top. Both the merry-go-rounds have music boxes attached just like the big whirligigs, and the children have music with every revolution."

Steam Machines

Early merry-go-round located in a picnic area on the railway grounds.

WANTED -- TWO YOUNG MEN AT REED'S lake; one that is an engineer, for steam merry-go-round. Joseph Horn. 164 Ottawa

In 1900, the park had steam equipment to run a more sophisticated carousel as was indicated by this ad in the *GR Press*, above.

But in 1903, the railway company got serious about offering a merry whirl to visitors. They contracted with the T. M. Harton Amusement Company of Pittsburgh to construct a building and install the equipment. The new device cost between $10,000 and $12,000. The octagonal structure measured some 80 feet across and 25 feet high. The merry-go-round was 50 feet in diameter. The secretary of the Harton Company superintended its installation.

The reporter from the *GR Evening Post* thought the new carousel was, *"a magnificently equipped merry go round, and except that it is much larger and more elegantly furnished than anything of the kind that has ever been put up at the lake, it differs little from the old fashioned kind."*

A view of the new building and streetcar walkway.
The fountain was built in 1910 as part of the "New Ramona" when the theater was expanded.

157

The Early Carousel

Merry-go-round, Reed's Lake, Mich.

The carousel installed in 1903 was also steam powered. In 1906, it was converted to electricity.

Shortly after the new amusement opened, surprisingly perhaps, an accident occurred. This article of June 29, 1903 from the *GR Press* describes it.

SMALL BOY INJURED

Thrown From the Reed's Lake Merry-go round—Father Also Hurt.

Yesterday afternoon Tunis Quick of 44 Page street was riding on the merry-go-round at Reeds' Lake with his little son. The machine had about reached full speed when the centrifugal force threw the boy from the wooden horse and rolled him to the ground with considerable force.

The little fellow was injured about the head and groin by the fall, and his father, who leaped after him without sufficient preparation, was dashed to the ground by the rapidly moving platform and injured about the face and shoulder. Quick was not greatly hurt, but it is feared that the boy may be seriously injured.

For all its splendor and pedigree, this contraption only lasted three years before it was upgraded with new animals and electricity instead of steam. But, in 1908 the *GR Press* announced that,

"The merry-go-round and its wheezy organ have disappeared. The building will be used for other purposes."

Also, *"The old merry-go-round with its doleful grind organ has disappeared, although the building still remains. This building will be turned into a waiting room, its proximity to the car landing and its outlook over Reeds lake making it admirably adapted to this purpose. A candy pulling machine will be installed there."*

While this apparatus was equipped with an organ, apparently it was not held in much regard.

The McElwee Brothers

Part of what made Ramona Park remarkable was the talented people who were involved. The McElwee brothers' ingenuity, integrity and longevity were responsible for much of the success of this amusement park.

Growing up in the town of McAdoo, Pennsylvania, with their coal miner father, and being also involved in the mines as "slate pickers," John and James could not fathom a lifetime of that activity. They strived early on to develop their musical talents, and

OUR FIRST ENGINE

after joining a show band, toured the country in circuses and carnivals. Eventually they bought a small carousel which went with them on their journeys, thus starting their own merry-go-round business.

Becoming weary of traveling, they turned to amusement parks and increased their holdings to include merry-go-rounds installed in several of the parks in the Midwest. The whole family was living in Detroit by 1910 where the brothers were involved in Electric or Riverview Park.

The merry-go-round that was installed in the octagonal building at Ramona in 1909 belonged to the McElwee brothers. John was living in Grand Rapids by 1911 and was joined by James the next year. Their associations in Detroit amusement parks led to their bringing the Derby Racer to Grand Rapids in 1914, and the McElwee Brothers Amusement Company was in full swing by 1917.

John and James McElwee held that their customers deserved the best and safest possible equipment. The best security companies were engaged to inspect the equipment. The brothers kept watch on amusement parks around the country and sought to bring to Ramona the latest devices. Of John it was stated that *"he is an old circus man who doubled in brass many years and in many climes. He knows what folk bent on a holiday desire."* When he was manager of the park, he traveled to several cities looking for a ride more thrilling than the Derby Racer but returned home having found none. Several years after the Derby Racer was built, John McElwee had roller coasters built in Dayton Ohio and Narragansett Pier Rhode Island, but they were not very successful ventures.

Over the years, the McElwees brought in and managed the merry-go-round, Derby Racer roller coaster, Mystic Chutes, airplane swings, fun house, caterpillar and penny-arcade machines.

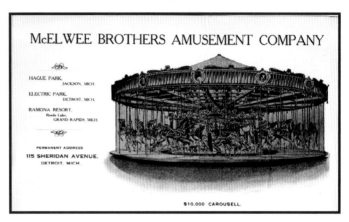

McELWEE BROTHERS AMUSEMENT COMPANY

HAGUE PARK, JACKSON, MICH.
ELECTRIC PARK, DETROIT, MICH.
RAMONA RESORT, Reeds Lake, GRAND RAPIDS, MICH.

PERMANENT ADDRESS
115 SHERIDAN AVENUE, DETROIT, MICH.

$10,000 CAROUSELL.

John McElwee
Baritone and Trombone

PER. ADDRESS
KELAYRES, PA., OR "BILLBOARD"

JAMES McELWEE
CORNETIST

McELWEE BROS. CAROUSELL CO.
PERMANENT ADDRESS
115 SHERIDAN AVE.
DETROIT
GRAND RAPIDS
JACKSON
DETROIT, MICH.

McELWEE BROTHERS
GOOD FOR ONE RIDE
Merry-Go-Round
3667 | 6 FOR 25c

THE ARGUS TICKET CO. CHICAGO

RAMONA RESORT
GOOD FOR
ONE 5c RIDE
MERRY-GO-ROUND
9669

Fun for All--

When Visiting RAMONA PARK Get All There Is in the Way of Enjoyment and Thrills!

The Derby Racer

NOTHING BETTER ANYWHERE

85-foot dip, with 70° grade. More thrills per second than ever before.

The Mystic Chutes

New scenes, in addition to favorites of old, such as Lovers' Lagoon, Spooky Nooks, Etc.

Merry-Go-Round

The Old Reliable

Aeroplane Swings

A Ride Through the Clouds

The Fun House

All the Fun You Want

NOTE:—City Ordinance imposing $50 fine for improper riding will be enforced

The McElwee Carousel

Shortly after the new amusement opened, the July 29th, 1909, *GR Press* article about the new carousel stated:

"Not the old fashioned merry-go-round with the alternate stiff little horses and sleighs and the cracked voiced grind organ in the middle, which we patronized in our youth, but the magnificent $10,000 indoor wheel that is furnishing the leading amusement to visitors, both old and young at Reeds lake.

"Here one may ride on a staid carriage horse, or a prancing racer, while the youngster with an adventurous spirit, clings to the long neck of a speckled giraffe or takes a fearsome journey on a huge lion. Some of the horses do not wave up and down, though in appearance they are just the same as the ones with the extra motion. It is amusing to watch the facial expression of people who get on a horse and then find that it is one of the quiet kind."

In 1910, the building was also used in the winter as a waiting room for trolleys bringing skaters to the lake, and it was kept heated. Before the opening of the 1912 season, the octagonal building, originally fronting on the loop for the railway, was moved with its carousel to the place in the midway where it stayed until the park closed. At its new location, the building was set upon a concrete floor, quite an improvement. Park officials chose to move the building because they felt that disembarking passengers should have an unobstructed view of the lake.

CHILDHOOD'S PASTIME

GROWS INTO ELABORATE AMUSE-
MENT FOR GROWN-UPS.

People Go Wild Over New Merry-Go-
Round at Reeds Lake
Resort.

Original location - "1"
Final location - "2"

View of the carousel building in 1912, in its new location.

The Joy Wheel

In the 1910 season, for the adults who didn't want to be seen riding the whirligig, or for anyone who thought it too tame, the Joy Wheel was installed at Ramona Park, housed in its own building at the north end. This description gives a good glimpse into the joy-wheel-world:

"If you pride yourself upon your stability, your ability to maintain your position under all circumstances, just go out to Ramona and try the Joy Wheel. If you don't you miss a great sensation, a lot of good fun. The Joy Wheel is a polished wood platform which revolves rapidly in the middle of a pit about thirty-five feet across. The wheel is eighteen feet in diameter and when it starts to going round you've got to get off sooner or later. And you won't stop to pick your landing place nor your manner of landing. Centrifugal force will send you whirling, tumbling and laughing out against the padded cushions at the edge of the pit. A carnation is hung above the center of the wheel and lowered within reach after the wheel is in motion. Whoever can grab it keeps it, but it is no small trick to keep on the wheel and reach up for the carnation at the same time. A trip on the Joy Wheel will give you lots of excitement, plenty of exercise and a world of laughter at yourself and your neighbor. Just to stand at the rail and watch the others is worth the price. But get on the wheel, you'll not regret it."

This old-time entertainment had its drawbacks as attested to by the fellow who suffered the ignominious injury of a broken leg incurred from being thrown off the device. The joy went out of the wheel after three seasons, the building tumbled down of its own volition, and the wreckage was cleared to make room for the pony livery in 1913.

A Ride on the Carousel

"How about the roller coaster?" my father says but I shake my head.

"I want to go on the carousel," I say. Dad frowns and I know he wishes that I was more adventurous, more daring.

"I need to ride a brown horse," I tell him. "Nobody chooses the brown ones so they feel sad."

My younger brother says, "I want to ride on the lion."

Bob prefers the lion because it doesn't move and I decide to not tease him about this because he knows I'm afraid of the roller coaster. Each time we come to Ramona Park I hope I'll be more brave but I'm not.

Inside the carousel pavilion, the music is blaring and the horses are galloping around and around beneath the colored lights and flashing mirrors.

I hold my paper ticket in my sweaty hand until the carousel stops and it's my turn. While other children run toward the white horses and black horses, I walk around the circle until I find a tall brown one with a curving neck and arched tail.

A man in a red cap helps me climb up into the slippery saddle. "Hang on tight," he says and I grab the brass pole. I only need one hand.

The music begins and the brown horse moves up and down, up and down, faster and faster, until we're flying, soaring, riding the wind. Somewhere in the crowd, I see my father. He is smiling now and waving.

I wave back.

Karen Anderson,
Traverse City Record Eagle

An Attraction for All Ages

Newsboys in 1943

Ladies posing for a publicity photo

162

Over the years, besides regular maintenance to the building, subtle changes were made. The exterior walls received a rough coating to simulate stone to match the other buildings. In 1916, a cupola was added to the top of the sectioned roof lending a Japanese effect to its appearance. The machinery and motors were replaced from time to time. By 1918 it was advertised to be the finest in the country with every horse being a "galloper."

Among those that did not move were the lion and the chariots which were always available for the less adventurous.

Jim McElwee and Mrs. Stankey in the carousel ticket booth.

James McElwee, who was something of an artist himself, kept the exquisite animals painted. In one season he would use up several gallons of gilt and silver finish. This close-up of a black horse shows some of the intricate detail in the carving, and the effects of constant use.

View of the lion and the chariot behind it. The lion is known to still exist in the hands of a private collector.

Phil McElwee and son riding in the chariot

Even the gentle merry-go-round had its warnings.

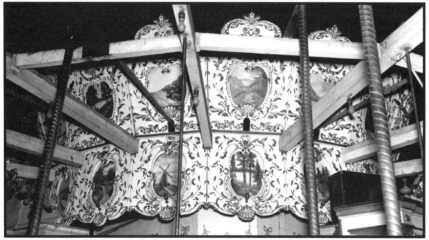

The Ramona carousel was more than a ride, more than wooden animals and music. It was a work of art.

Another glimpse of the ornamentation that graced the center.

End of an Era

This advertisement from Billboard Magazine, May 14, 1955, tells the story. When the park closed, everything was disposed of in one way or other.

FOR SALE — 3 ABREAST MERRY-GO-Round, large park machine in good condition. 42 hand-carved jumpers, 8 stationary and 2 chariots. James P. McElwee, 1529 Robinson Rd. S.E., Grand Rapids 6, Mich. GL 40064.   my14

This ghostly picture from the *GR Herald* depicts the somber occasion in September 1955, when the octagonal carousel building was torn down. The merry-go-round had been sold, the mechanisms, animals and organs packed up and shipped off to the new owner, and all traces of this exquisite device were removed.

The following text accompanied the *GR Herald* photo. It reflects the feelings of all the people who ever attended Ramona Park.

"Ever celebrate Labor Day here? If you're a native of Grand Rapids and out of the kindergarten class, the answer probably is, "Yes." For here, where a motionless and silent merry-go-round stands solitary guard, was once the hub of activity for every Summer holiday in Grand Rapids – Ramona Park.

"At the height of its glory Ramona, now all but razed to make way for a shopping development, once drew crowds as high as 70,000. On Labor Day and every other warm-weather holiday it was the center of family recreation.

"Ramona Theater in its day had the best vaudeville entertainers in the country and the derby racer and other rides delighted thousands of West Michigan kids. There were picnic grounds for family dinners. The miniature railroad probably gave more pleasure per foot of trackage than any other line in the country.

"Sure as the afternoon drew on, there was the balloon ascension. Maybe there were fireworks at night. Weary merry-makers left after a full day's adventure and were only a street car ride from home. It couldn't have lasted, of course. Holidays are spent farther afield now, in cottages and motels scattered over half a State.

"But in many a local citizen's memory Ramona still lives, gay and insouciant, the Never-Never land of two generations."

Mr. Norm Knapp worked in the park off and on in the late 1940s and part of the 1950s. One of his jobs was to check on the galloping horses to make sure they would move. He was a part of the crew that took apart the merry-go-round building and its contents in 1955. He recalls finding 113 Indian head pennies under the organ as well as tickets for a 1947 Nash, that was given away that year. It is his recollection that the carousel was sold to an amusement park in Camden NJ, and that it was packed away in a local garage until shipment could be arranged.

Carousel Organs

Of the thousands of people who rode on the beautiful Ramona Park Looff merry-go-round with its hand-carved animals, how many noticed the organ music?

People visiting the Reeds Lake resorts in the late 1800s would certainly have noticed. Disparaging words were uttered in newspapers when they described the sounds emanating from the old hurdy-gurdies such as the *GR Evening Leader* reported on July 7, 1890:

"The Street Railway company has done all in its power to make the place attractive and is giving the people unexcelled transportation facilities but the company, alone, cannot save the place for the people. One nuisance that has come with the present season is a merry-go-round that has a noisy attachment. When the band is playing its sweetest and most popular selections, this noisy attachment that doesn't have a semblance of music or harmony, is running. There should be some understanding between the band and the merry-go-round proprietors. When the people are given an opportunity to enjoy music they should not be obliged to hear the awful strains from the machine attached to the merry-go-round. Just who is to blame for the attraction that detracts is not known, but the resorters have but one opinion of the automatic music chest – it is a nuisance, especially when real music is being served."

Other descriptive terms such as, "droning intermezzo," "wheezy organ," and "cracked voiced grind organ," provide a pretty sordid depiction of the sounds that assaulted visitors. But, carousels needed the accompaniment of music to "round out" the full experience of the twirl.

The 1903 Harton carousel did have two mechanical organs, one which was loud and one that produced more subdued tones. But they weren't good enough to accompany the McElwee merry-go-round. In keeping with their motto of "only the best," they ordered two organs in 1909 from the Muzzio Organ Works. The Muzzio company dealt in imported instruments made by Frati and Gavioli, previously owned instruments, and those which they manufactured. The McElwee brothers were still living in Detroit at the time, involved with Detroit amusement parks, but at least one of those organs from Muzzio was installed at Ramona.

According to the *GR Press* reporter in an article that announced in 1909 that the new carousel was ready to open,

"The biggest surprise, however, is the music. The organ cost $2,000 and is the best on any merry-go-round in the country, with the exception of one at Coney Island, which was built by the same makers. The selections are from grand opera – Wagner and Verdi."

Above right, letterhead from correspondence sent to Jim McElwee regarding the purchase.

Below right, bill of lading.

By the 1917 season, the Ramona carousel sported three organs, some needing paper rolls to play. At that time a single roll cost $14 dollars and the *GR Press* reported that, **"Every season new rolls are bought and since the McElwee carousel has been at Ramona park, several thousand dollars has been spent in music alone and this part of the ride is seldom noticed."**

The use of paper rolls as a method of playing the instruments was not original to the organs. Initially, the organs were the barrel style, which used cylinders with pins to produce the music. Then they were converted to play from perforated cardboard books of music. By 1917, another change had been made to at least one of the organs to play from North Tonawanda endless rolls. Not only was the purchase of the latest tunes costly, but the organs themselves had to be kept maintained from year to year. After all, they were housed in a drafty, damp building and had to endure extreme changes in temperature.

Mention was made in the *GR Herald* in 1926, that the Ramona merry-go-round was the only one in the United States that carried three organs. In the later years of the park, the organs were bypassed altogether, and the music was produced by a phonograph playing records of organ music.

The carousel was dismantled and shipped off to its new owner in 1955. Sometime between then and the year 1963, the three organs were put into storage in a shed in Gulf Shores, Alabama. That was when Paul Eakins, proprietor of the Gay Nineties Village in Sikeston, MO, found the three organs in more-or-less rotting condition. This mechanical engineer, formerly in the heating and plumbing business, had turned his skills toward restoration of nickelodeons and mechanical organs, so he was delighted with this find. According to Eakins' grandson, Chris Carlisle, **"two of the three organs were in pretty good shape, but the [other] was in boxes and baskets when it was delivered to the workshop."**

The three organs were given appropriate names, which they still bear in 2012. Chris further states, **"'Madam Laura' was sold to Walt Bellm's Museum in Sarasota, Florida, around 1972-73, where it sat for many years dying a slow death. Three years later the majority of the [Bellm] collection was sold to Disney World. Over a period of two years, 14 trailer trucks hauled the collection down to the Disney World warehouse. 'Sadie Mae' went in 1976 and 'Big Bertha' went in 1978, after she had all of her music recorded. 'Big Bertha' is still at Disney World, but 'Sadie Mae' is now in the hands of a private collector."**

Sadie Mae

The organ that became Sadie Mae, as seen on the Ramona carousel.

According to Robert Moore of Orlando Florida in his essay, Fair Organs in Ramona Park, Grand Rapids, Mich., **"'Sadie Mae,' once thought to be a Gavioli, is now known to be a DeKleist, and was sold to Walt Disney World. It provided the music used in one of the parades for a period of time. It was in storage for several years and later sold into a private collection, Bob Gilson's, I think, but I am not sure."**

This from Ron Bopp in 2000 in his writing, *"Paul Eakins' Gay 90's Organ Collection."*

"My interest in this hobby began in 1970, just about the time when the museum was in its last year of operation. My family lived in St. Louis and a trip downtown to the Arch, Busch Stadium and the Gay 90's Melody Museum was inevitable. Later in the year, the museum closed its doors to be followed by a flyer in the mail advertising all of the instruments. The saddening by this sudden termination of a new friendship was made only worse when I saw that my favorite instrument of the whole lot, Sadie Mae (the pink fairground organ), was for sale for much more than I could muster, a staggering $8,000.

"This organ contained 20 brass trumpets and 10 brass trombones as well as violin, flageolet, piccolo, clarinet, flute, cello, bass and accompaniment pipes. It was originally played from a pinned barrel but later converted to play Gavioli book music. It subsequently went to Disney World as did most of the Eakins collection."

When the Disney company was preparing to honor the United States on the occasion of the bicentennial, it went to great lengths to create a pageant that included appropriate music. The planners sought the band-organ sound and began a search two years prior to the start of the ceremonies. It was determined that "Sadie Mae," discovered in the Sikeston museum, would fit the bill. There was a problem, though. This organ played from the old punched-hole paper "books," only one person in the world continued to make them, and he lived in Belgium. Undaunted, the Disney people engaged the fellow to make the devices from their own musical arrangements.

Sadie Mae was taken apart and shipped to Nashville, reconstructed, and tapes were made of her music. The sounds were embellished with a synthesizer. After the finish of the parade, the sounds of Sadie were combined with sounds of a live band, and a record album was produced called, *'America on Parade.'*

Above, Mr. Paul Eakins holds one of the paper books used in the Sadie Mae.

Left, the back of the Disney album, *'America on Parade.'*

'Sadie Mae' pictured at the Gay Nineties Village with Paul Eakins, restorer.

Her large collection of trumpets has earned her the epithet, "Loud Mouth."

168

Madam Laura

At Ramona

The second Ramona carousel organ is now in the hands of Chris Carlisle, grandson of original rescuer and restorer, Paul Eakins. Chris continues with his grandfather's passion for mechanical music makers and he is making the history and music available to the public via the internet, on his website, bandorganmusic.com. Chris acquired the "Madam Laura," named for his grandmother, and restored the organ once again to its (her) former grandeur. Her journey to this point is told by Chris:

"Madam Laura was originally a 94 Key organ. She was originally built in France in the late 1800s. The organ was converted to 87 Key cardboard music books in July of 1914 by the firm of C.Eifler in Darby, Pa. In the early part of this century she played on a huge Carousel in an amusement park in Grand Rapids, Michigan until the early 1950s. Then she was sat in a shed for over a decade until she was bought in 1963 by Paul Eakins. The organ has 8 Bass notes, 10 Accompaniment notes, 17 Clarinet notes, 17 Piccolo notes, and 20 Saxophone notes. She currently has 206 pipes. The size of the organ is 8 foot 11 3/4 inches high, 10 foot 6 inches wide and 46 inches deep.

"Madam Laura has been featured on numerous recordings, appeared at the Gay 90's Village in Sikeston, Missouri and the Gay 90's Melody Museum in St. Louis, Missouri. She also appeared at many state fairs and expositions.

"In the early 70s, the organ was sold to the Bellm's Music and Cars of Yesterday museum in Sarasota, Florida. She was imprisoned at the museum where she was abused and neglected for many years. This neglect led to her being infested with wood boring worms that almost destroyed her. In 1999, she was sold to a private collector."

Left, Madam Laura in 1963.

Lower left, the figures being restored.

Below, after Mr. Eakins' restoration.

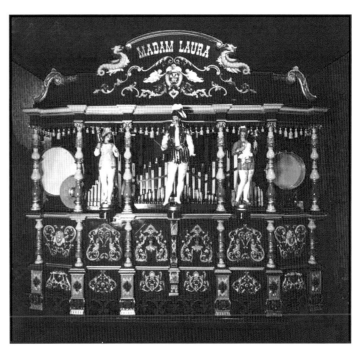

Left, the organ being moved in October 2004
Above, shown in pieces.

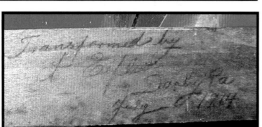

www.BANDORGANMUSIC.COM

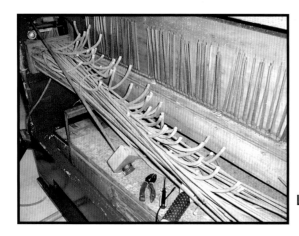

Upper left, proof of conversion to
cardboard books.
Lower left, exposed workings during restoration.
Above, as restored by Chris Carlisle, seated.

Big Bertha

The third of the carousel organs is undoubtedly the most famous because of its owner in 2012, the Grand Floridian Restaurant in Disney World, Orlando. This organ has been the subject of some controversy regarding its origin. The photograph taken at Ramona shows the name, Muzzio, on it. That particular business was a broker, not a manufacturer.

According to Ron Bopp, in *"Paul Eakins' Gay 90's Organ Collection"* from July 2000,

"The first was Big Bertha supposedly an 82-key Limonaire fair organ that featured a buxom director up front along with two bell ringers. Several organ authorities agree that this was not a Limonaire, however, and historian Tim Trager suggests that it might have been a Frati as it is similar to the large Frati at Knoebel's Grove in Elysburg, PA."

The following is a detailed description of this organ from Chris Carlisle.

"*She was purchased by Paul R. Eakins in 1963, and over 2500 man-hours were spent in completely redoing the organ from August 1963 to June 1966. During 1978, the fifth change in the method of programming was made for Big Bertha, ... now plays from #165 Wurlitzer Military Band Organ rolls.*

"*Big Bertha plays 369 pipes, a bass drum, a snare drum, two bells, tympani, double castanets, cymbals, a triangle, and a set of 18 bells. The very ingenious snare drum action stems back to the great Leonardo DaVinci who designed this type of arrangement. The triangle perforations now activate the two comely bell-ringers. The Director, Big Bertha, is in time with the bass drum. The piccolos now play intermittently with the trumpets. When the piccolos are playing, the bell-ringers play in unison with the bass drum.*

"*The leader holds the baton with her right hand, and when she turns her head to the left, directs in time with the bass drum; when she looks straight ahead again, she raises her left hand. She is flanked on either side by a bell-ringer. The three figures are beautifully proportioned and resemble real people. Hand carved, the embellishments are colorful and elaborate. On the top grille is an unusual figure-head resembling Columbus. Two charming cherubs with carved gossamer drapings also adorn the grille. At the lower center of the facade is a very savage-looking gargoyle. These are all fine examples of the highly specialized art of wood-carving.*"

Big Bertha shown on the Ramona carousel, purchased from Muzzio & Son.

A section of Big Bertha as she was when Mr. Eakins purchased her.

Back of Big Bertha when she was at the Gay Nineties Village

High above the entrance to the dining room in the Grand Floridian Resort, sits Big Bertha.

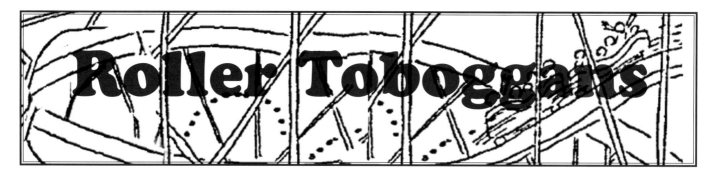

Roller Toboggans

What is it that causes the human to crave the sensation of plummeting downward at high speed, at the mercy of gravity? Riding downhill on "coasters" on snow was a recreation that required no power other than stamina to make the trip back up to the top of the hill. In 1893, the Grand Rapids Common Council granted youngsters the privilege of using the snow-covered Fulton Street Hill for their "coasting." It was with the understanding that the children would *deport themselves in a seemly manner*" that the permission was granted. However, the neighbors complained that the youngsters were too noisy in their reveling and this activity resulted in several accidents as well, so the practice was halted. Sleds and sleighs were called coasters at that time.

How It All Began

The first mechanical downhill slide on tracks in the United State was developed in 1827 in Mauch Chunk, PA, to transport coal from the mine to the coal chutes. The coal was accompanied on its journey down this inclined railway by a brakeman to slow the train at the bottom and by a mule which hauled the car back up the hill. Occasionally this train took on passengers for the ride since it was scenic and exciting. This led to the development of the switchback railway for amusement parks. LeMarcus Thompson's Gravity Pleasure Switchback Railway opened at Coney Island New York in 1884. Two side-by-side, 600 foot wooden tracks ran between 50 foot platforms. Thrill-seekers rode in a car downhill until it stopped coasting, then disembarked while attendants pushed it to the top of the second tower for the return trip. The $1,600 cost of construction was recovered in less than a month.

The Switchback

Remarkably, there was a switchback railroad at Reeds Lake in 1888, just four years after the first one appeared at Coney Island. Cedar Point started its Roller Coaster heritage with a switchback also, but not until 1892. An article from the *GR Evening Leader* in 1890 mentions,

"Mr. A.L. Hathaway, one of the oldest and most popular conductors on the Lake Shore railroad, has concluded to take a rest from active railroading this season and will personally superintend the switchback road which he purchased last spring. Mr. Hathaway and men were found at work upon his gravity line and it will be in find condition for the summer business. The frame work has been painted white and the cars and track thoroughly overhauled and made strong and safe. The switch back furnishes an inexhaustible source of exciting and innocent amusement for young and old at a very small

price, and it will continue this year to delight thousands again for he who rides once is bound to ride again."

There is no more mention of this amusement after the 1890 season, but Mr. Hathaway is found in Muskegon in 1891 running the switchback in Lake Michigan Park. A description of that amusement from the *Muskegon Chronicle* says,

"The car holds 10 passengers and the track is 450 feet long. It is operated by gravity, the impetus received by the car by the system of down grades being sufficient to carry it up at the opposite end of the track to the same elevation as that from which it started. The return course is the exact reverse of the first. The ride out and back is a novel experience as the car plunges at a rapid rate."

Photo from 1888 of the railway company switchback ride.

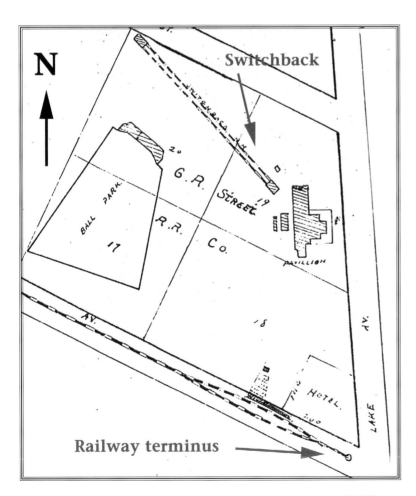

Portion of a railway map from around 1888. The large trapezoid with its four sections was the property owned by the railway at that time.
The road to the east was Lake Ave (Lakeside), on the south, Michigan (Wealthy) and on the north, Barnard (gone).

The map shows the location of the first railway pavilion, the switchback railway behind it, the ballpark in its original position and the Lake View Hotel property on the corner of Lake and Michigan.

At this time the steam dummy was still in operation and a turntable for the locomotive was indicated at the terminus.

The Figure Eight

In 1903, the year when Coney Island-style attractions turned the Reeds Lake resort into an amusement park, the "toboggan slide," or "roller toboggan" alias "the figure-eight" was introduced. Ingersoll Construction designed and installed it.

The announcement of the construction came in November of 1902, when the *GR Press* description of the new amusement gave readers this advanced notice:

"The great straggling framework extends from an attractive entrance pavilion far out into the large lawn. In the center is the engine house. Patrons of the toboggan climb a short flight of steps to the main floor of the entrance pavilion. There they are seated in comfortable, cushioned, four-seated cars. An attendant starts them on toward a steep incline, an endless chain picks the car up. It is pulled to the top of the incline and then it starts alone on its long journey, gravitation being the sole motive power. It shoots down sudden dips, mounts little hills, and then scoots over long level stretches high in the air. Back and forth it shoots, twists, dashes and rolls making three complete figure eights before it glides smoothly into the home stretch and is brought to a stop. The toboggan works like clockwork. The cars will travel from the bottom of the incline to the top in sixteen seconds and they run at such speed and intervals that, if necessary, eleven can be kept in operation at the same time. It has its own power plant for the four hundred electric lights that illuminate it."

This old roller coaster grew significantly in 1909, earning the title, "Giant Coaster." The length of the ride stretched to 3,500 feet with some "thrilling dashes" added. The

greatest speed of the ride was in long, straight glides which included several sensational dips. Not only was it equipped with new cars, but a special, private car called "Little Honolulu" was available. Rebuilding the track also provided additional strength. Two years later, coaster manager Austin McFadden added his newly invented roller bearings to the wheels giving the cars even greater speed. It was then billed as the fastest roller coaster ride in the world, because none other was so equipped.

However, the Giant Coaster only held its own for two more years as it was soon forgotten when its replacement, the Derby Racer, was presented to the world at Ramona Park in 1914. Nobody could forget this new attraction.

The Figure-Eight   Theater   Merry-Go-Round

RAMONA CIRCLE REEDS LAKE.   GRAND RAPIDS MICH.

As Ramona Park looked from 1903 through 1911

174

The Derby Racer

The famous Derby Racer opened at Ramona Park on Sunday, May 23, 1914. This long awaited day finally arrived after more than a year of preparation. The Ramona Park grounds changed significantly over the off-season period leading up to this event. More land had been purchased by the railway company, three acres between the old figure-eight and the back yards of the houses on Lovett. The Laughing Gallery and The Old Mill, which had become a "shoot the chutes," were also removed to make room for the great coaster.

Construction

This immense construction project, initiated by the McElwee Brothers, required 18 carloads of the very best lumber to be had, long-leaf yellow pine. A year before construction was to begin, Mr. R.M. Schornstein, local lumberman, made a trip south to the "Dixie" forests, to select just which pine trees would be harvested. The *GR Herald* reported on May 24, 1914 that, in addition to the lumber, it took 13 tons of bolts and 30,000 feet of steel to create this Goliath of amusement park rides. While other such structures were nailed together, this one was to be bolted. It was boasted that, ***"Every inch of the trestle is built solidly enough to carry a railway train."***

Ingersoll Amusements, the foremost construction company of its type in the country, was hired to do the design work and supervise local railway company employees who did the building. Construction was started on March 1st and it took a whole army of expert carpenters, masons, and mechanics of all kinds working to complete it in time for the opening in May. Foreman William Goldner was one of those.

At the opening on the 24th, the *GR Herald* stated,

"The Ramona Derby Racer Company is incorporated for $50,000. McElwee Brothers and their immediate relatives will operate and manage the affair. The president of the corporation is John J. McElwee. Mrs. Lillian McElwee is vice-president, and the secretary is James P. McElwee. The McElwee Brothers are also proprietors and managers of the Merry-Go-Round which has been so successfully operated at the park for the last 5 years.

"These young men are entitled to a great deal of credit for their energy and business ability in building up the amusement enterprises which they own and have operated throughout the country."

Ingersoll Amusements

Frederick Ingersoll, designer of the Derby Racer at Ramona, was a person of national fame, lauded as the man most responsible for the spread of amusement parks over the world. His father, LeGrand, was a railroad man for years but quit his job and turned to his inventions. Fred also loved to tinker and directed his energies to amusement park rides. He and his older brother LeForest went into the construction business, based out of Pittsburgh, around the beginning of the 20th century. Fred's specialties were roller coasters and scenic railways. His company was engaged for the construction of the Figure-Eight at Ramona late in 1902. Fred was called on again to design and build the Derby Racer at Ramona Park, his sixth by that name.

The Ingersolls were instrumental in building amusement parks on all the inhabited continents. Many of them were known as "Luna" parks or Electric parks or "White Cities" because of the profusion of lights adorning them. The Ingersoll company is credited with having built over 275 roller coasters over the years.

The "Derby Racer" at Ramona was the one hundred and thirtieth ride that Mr. Ingersoll was involved in and he said that it was the best one he had put up, having even more new features than the one which he had just completed in Detroit. He pronounced it his masterpiece.

JOHN McELWEE, PRES. AND TREAS.   JAMES McELWEE, SECRETARY

Ramona Derby Racer Company
RAMONA PARK
―――
Grand Rapids　-　Michigan

Laying out materials behind the dance hall.

Humble beginnings.

Hoisting a section into place.

Beginning to take shape.

Working on the back end.

Working on the entrance.

The gang stopping work for a photo shoot.

Finishing up on the back end.

The western-most part from a different viewpoint.

This photo, taken from the roof of the theater, shows the nearly finished Derby Racer. Close inspection reveals the scaffolding in place around each of the towers and the fact that the name has not yet been applied to the area above the entrance.

The entryway conformed in style to the architecture of the front of the Ramona Dancing Casino. The whole effect was Spanish and suggestive of the missions of Southern California. This choice of design was probably inspired by the setting of the novel, "Ramona." The plaster also matched that on the dance hall and theater. Each of the two towers rose to the height of seventy five feet, and flanked the large covered waiting room, the starting point of the thrilling trip.

It was a double track affair, hence the name, racer. There were 18 cars running in trains of three and the trains ran in pairs, racing with each other side by side. Initially the cars made the mile-long trip every two minutes. Another feature in 1914, in which Grand Rapids people had an advantage over other large cities, the price was only 10 cents, while in Chicago, Belle Isle, and other large amusement places, the coaster cost 15 cents. A description from the *GR News* stated,

"Parallel tracks the best of a mile long wind in and out and round about over a stout scaffolding, dropping into holes like the Grand Canyon of Arizona, sliding up inclines like the side of the new Pantlind, until your back hair stands out straight behind instead of straight up, and on these tracks, as you have guessed, two trains of cars are started at the same moment. You may think your train has won until the last moment, when you find that there is one more turn to round, and you, alas, are on the outside track. You hit the turn with a cozy lead, grinding ahead, when your rival car crawls up to your elbow and shoots past inside you to victory. You hang onto your brand new straw hat and yell the top of your head off, and then buy another ticket."

The Race Is On

This view shows two "trains" evenly matched. Note in the background,
right, is the back side of the Mystic Chutes scenery wall.

In this view, one "train" has pulled ahead of the other.
Note how the nearest tracks go beneath the surface of the ground.

As if this new sensation needed any assistance in attracting customers in its first year of operation, park management offered a Ford touring car to some lucky racer rider to be determined by a drawing at the end of the season. For several weeks prior to the September 12th event, the car was on display at the concession entrance. When the big day rolled around and the ticket was drawn, the winner was 14-year-old Alice Eldridge, who proudly rode home in her prize.

RAMONA PARK
DERBY RACER
Keep this Ticket it may be the lucky one.
FORD TOURING CAR to be given away SATURDAY NIGHT, SEPT. 12, 1914.
22683

Jack Rabbit

Two years after the opening of the Derby Racer at Ramona Park, it was dubbed, Jack Rabbit. The name was emblazoned across the ornamental front of the structure and later, a pair of chasing rabbits joined the design. It was advertised that several new dips were added in 1916 as well.

Ever on the alert for new ways to attract customers, John McElwee traveled in the fall of 1926 to several cities, hoping to find a more thrilling ride than the Derby Racer, so he could purchase a similar one. His search was fruitless, for his roller coaster was as speedy and as thrilling as any he investigated.

After thinking about it, one day Mr. McElwee had an idea which he worked out, with the result that the Derby was rebuilt during the winter and when it was opened for its pre-season rides it possessed a much steeper dip. Ramona could now boast that its roller coaster had an 85-foot dip, 400 feet long, and at its lowest point was five feet below the ground. It was advertised as the steepest one in the country with its 75 percent grade.

Derby Sounds

Anyone who visited Ramona Park, whether he or she ever rode the roller coaster or not, can bring to mind the sounds of the Derby Racer. The telltale clicking of the "dogs" grabbing a car loaded with thrill-seekers as it was hauled up the initial incline; the wood creaking as the car with its heavy burden rose higher and higher; the deadly silence occurring in the transition from the rise to the fall; the screams of the passengers feeling the tug of gravity as the car plummeted into the depths. People living anywhere near the park fell asleep at night listening to these sounds, especially the screams.

At least one person was not lulled to sleep. In 1920, Mr. John P. Sayres spoke his piece by bringing suit against the Derby Racer Company, claiming his peace was being disturbed by the mammoth coaster.

The *GR Press* reported in 1920 that the jury on the case made the following decision:

"A verdict of no cause for action was returned by a jury in Judge John S. McDonald's court in the suit brought by John P. Sayres against John McElwee, proprietor of the Derby Racer at Ramona park, seeking damages for the annoyance which he alleged the racer caused him. Sayres charged the racer was too near his home in East Grand Rapids and that the racer's business not only hurt his nerves, but also his property and lessened the probabilities of selling it. The counts of the declaration against the property were dismissed by Judge McDonald. The jury after hearing the testimony could not find that Sayres' nerves had been damaged enough to warrant payment of any damages."

Maintenance

The Derby Racer was green. It had to be painted periodically to preserve the wood, and to make it look nice. It took forty six barrels of paint to cover it initially. In 1921 a sprayer was employed for this task and the job was completed in four weeks. With the help of this "modern" convenience, only twenty-five barrels of paint were used. It took four men, however, two for spraying and the other two for building and moving the scaffolding.

The original wood was long-leaf yellow pine, said to be especially well adapted to work where a lifetime of service is desired as well as a material that would withstand unusually severe strain. Over the years, crews would walk every inch of the structure looking for boards that had weakened and needed to be replaced. Mr. Jim McElwee made the remark in the 1950s, that probably not one inch of the original wood was left.

Bolts, not nails, held the structure together. These had to be checked and tightened regularly. The tracks were oiled every afternoon in preparation for the evening crowd. This was to make the cars run as fast as possible. Sometimes this was done by the crew who leaned out over the front of the car and held oil cans over the track as they sped around.

According to Mr. Warren Hecker, who worked on the coaster in the 1950s,

"First thing in the spring, if test dummies were used [for the first trip around the track] *it*

was probably US, that is, the staff. It would not be unheard of to send an empty train one time around, just to make sure no sections of track were totally missing over the winter, but then my guess is, a small team of workers, probably Hugh McElwee and a couple of others, would take a ride and make sure that all was well.

"As I mentioned, when the second train was put on the 'other' track for holidays, due to rust on the flat rails, the car would likely not make it to the top of the second high grade, and that was when we got out and rigged the block and tackle and hauled the cars the rest of the way up. Meanwhile, the kerosene oilers were going, attached to the front bumpers on each side, with a small line to pour a light stream of kero onto the tracks ahead of the front wheels. After about the 2nd or 3rd run, all was okay, and from then on things got faster and faster, until the maximum was reached."

Crewmen performing timber repairs. The walkways between and either side of the tracks are visible.

Note the roof of Blodgett Hospital in the distance

182

Crew members making routine
structural repairs.

Jim McElwee and employees.

Much behind the scenes work went into insuring the safety of
riders of the great Derby Racer. This photo shows what the
structure looked like from beneath.

Safety First

The McElwee Brothers vowed that it would be the safest and best built ride of its kind anywhere. It was extremely important that in the opening season, no riders should be injured. The cars were open only on one side and those openings, being on the inside, were only eight inches wide, enough for a person's feet to get into the car, but too narrow to fall through. At the top of each dip was a system of brakes, controlled from the starting platform, by which the progress of the cars over any part of the track could be governed. Initially, two lookouts were on the watch for anything that might cause the slightest trouble. Between the two parallel tracks and outside of them were walks, altogether three walks went completely around the course.

Starting with the first cars to travel the course on opening day, the warning was issued, **Do Not Stand Up!** Even so, in the first month, six men were arrested and fined for risking their lives by doing that very thing. While it may have seemed most harsh for people to be prosecuted for this offense, protecting people from serious injury or death due their own foolhardiness was necessary.

"It is just this way," explained John McElwee, proprietor of the big amusement feature when discussing the arrests. *"We have had no accidents yet and we do not propose to have any if we can help it. The coaster, in spite of its thrilling speed, is safe. We have spent a lot of money to make it safe as well as enjoyable. No sensible or sane person would desire to stand up as the perfectly safe enjoyment of the race is sufficient if the riders comfortably occupy the roomy seats. Not a train starts on the ride before the occupants are warned to hold their hats and keep their seats. We do not propose, however, to have our coaster injured by those who do not know enough to take care of themselves and so we have resorted to prosecution".*

Nonetheless, in August of that first year of operation, a death occurred when a man stood up and leaned over toward the seat ahead and was thrown out. Then he was run over by a second car which was loaded with people, and the body fell to the ground.

Early in 1915, by special enactment, the East Grand Rapids council passed an ordinance making it unlawful to stand up in a moving car of the Derby Racer. However, from time to time it was still necessary to impose heavy fines, up to $50 on violators. McElwee pointed out that the structure was built with a greater factor of safety than required in bridge engineering practice, and that the rails were laid with an idea of meeting the greatest stresses or emergencies that could be imagined. The cars themselves were all steel.

Newsboys on an annual outing, showing off for the camera

In 1917, the *GR Press* stated the following:

"On the Jack Rabbit racer, service comes above everything else. A force of fourteen men constantly is on the job. Safety is the watchword with the racer. All of the cars which travel over the steel rails are made of malleable steel with chrome nickel shafts and phosphorous bronze bearings. They are outfitted with all modern safety appliances, all of which have been tested and found adequate."

Further efforts by the management to insure safety were indicated in a *GR Press* article in 1926:

"Workmen under the supervision of the United States Fidelity and Guaranty company have finished inspection of the roller coaster to assure patrons safe riding during the season. As a matter of fact, representatives of the insurance company report the Ramona racer to be one of the safest in the United States. In order to make assurance doubly sure, workmen employed upon the racer have added an extra guard rail that will extend eight inches above the front safety rail on the cars to further protect front seat riders."

Tragedy Strikes

From the very beginning, signs were posted that stated, **"Hang on to your hat and don't stand up."** The removal of hats and caps by the force of the ride was laughable, but the standing up part was not. Over the years, there were four people killed from being thrown out of their cars due to forces acting on them as they stood up. They were all adults. To young boys, it was a challenge to stand during the most dangerous parts of the ride, but they were apparently short enough and light enough to be able to withstand the forces acting upon them.

And Away We Go...

Loading up; starting out; looking ahead; looking back; the view from up there.

Viewing the lumber labyrinth.

The ride is over. Ready to go again?

Sundry

This *GR Herald* photo shows that the Derby Racer could produce thrills in another way.
The aerialist is the Great Prince Nelson who was engaged for special theater shows.
The Elks' Mardi Gras event was held in September, 1922, after the regular season had ended.

The Tracks

"The D.R. tracks, you must understand, were not 3-dimentional, as in train tracks we commonly think of, but were simply strips of steel, I would judge to be about 2.5" wide and probably less than a quarter inch thick. These strips were laid end to end, and butted without overlap, and I suspect screwed down with fairly long flat-head wood screws, into a massive support structure... those supports were then further supported by the various timbers shaping the entire structure. The strips of track were plain steel, and would rust when not in use, especially if for a long time." - Hap Hecker

"Hang On To Your Hats..."

This was the humorous part of the serious warning spoken to every rider about not standing up. In the later years it meant little because fellows didn't wear hats so much. But early on, it was even the subject of a newspaper article. The *GR Press* told about this:

"*The terrific speed of the twin trains over the mile of twisting, dipping and soaring rails of the coaster, together with the almost hysterical enthusiasm that reigns in the cars does not contribute to stability of headwear. On busy days there will be a shower of hats from the heights where the parallel tracks are carried upon lofty trestle work. Since safety first is the one big slogan of the concession management, no one will be permitted on the ground under or near the trestle except employees whose business takes them there. For this reason it will be impossible to recover hats promptly on rush days and so the management will issue caps to those who lose their headgear in the cars and will collect and care for the lost hats until the next day when they will be returned.*"

Under the Tracks

People who worked in the park were the only ones allowed to go under the tracks. A couple of anecdotes follow:

Park employee, Ham Berry: "*The Derby Racer (aka Roller Coaster), by the way, I never did ride that device - -didn't trust it (even as a kid). Although they ran test cars with dummies around every spring, if one walked underneath (as we did to find stuff that flew out of peoples pockets) one couldn't help but notice that the counterweights for the braking devices were actually regular buckets filled with old bolts, etc. and the bottoms were very rusty.*"

Park employee Dick Ryan: "*For the Derby, guys would hang out underneath and throw water balloons at anyone who stood up while riding the cars. If the individual complained to management about being bombarded, they would be admitting to the guilt of standing up, and the manager was not sorry about the drenching.*"

The Fifty-Cent Piece

Memories of the thrills of riding the Derby Racer are still fresh in the minds of former Ramona Park visitors. Probably memories of waiting in line have faded away. But some might remember seeing a half-dollar lying on the floor in the approach area and trying to pick it up only to find immovable. That coin has a story as well.

"I dunno where, or who exactly, but likely one of the Baker boys may have had hand in it, and likely with the blessing of young Huey McElwee, who was not beyond a good joke, himself. A flat-head or square iron stove bolt, of about 2" length, and a size of about 3/8": a dab of silver solder, which would stick well to the coin, and in effect weld it to the bolt head, a brace and bit and a 3/8" hole, and someone to go under the platform to slip on a flat washer and the matching square nut for the bolt, an it was a job well done. And a rather harmless joke, too."
- Hap Hecker

187

The entrance as it was built.

The entrance at the end.

Off-season view of the Derby tracks seen when traveling west on Wealthy Street. The desolate aspect portrays the close of another season. Note the stone pillar.

Two giants of Ramona Park history, taking a last look at the glorious "Jack Rabbit" Derby Racer.

James McElwee, left Louis J. DeLamarter, on the right.

RAMONA DERBY RACER CO.
RAMONA PARK
GRAND RAPIDS, MICHIGAN

Mail address:
1529 Robinson Rd., S. E.
GRAND RAPIDS 6, MICH.

Frbruary 16 ,1955

Seidman and Seidman
407 Peoples National Bank Building
Grand Rapids, Michigan

Dear Sirs,

December 31st,1954 is final for Ramona Derby Racer Company. There is nothing left to liquidate.

We got a good price for the Phoenix building, or Naval Armory, from the Real Estate company platting Ramona Park. They are paying the Capitol Wrecking Co. $2,500 for wrecking the Derby Racer and buildings, the wrecking company keeping all material.

We would lose about that amount if we were to wreck the ride ourselves, owing to the high cost of labor.

Capitol started tearing the ride down last week.

Yours truly,
RAMONA DERBY RACER CO
James P. McElwee

Yellowing letter from Jim McElwee, just a matter of business at this point in time, but a matter of great sorrow for those who loved that ride.

"D Day"

Derby Demolition,
Dejection,
Destruction,
Devastation,
and fans are forever
Deprived.

Business Matters

As long as Ramona Park existed, the property on which it resided was always owned by the transportation company. Through the years the scope of the company evolved from street railway to electric and cable and then motor coach, but it was the same company from 1875 through to the end of the park in 1954. Ramona was a separate business entity having its own designated general manager, and the park brought a great deal of revenue to the transportation company. The various concessions, rides and food were owned by private individuals who obtained leases to operate on Ramona property and who were responsible for paying taxes to the city of East Grand Rapids.

Ramona Amusement Corporation

Throughout their years of association with amusement parks, the McElwee Brothers formed companies to handle the business of their various ventures. They operated the Derby Racer, Carousel and Mystic Chutes through separate companies, for example. Likewise, Harry Glidden set up a company to handle his miniature railroad. A different sort of venture was set up in 1921, as is outlined in this notice from Lansing, August 11:

"Incorporation of the half million dollar Ramona Amusement corporation and approval of it by the State Securities commission today is the first step toward revolutionary changes in

the ownership and management in amusement concessions at Ramona park, Grand Rapids.

"The Ramona Amusement corporation proposes to take over all the big rides at Ramona park and the lake front rights and eventually may lease Ramona theater and the casino dancing academy as well, although these two latter enterprises will remain for the present under the direct management of the Grand Rapids Railway Co."

It was published in September that year that the approval was for 54,000 shares of non par stock.

The image in this advertisement shows the proposal for the waterfront portion of this venture.

The next step was to sell the idea to stockholders. Newspapers published huge advertisements telling potential customers of the rewards of "Owning Your Own Playground." The assets would include the Derby Racer, Carousel, Mystic Chutes, Venetian Swing, Aeroplane Swing, Penny Machines and the Miller Boat livery. The old Phoenix Club building was also part of the deal as was the proposed swimming pool **"with filtered water."**

The proposed directors of this new venture included Charles H. Seaman, general manager of Consolidated Theaters Inc., Clay Hollister, bank president and Louis J. DeLamarter. When the corporation finally appeared in the Grand Rapids city directory in 1924, the president was listed as John McElwee. The entries continued until 1928.

It was apparent that the company existed, but did not accomplish everything initially intended.

Another part of the appeal was to publish the monetary success of those concessions that were to be included:

EARNINGS

The Derby Racer has earned over $300,000 gross in seven years.
The Merry-Go-Round has earned $8,000 to $10,000 per year for past seven years.
The Mystic Chutes, built this past summer and operated less than half the season, earned an average of nearly $150 (net) per day for the 27 days in operation.
The other concessions have been consistent earners for different periods they have been in operation. Miller's Boat Livery has been a steady producer for 25 or 30 years.

STOCK ISSUE

We offer 35,000 shares (no par value), full participating stock of this corporation at $10.00 per share.

Based on previous years' profits we estimate this stock will show an earning of 15 to 20% per year.

Ramona Park Corporation

In the 1930s and 1940s the concessionaires at Ramona signed contract agreements with the transportation company that specifically outlined their obligations. Then, in the late 1940s, another corporation was formed called, "Ramona Park Corp." It operated the park under a three-year lease from the Motor Coach Company.

This photo shows the building that housed the park manager's office. It was located near the Fun House and Kiddie Land.

Mirth Places

What is it that causes the human being to seek the mysterious, to venture into the unknown, to yearn to be frightened? The intrigue of amusement park fun houses drew in visitors to experience those sensations, and instilled the desire to return time after time. Ramona Park had its share of houses of amusement over the years, the nature of the mysteries found inside varied, but the attraction remained strong.

When Ramona made the transition from theater only to an amusement park in 1903, there were three separate houses of fun. They were built in the vicinity of the railway turnaround, two flanking the merry-go-round building. The **Laughing Gallery** contained an array of mirrors *"that distort the human body into all sorts of ludicrous shapes, a trip through it will be as much a dream of grotesqueness as was Alice's journey through the looking glass."* The Georgia pine building's estimated cost was $3000. It was built by local workingmen, and was lighted up at night. Initially, a trip through this adventure cost 10 cents. In

1905, the name was changed to The Palace of Mirth and some new features were added.

In 1910, the building housed the "Strange Girl" and her snakes for a while, then provided display space for an illusion of the living statue order. The viewer looked upon the bust of a very much alive girl shown resting on a table with the appearance of having been cut in two. The mirrors were still in place elsewhere to bring laughter to those who had become horror-struck.

The building disappeared for good in 1914 to make way for the Derby Racer.

View of the Laughing Gallery after it became the Palace of Mirth. It is seen here decorated for a Japanese Fete.

Note the figure-eight track looming behind.

The **Cave of the Winds** was situated to the north of the merry-go-round building, an odd-looking structure on the outside. It had the appearance of a large grotto with dark narrow passages opening between walls of limestone rock. The inside must have been truly strange to those who dared venture in. Built by an amusement construction company from Detroit, it was similar to one found at Coney Island.

"Once inside, the visitor finds himself traversing the narrow passages of a cave. As he walks along sharp gusts of wind catch him most unexpectedly coming from all directions, above, below and on the sides. The real secret of the cave is not disclosed in advance to visitors and the management promises all sorts of surprises to those who visit the place."

Cave of the Winds

House of Trouble, next to the Carousel

Erected by the same construction company as the "cave" was the **House of Troubles**. Each of the two buildings cost about $2,000 to build. The descriptions of this amusement included,

"... the visitor will probably also find amusement as well as trouble. This place consists of a maze or labyrinth of narrow passages lined with mirrors and forming a very difficult puzzle which one must solve before he can get out of the place."

This building stood just to the south of the merry-go-round. Before long, these two buildings of mirth faded into oblivion.

View of railway loop, showing Cave of the Winds, on the left, Merry-Go-Round building and House of Trouble, behind the streetcar.

193

Trip Through the Human Laundry

For some reason, the prospect of becoming a piece of laundry appealed to youngsters. In 1908, the first electric washing machine was invented, a rotary drum affair, and that was the same year the **Human Laundry** appeared at Ramona. It was installed in a building formerly housing the aquarium. The introductory newspaper description of this contraption said it was *"where persons are washed, ironed, blued and dried without removing their clothes."* A similar amusement at Indianola Park, described it as *"a popular fun house that tumbled park-goers head-over-heels like so many dirty dish towels and then wrung them out between giant rollers."* One of the best parts of it was the slide which was used later in the children's playground on the beach.

Hurrying to the human laundry.   —Staff Photographer.

The manager of the operation was Dennis McCarthy of Leland Park fame, and he guaranteed that the ironing and washing would leave nothing but smiling and happy countenances. For the GR Press Newsboys' picnic in 1908, the paper reported, *"They got there before the attendants and so enthusiastic was the rush that they went right through the solid door and through the entire works before the surprised staff appeared on the scene."* For all the mirth it may have generated, it only lasted the one year.

HALL OF MYSTERY

Another short-lived place of mirth was the **Hall of Mystery**, also called the Palace of Illusions. Located in the northeast corner of the grounds, in part of the old billiard hall, there was a well-equipped stage in a tiny theater auditorium. The illusionist, Harry Sears, gave performances of magic every day with frequent changes in the bill. He was a pupil of Kellar and became widely known himself. A little too widely known, actually, because he disappeared from the palace for a few weeks whilst he performed elsewhere. The "Palace" itself even disappeared after this season.

Small booth for the reading of the palms. Perhaps sometimes the outcome not so mirthful?

The following description appeared in the *GR Herald* in 1892, indicating the existence of a very early form of fun house.

That Mysterious Chamber.

Reed's lake possesses one of the most unique and puzzling places of entertainment to be found at any resort, east or west. It is contained in the handsome structure in the pavilion grounds which is called the "Mysterious Chamber." It consists of a limitless expanse of broad halls and spacious appartments which form a vast crystal labyrinth into which one may wander for interminable distances. It illustrates one of the most marvelous facts of science and deserves the patronage of the refined and educated classes as well as the seekers after recreation and wonders.

The Fun House

After the introduction of the Derby Racer to Ramona, interest in the house of fun ilk waned. But in 1924, the appearance of the new "House of Mystery," thereafter to become known as "The Fun House," was the beginning of a 31 year run of this kind of amusement for Ramona visitors. The illustrious McElwee Brothers were responsible for introducing this epic delight to Grand Rapids enthusiasts.

Predecessor of the Fun House before the Clown-Face appeared.

House of Mystery Would Bring Thrill To Most Hardened

The House of Mystery, called the "Fun House" for short, is a place in which one must suppose even a marble statue might get a thrill, and Ramona patrons are taking to this new amusement enterprise like a duck takes to water. It's a gamble from start to finish whether the patron is going to really believe he or she actually encounters all the surprises which are contained within the walls of this structure. It's one of the McElwee devices and the McElwees are noted for bringing only devices of proved merit and superenjoyment to Ramona.

June 28, 1924

"No season at Ramona, especially on Fun Street, would be complete without Harry Lavardo the Fun House Cop" 1929 - 1931

Ad from June 27, 1925 showing the features of the early attraction

The Slides

The popularity of this amusement was evidenced by the fact that the very next year, 1925, the house was, *"enlarged to meet the demand that taxed its patronage last year."*

A two-story addition was put on the back of the building to accommodate the two slides, 38 feet high and 38 feet long.

Two GR Press newsboys on the steeper slide, on their magic burlap carpet, coming over the hump at the end which was there to slow people down. Notice the walls are covered with stiff cardboard-like paper, held on by thin wooden strips.

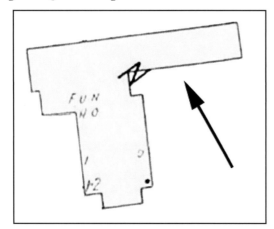

Sanborn fire-insurance drawing of the fun house after it was increased in size. The slides went across the back.

The descriptions printed in the newspaper said, *"A burlap pad plays the role of toboggan and the tobogganist takes a dip down and a dip up and a big slide to land upon a soft pad. You take your piece of burlap sacking, write your own ticket and generally find that you didn't light at the bottom the way you expected to land. There are never enough burlap pads, either, so popular is this latest McElwee contribution to Ramona, described as the thrill of your life. Crowds that gather on the outside to peer through the slats at those who take the ups and downs of the two 38-foot slides bear witness to the success of this new addition."*

Written by "Hap" Hecker who worked in the park in the early 1950s.

"I looked after the welfare of those who climbed the extra steps to ride one or both of the slides - as many times as they cared to, until they were too tired from climbing that long flight of steps, just south of the 2 slides. The north slide was the steep one, a single drop, seemingly straight down for a long ways, then the one "hump" to go back up, and over, until slowing and stopping at the foot of the slide. Getting off, and/or stopping there, was up to the rider. Often we requested they bring their burlap sacks back up, but often they let them lie, and during a lull, we would jump one of the slides and go down after them. We were actually able to climb BACK up the steep slide, but it was very difficult, unless barefoot. The secret of walking back up the bumpy slide

About That Cardboard...

I can almost smell the old Fun House. I think I worked there one entire season, or a good part of it until I was upped to the air-rifle range. Knew Claude Baker well, the old-timer who ran the fun house. My little domain was atop the slides, neatly stacking the burlaps, placing and holding them on the slide while helping one, two or three side by side to sit down, then a gentle shove and off they went, screaming all the way down. Remember once when friend, Buddy Baker, the old man's youngest, came over after skating, and had his skates in a typical metal roller-skate box. He didn't want to climb the steps again to retrieve them, so he put down his case on the burlap, sat atop it (like a horse) and "took off." Literally, when he went over the first bump, he went airborne, and his head actually put a small hole in the cardboard ceiling panel before he dumped in a wild heap on the lower landing of that steep slide. I jumped on the slide and flew down to see if he was all right. He was! Those Bakers were indestructible. But the hole remained in the ceiling for some time afterward. --- Hap Hecker

(easiest to do) was momentum, getting momentum to go up and over the bumps, then run down the next little valley, and up each succeeding hump until at the top, with a last burst of running to make it without falling and sliding all the way back down, bumpity-bump, bump, which occasionally happened.

"The steep slide was against the north wall, and at the end was a 14 ft. long by 4 ft. wide hunk of heavy sheet steel, which bounded when you hit it at the end of your ride. It was intended to slow you down, or stop you quite suddenly. Riders never seemed to fly off the end of THAT one."

196

The Mirrors

Fun house features came and went, but the crazy mirrors were an attraction that was a part of Ramona Park from the very beginning. Incorporated into the journey through the mysterious building, the mirrors caused people to laugh at the grossly distorted images of themselves and anyone else standing nearby. *"Even the handsomest sheik or beauty prize winner cannot escape their topsy-turvy changing without losing some of their aura."*

It is reported that when the Fun House was dismantled in 1955, the mirrors went into the foyer of the Wilcox Mansion.

A spoof of the mirrors was written in the *GR Herald* in its full-page promotion of the park in 1925:

> **Those Freak Mirrors**
> If there's anything in this suggestion stuff, fat women and thin men ought to spend a lot of time in the "Fun House." Might not be a bad idea for Manager Boon to advertise his freak mirrors as better than the "do it to music" exercises for those who wish to take off or put on fat.
>
> Anyhow, if they don't actually change your weight, they certainly give you a hearty laugh and your friends a heartier one, if they happen to be along when you look in the mirrors in the "Fun House."

GR Press Newsboys admiring themselves.

The Floors

The slides and the mirrors were attractions of the fun house that most linger in the memory. There was also the giant wooden wheel, part of the pathway through the house, that a visitor had to cross in order to keep going. The wheel was mounted at a slight incline so that stepping on it caused it to rotate making it difficult to walk on. Another such feature was the moving floor, up and down according to the placement of the feet. Mr. Hap Hecker, who worked in the fun house, provided this description:

"Loose change found its way into the interesting little crack at the bottom of the angle wheel, built in a room with the floor at about a 30 degree angle. No motor, but by walking one edge of it, you could get the thing moving, then faster and faster until you were running on it. With practice, we could step off into the very small area beside the wheel, only on one side and the bottom, or, back onto it again. If we happened to be in that area when guests were going through, we often treated them to quite a ride, with lots of laughing, and screams.

"The electrical wiring in the Fun House was by today's standards, a disaster, often knob and tube wiring, etc., It seemed safe enough in those days, and there was never problem in the Fun House. There were large leather belts that moved ancient levers, etc. that made the moving floors move, but some of the moving floors were simply hinged, and by walking on the UP part, it suddenly went DOWN, causing you a little balance problem.

"As for maintenance of under the floor equipment, let me just say that there were a lot of moving parts that had to be checked on a regular basis, things to be oiled, greased, and inspected. There were also leather belts, and a few motors to run them."

Entryway to the Fun House as it looked in the 1950s

Claude Baker, manager of the fun house, 1950s

"The Ramona Fun House seemed to run itself! At least it seemed that way to most people. There was a young lady in the ticket booth out front, whom most people never even noticed as long as they got the right change back. If you looked closely enough, you might see old Claude Baker, the head guy, sitting in his chair beside the wall, and with his hand on the air valve mounted on a pipe that came up out of the floor. As people walked by, "Bake" would quickly press the handle down and the loud hiss of compressed air could be heard by anyone in the vicinity, and sometimes even beyond that. If anything went wrong in the fun house, it was "Bake" who was there to attend to it; fix a broken belt, make repairs to a faulty electrical circuit, or replace a critical light bulb. I don't remember his ever not being there. By day he did various maintenance work, oiling, greasing of moving machinery, and reporting any major difficulties to the Park Office and Don Williams.

"Some corridors were very dark, and often these had secret panel doors in them that patrons were not supposed to know about, and likely never did. But this is how we got to short stairways or ladders leading below that area to where the moving machinery was located. There was also a choice, for those who knew the fun house, where-by one could go through it faster, avoiding some of the areas we kids felt "less exciting." And so, as far as I know, there were only 3 people on duty in that place at any time. I even took my pet raccoon up to the slide area when I worked, but often he hid in a hole in the wall, between the windows. I had to watch him like a hawk, so he would not jump out the window to one of the big old trees that nearly touched that 3-4 story-high place."

--- Hap Hecker

Upper left: Entrance showing Kiddie Land rides
Lower left: Fun House in context of other buildings
Above: The sad clown, silenced for the winter and then forever in 1955.

Miniature Railroads

Many, many people who traveled to Reeds Lake, went by rail. And, it makes sense that since the amusement park was owned by a railway company, there should be a ride offered to the children on a miniature train inside the park. It became a ride that attracted all manner and age of folk. It was safe for the youngest and oldest, and could hold the interest of anyone aboard as it traveled around the park. From the earliest little train to the last one to enter the scene, this attraction entertained thousands of passengers through the years. Thankfully, that last little engine wasn't side-tracked just because Ramona Park closed down.

How it All Began

One of the earliest miniature locomotives was not intended to be a toy or an amusement. Steam locomotives were starting to draw attention in England, and a few of them were being brought into America by 1829. About then, at the West Point foundry in New York City, a steam locomotive was constructed, but it did not function. In order to draw attention to this new type of engine as a possible replacement for horse power on the railroads, Franklin Peale, proprietor of the Philadelphia Museum, engaged Mr. Matthias W. Baldwin to construct a miniature locomotive to be put on exhibition. Mr. Baldwin, a jeweler and silversmith by trade who began to branch out in the early 1820s into making mechanical devices, took the challenge. On April 25, 1831, in the museum, this tiny engine made its rounds on a circular track made of pine boards covered with hoop iron. There were two small cars with seats for four passengers. The fuel was both anthracite and pine-knot coal

and the exhaust steam was discharged into the chimney, increasing its draught.

Because of the success of this model Mr. Baldwin was commissioned to build a full-sized locomotive for the Philadelphia, Germantown and Norristown Railroad Company for a six-mile railroad. Having no real blueprints or instructions, Mr. Baldwin created his own by inspecting a newly imported locomotive from England, which was being stored in its original state – unassembled. Despite great hardships in not having tools suited for the tasks or men with skills needed for construction, "Old Ironsides" emerged from Mr. Baldwin's shop in November, 1832, and successfully ran the rails. This "experimental" locomotive stayed the course for more than a score of years.

The first steam locomotive put on the tracks between Ramona and the city of Grand Rapids in 1881, came from the Baldwin Works in Schnectady.

The First Train

According to early advertisements for the 1902 season, there was a miniature train on the Ramona grounds. There was a feeble photo of it in the newspaper, but it was not described in any forthcoming articles about Ramona. In 1903, when the figure-eight roller toboggan was built, it was simply stated that the train was removed to make way for the new attraction.

When Ramona Park was in full bloom in 1906, a miniature railway was among the new features introduced for the season. Its station was near the old mill entrance. Whether it was the same train as that of 1902 is not known.

This train had open cars with benches and if the train didn't go too fast, was perfectly safe. However, there was at least one incident where a passenger was injured while on the train. Officially he wasn't a passenger, for, as was stated in the verdict on his lawsuit, he was trespassing. This man, on his lunch hour, bicycled to the park to eat, and seeing the train, asked if it were getting ready for a ride. Even though he was told that it was not open for business, because there were workmen sitting in the cars, he climbed into the last car to eat his lunch. The train started up to take the workmen to the other end of the tracks, and the man in the last car hit his head on a post as it went around a curve. It is from the report of this legal action in the *Northwestern Reporter* in 1916, that a description of the layout is obtained:

"The miniature railway occupied an oval space 300 feet east and west by 100 feet north and south. There was a station at the east end, and a miniature tunnel, with mountain and other scenic effects, at the west end. The railway gauge was about 14 or 15 inches, the rails were laid upon plank ties, and there was a natural slope to the ground from the station to the north. The equipment consisted of a diminutive locomotive engine, tender, and (three) small, open cars, carrying three grown people each."

Left, GR Press Newsboys crowd around the train waiting for their turn to ride.

Below, a story about improvements to the train made in 1914.

In 1910, for the Japanese Fetes, the tunnel for the little train was hung with grape vines, about 20 loads of foliage, and above was placed a gigantic Japanese dragon.

In 1912, the use of the little train was suspended for a couple of years, but it came back strong in 1914. In 1915 the *GR Press* reported:

"Among the amusements for the children will be an improved scenic miniature railway. The track will be extended and the little trains will run through a scenic tunnel, also into a fairy city wonderfully decorated and lighted, and there will be many surprises before the end of the journey is reached."

Later in the year, the juvenile tourists were treated to a trip through Switzerland.

RAILWAY STATION FOR CHILDREN AT RAMONA

The miniature railway at Ramona park has a new station. It is a real station, too, built in the fashion of all the buildings of the new Ramona, and it has its waiting room, its ticket office and telegraph office—all in miniature. It offers to its juvenile patrons all the comforts and conveniences that a railway station should offer and will doubtless be much appreciated by them since everything about the place is just their size.

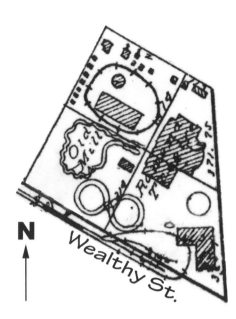

Above left, 1907 map of Ramona Park showing the circular mini-train track, the Old Mill ride, the figure-eight coaster track, the theater pavilion, the streetcar loop on Michigan (Wealthy), and, on the southeast corner, the Lake View Hotel.

Above, right, this popular postcard view shows the train that wound through the park from 1906 through 1921. The porch of the theater is in the background.

The miniature train and its three cars taking a tour around the deserted park. Visible in the background, just above the engine, is the bear cage. To the right of that, some of the midway concessions. Between the engineer and the lake is the Lakeside Club and on the right, the north side of the Ramona Theater.

The Glidden Trains

The next train began its tour of duty in 1922. It was described as a *"toy scenic railroad which writhes for a mile among the other attractions."* This locomotive was not considered to be a toy by its owners. Themselves employees of the Rock Island Line out of Cedar Rapids Iowa, Harry D. Glidden and Fred Hillman formed their own company as contractors, president, board of directors, engineer, fireman and conductor of this line. The *GR Herald* reported on the 21st of May, 1922, that this train was *"an exact reproduction of that which operates at Riverside Park, Chicago."*

The article further states:

"The terminal is close to The Whip and the route lies under the Mystic chutes and back of the Derby Racer. Five cars, accommodating 40 persons, are hauled by the diminutive locomotive.

Complimentary Ride
RAMONA RAILWAY
Grand Rapids
Except Holidays

Experience with this kind of a line, the proprietors aver, is that the adults are just as rabid as the youngsters.

"The line is the smallest incorporated one in the world and has to make an annual report to the interstate commerce commission.

"Mr. Glidden devoted all his spare time during four years to the construction of the locomotive, which is the nearest thing to perfection yet assembled in its line. It was all put together at Cedar Rapids, Iowa, in what he calls a tinker shop.

"The 999 weighs 100 pounds over a ton, gets up 170 pounds of steam and has a tank which holds 90 gallons of water. Skeptics as to the capacity of the tank will be permitted to fill it by the bucketful."

Number "999," the first Glidden train, the "G & H" line.
Note the double tracks and the Whip and Merry-Go-Round in the background.

A couple of years after Mr. Glidden joined the esteemed proprietors of Ramona Park amusements, he bought out his partner and established a business that involved his whole family. In 1928, the *GR Press* stated, ***"The railroad is the smallest under I.C.C. All tariffs and schedules are received by Glidden the same as by any other railroad operator. This tiny railroad is the only one of its kind in the United States."***

Mr. Glidden had double tracks laid around the park. He also added a second engine to insure that the ride would never be shut down due to engine repairs. Patrons could tour the entire park grounds and "Stop-Look-Listen" signals alerted pedestrians to make way for the approaching train. The Glidden family endeavored to make this miniature railway a very realistic reproduction of its giant counterpart.

The second of the Glidden locomotives, the "1045."

Photo shows both of the miniature locomotives. The front one, the "999," has the name "Ramona Railway" while the second, the "1045," is the "Rock Island."

The "1045," Ramona Park's version of the "Rock Island Line" seen as it skirts the midway.

Ramona's New "Baby" Locomotive

For the opening of the 1937 season, a new miniature locomotive was introduced, the "5001." This engine was larger than its predecessor by a half ton, one quarter size of a regular Rock Island locomotive. Wagner & Son of Plainfield, IL, manufactured this 3-foot high, 7 1/2 foot long dynamo that generated 40 horse power with a 175 pound head of steam. The only other miniature train besides this which was equipped with air brakes was located at Niagara Falls. By this date, in the 16 years of experience of Mr. Glidden at Ramona, he estimated that about three fourths of his passengers were grown ups who also were fascinated with the mechanical operation details of the model. An average of 50,000 riders enjoyed this amusement each year.

Besides being a veteran railroad man and conductor for the Rock Island Line, Mr. Glidden was an inventor as well. Some of his railroad-related designs received US Patents. So it was natural that the "5001" was built on his design. He drew up the patterns and finally machined the finished parts to assemble the engine. It was able to attain a speed greater than 30 miles an hour and pulled a four-car trainload around the track. The locomotive was hand-stoked with egg-lump coal.

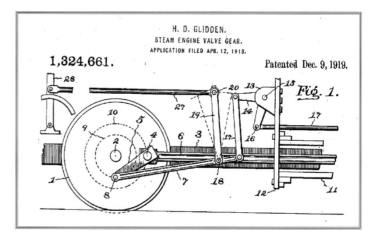

This photo gives a good view of the station.

Loaded fully, the train, drawn by the "5001," pulls away, ready for its journey.

On the left, a lucky little lady gets to sit in the tender.

Little girl on the right waits to board the train.

Ramona Railway train making its way around the Derby Racer and Ramona Gardens

By 1940, Harry Glidden and family had moved to Grand Rapids, to 544 Lovett. This was ideal because there were two dwellings, one occupied by Harry, his wife and younger children, and the other by son James and wife.

The back yard of the Lovett house abutted Ramona Park property. With the second dwelling situated alongside the fence, it was an easy place to house the locomotive. The family lived upstairs.

According to neighbor Chuck DeVries, in the lower part of the rear building was a complete machine shop with every imaginable tool. This was where Harry worked on his engine or made repairs to the cars. It was also a place to keep the "5001" safe.

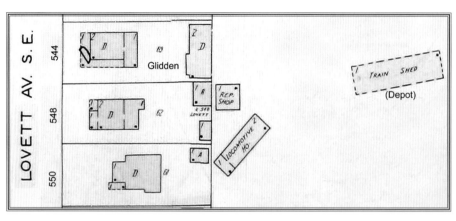

Ladies from the Baby Welfare Guild pose for publicity photos next to the locomotive at the Glidden train barn.

Even though Mr. Glidden kept his machinery in top running condition and had annual inspections, it was still possible for the locomotive to occasionally jump the tracks. This photo shows the process of "re-railing" the engine.

—Grand Rapids Press Photographer.

CHARMING CHOO-CHOO—Two veterans of 40 years of real railroading, Harry D. Glidden, sr., right, a conductor, and Henry Brown, an engineer, run the Ramona railway whose miniature locomotive chugs merrily around a half-mile of track through the park. Glidden is the owner. Do the children love the ride? Yes. But Glidden says 75 per cent of his patronage is adult.

The "5001" up on a trestle for
maintenance or inspection.

Moving On

When the Grand Rapids Motor Coach Co. was ready to shut down Ramona Park, Harry Glidden was not ready to shut down his railroad operation. Instead, he sought to find another area where he could install his railroad. The first step was to remove the tracks and ties and make everything ready to be moved when the time came. When the *GR Press* article appeared, January 11, 1955, his concession was the first removal operation after the closing of the park. At that time he did not know what was to become of his railroad but he was looking at Lamar Park in Wyoming township, Johnson Park along the Grand River, and a farm east of Grand Rapids that was for sale. The article that accompanied the picture below stated, ***"Meanwhile he is profiting by the clear weather to take up the miniature rails and ties, using miniature work-train cars he designed and built. His shiny engine, an exact scale model of a steam locomotive, sits idle in the roundhouse. It has run its last mile at Ramona."***

—Grand Rapids Press Photographer.

END OF THE LINE—AT RAMONA—Harry D. Glidden, sr., center, owner of the miniature train at Ramona park, helps take up the half mile of track over which millions of joy-riders have traveled. At left is Bert Harwood. Fred Kruizenga is at right. The three expect to have the rails and ties stacked by the end of this week.

Train Lowell Bound
Ramona Limited to Chug Again in 1956

In February of 1955, Mr. Glidden received 31 letters from sixth graders in a Wyoming Park school, indicating their wishes for him to choose Lamar or even Johnson Park. In order for that to happen, "officials" would have to approve it. In the end, the request was refused.

Ultimately, he decided to run the operation on his own and an entirely new location was chosen on the west side of the nearby town of Lowell. The whole train, tracks, station and all the accoutrements were taken out to the new park. The July, 1955, article in the *GR Press* making this announcement told readers,

"Kent county's only steam-powered passenger train—the former Ramona Limited—is moving to a new site.

"The little steamer which has hauled countless thousands of Kent county residents and visitors and celebrities from afar will be open for business next Memorial day in a new park west of Lowell, Harry D. Glidden Sr., owner, conductor, maintenance superintendent and engineer announced Monday.

"Our new location will feature a track about 1,000 feet longer than the old right-of-way," Glidden says, *"and will run a loop from the 200-car parking lot on M21 to the Grand River, several hundred feet along the shore, then back to the terminal and the parking lot. The land is wooded and in setting up the right-of-way and the picnic grove and other attractions within the tracks we plan to make every effort to preserve the natural beauty of the site."*

Harry Demond Glidden Sr. had two sons living in Grand Rapids, Harry Jr. and James. Besides the train business at Ramona, these three were involved in the Glidden Hardware store in East Grand Rapids. By the time the park closed and the train was moved to its Lowell address, the elder Harry was approaching 70 years of age. The young Harry inherited his father's interest in the trains, and along with Ed Bytwerk and Lyle Rigney, ran the Lowell Railway. They operated it until the end of the 1964 season. Harry senior died in 1969.

The "5001" became the "5002" when it went to Lowell, Michigan. Steam up, it is ready to go.

The Graves Family

The next owner of the railroad property, train and all its paraphernalia was Ilin Graves, who, with his son Steve and other family members, continued to run the railroad. The services of Ed Bytwerk were retained as engineer and mechanic.

1972 photo looking east on Fulton toward Lowell. Arrow indicates Lowell Railroad entrance.

Above, the station with its red trim.

Right, family members in the red cars.

The locomotive with the red trim on the nameplate.

Engineer Ed Bytwerk operated
the train for the Glidden and
Graves' enterprises.

Spring cleanup, start-up
and repairs.
Note the little work car
behind the tender.

The Vierson Connection

Although Harry Glidden Sr. was an accomplished railroad man, mechanic, inventor and knew his way around a machine shop, from time to time he needed to enlist the services of a professional "boiler man." He became acquainted with the work of Neil Vierson Jr., proprietor of Vierson Boiler Repair Company, and a long-time association began between the families. Neil Jr., who developed a passion for miniature trains, was a second generation boiler artisan. At the suggestion of Harry Glidden Jr., Neil Jr. built a duplicate of the Ramona locomotive during the years 1974 to 1982. Harry did some of the machining for this replica but died before it was

completed. A second engine like it was started by Neil Jr. but he didn't live to see it finished so Neil "Bud" Vierson III stepped in and completed the work in 2006. The Vierson business has a track layout for their engines and cars behind the main building.

Neil Vierson Jr. also had two diesel engines of the same gauge as the Ramona locomotive, and took them to Lowell to run on the railway.

Above, Bud inspecting one of the Vierson reproductions of the Glidden "5001."

Left, Harry Glidden Jr. in the Vierson machine shop.

Tragedy Strikes

The Graves family sold the business to neighbor Keith Buck who owned a used car lot near the railway. The Ramona engine, tender and train cars were put into a storage barn as was one of the Vierson diesels. For unknown reasons, that facility caught fire and burned but the little engines were hauled out of the building before they were completely destroyed.

Burley Park Bound

The final rescuers of the miniature train were Dan and Judy Rogers of Coral, Michigan. Dan grew up in Grand Rapids and spent many hours of his youth around railroads and trains, watching them, riding on them when possible, and collecting train-related treasures. In 1985, Dan and Judy purchased an acreage near Howard City and opened the Burley Park Flea Market. Through the years, they kept track of the whereabouts of the Ramona train, knew about the fire, and commenced negotiations to purchase it for the new park up north. They started talks with Keith Buck in 1986 but could not generate any enthusiasm for a sale.

Dan and Judy were not the only ones interested in procuring the railroad. The Michigan State Historical Society and Amway were two of the others. Another, Mr. Hollis Baker of Baker Furniture went so far as to send an envoy carrying a check for $65,000 in payment for a deal that was struck, only to have it finally fall through.

Not giving up, Dan and Judy approached Mr. Buck several times during the next twelve years and finally hit on the key in 1998. Besides the offer of considerable funds, a deal that included their 1969 Corvette coupe was finally accepted. This approach worked so well that within three days they had bought themselves a train, such as it was. The Ramona engine and tender had been sitting outside in a field under a rotting tarp for fifteen years or so. The cars had burned up in the fire, but their trucks were still functional. By the summer of 1999, Dan Rogers had the

train running across the front of the park. In 2000, the season opened with the train traveling two and a half miles of track. Were it not for the help and hard work of Dan's friends, Al Larsen and Don Doxtater, this feat could not have been accomplished so soon.

This project was not just a matter of making a deal on paper and handing over the funds. Although the package was supposed to have included "all things train related" in the possession of Mr. Buck at the time, Dan came away with far less than was bargained for. He had to build another station, which he duplicated using old photos, excepting that his version has a peaked roof instead of flat. New cars were built for the trucks and platforms. A computer-whiz friend, using a photo of the cars when they were at Ramona and applying electronic magic, produced computer-drawn plans for their construction. The coal tender was in bad shape so a new top was built to fit on the undercarriage. And, of course, tracks had to be laid. Dan took up and transported the tracks from Lowell, but in order to accomplish the total layout, he acquired more track from the aborted Frontier Village in Brighton, some from a junk yard in St. Ignace, and another mile of new track that was made in Japan.

In 2007, the boiler finally gave out after seventy years! Thanks to information supplied by friend David Kemler, Dan obtained a new, replicated boiler from the J. S. Company, LLC, in Middlefield, Ohio, in the winter of

2012. This inspired him to completely restore the "5002" to like-new condition. It will be up and running once again for the 2013 season.

The old boiler, which was used as a the pattern for the new one.

213

Right, the "5002" in storage in 2008.

Below, in 2012 after extensive restoration.

The four train cars with the "5002" and its coal tender.

The part of the cars that was salvaged from the fire, left.

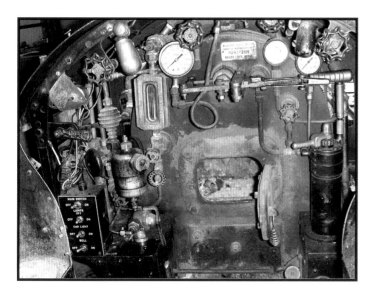

Before and after views of the "cab" of the tender.

About the coal: Fuel is anthracite coal, stored in the tender, which holds 50-60 pounds. The fire needs to be stoked several times during the 2 1/2 mile trip. The engineer releases a handful down the chute, and hand tosses it into the fire, as needed.

About the tracks: When Harry Glidden Sr. built his first railroad at Ramona, he made the track gauge slightly less than the standard 16". This was to prevent someone else from using his layout in the event he ever lost the contract.

Below, the pressure relief safety valves with inspection tags.

About the water: The boiler of the engine holds 40 gallons, the tender holds 60. When starting out with both tanks full, the train can make four 2 1/2 mile trips.

Burley Park Railroad Views

Right, Mr. Dan Rogers
engineer, rescuer and restorer
of the Ramona Railway.

The Ramona Park Railway: The little engine that could, and did, and still does. The only ride from Ramona Park that is still going.

The Old Mill

A type of amusement called "The scenic railway" took passengers on a train high enough to give a thrill when gravity took over and caused the cars to plummet downward. But, unlike the roller coaster or roller toboggan, the cars also went through indoor passages or tunnels. The first Ramona Park version of this was called the Old Mill ride. Instead of riding in rail cars, the travelers rode in little boats. There was no downward plunge, just a nice quiet cruise.

Austin McFadden of the Ingersoll & McFadden company of Pittsburgh, the man responsible for the figure-eight roller coaster at Ramona, was always on the leading edge in the amusement park world. He also brought the Old Mill ride to Reeds Lake.

The *GR Press* described this new amusement in April, 1904. *"The 'old mill' is an elaborate contrivance, and its installation will cost a considerable sum. It is somewhat on the principle of the scenic railway. The mill itself is built to resemble an old style grist mill which is operated by a water wheel. The wheel is a large contrivance which turns continuously with a stream of water passing through it.*

"This stream of water, after leaving the wheel, passes through a long, narrow canal, upon which boats are floated. There is a swift current in the canal and the boats, loaded with passengers, are given a lively and interesting trip for a considerable distance, the boats finally returning to a landing place in front of the mill wheel. The canal is winding and is bordered by artificial scenic beauties.

"Similar mills are operating in Lincoln park, Chicago, and at other outing places. The work of construction will be started as soon as the formal contracts are signed."

There was a pond in front of the mill where the boats started, then they entered the tunnel where they wound through brilliantly lighted scenery for about 1,500 feet. This was not unlike a "Tunnel of Love" type ride. The scenes were painted by professional scenery artists and were changed frequently to keep up the interest of the crowds. They were supposed to simulate actually being in places like Japan, an under-the-sea grotto, jungles and even heaven and hell. Working appliances also effected such features as fountains and moving figures. The trip took about four and a half minutes.

During the picnic for the Press newsboys in 1908, an incident happened in the Old Mill that made for a good story to be told to grandchildren.

"Each boat was filled with eager youngsters, who roused the echoes when they plunged into the dark passages and then 'oohed' and 'aahed' with pleasure and awe as they glided from the blackness into the numerous scenes that lend interest to the boat ride. One lad became so excited when he reached the lower regions that he fell out of the boat right in among the grinning demons. The boat went right on and left him, and it was a mighty scared and excited youngster who leaped with a wild yell into the next boat that came gliding by a moment later. His coming almost caused a panic, for the passengers in the second boat thought surely the evil one was after them."

217

The Mystic Chutes

"The Mystic Chute"
Newest Novel Sensational Ride
at RAMONA ALL SUMMER
Starting NEXT SATURDAY

Starting out the fifth season for the Old Mill, 1908, talk was begun regarding the thrillifying of this amusement. Compared with the improved figure-eight coaster, this ride seemed pretty tame. Elsewhere in the country, the new amusement "shoot the chutes" was receiving much attention, so Mr. McFadden had the Old Mill converted for 1909, and called it, "Mystic Chutes." An incline and drop into a pool of water was added at the end of the ride. After being run for a few days, it was temporarily closed while work was done to enlarge this pool for the ***"sensational plunge down the waterway."***

Written in the vernacular of a youngster, this account of the ride was printed in the *GR Press* in 1910:

"Kids that couldn't get in line [for the coaster] went over to the Mystic Chutes and made another line there. Say, that's some ride, th' Mystic Chutes. First you go riding in a boat through an underground river, seeing all sorts of scenes, and then you go up a hill, way, way up, and all of a sudden you go shooting down into a pond of water. Gee, I held my breath! Thought sure my day had come, but it hadn't. We just went splashing into that water and then shooting across it, like sliding down hill, and then it was all over and I wanted to do it again. Don't know which I like best, th' Giant Coaster or th' Mystic Chutes. Both are more exciting than a ball game."

When the Derby Racer appeared in 1914, the converted Old Mill was discontinued to make room for the new ride. For the 1921 season, however, the new and improved Mystic Chutes made its debut. By this time, Mr. McFadden had moved on and the McElwee Brothers had moved in. The new Mystic Chutes was constructed somewhat like the former ride, but in much greater proportion. The total length of the ride was nearly a half a mile. The incline was doubled in height to about 40 feet. During the construction, the corps of railroad workmen erected a small sawmill on park grounds in order to prepare the lumber.

The tunnel, or mill-race portion, was described as a ***"watery channel winding like a labyrinth through forests and mystic scenery, which the traveler traverses in about five minutes."*** Three big pumps circulated the water around the canal keeping the boats in motion by water force. The exterior was constructed in a rustic design to represent the old mill idea, with the waterwheel and other realistic effects brilliantly lighted. The boats, representing gondolas, held seven passengers. Through the years, some changes were made to the tunnel part of the ride, new scenery, different lighting, a "Spooky Nook."

It was told by a lady some eighty years later that she recalled riding on the Mystic Chutes with her parents as a very small child. She said she was really scared for the first part, the "dark" part, but when the boat plunged rapidly down the incline into the water, she loved it!

Entrance to the Mystic Chutes ride. Behind it on the right is the tower from the airplane swings and the entrance to the pony rides.

218

Entrance to the tunnel

Out of the dark tunnel into the light and climbing up.

Coming down for the splash

219

Above, the "gondola" glides into the pool. The Derby Racer is in the background, and the painted scenery backdrop is visible just beyond the pool.

Left, a peek through the fence.

Tragedy Strikes

Many resort buildings inhabiting the shores of Reeds Lake in bygone days were destroyed by fire. On the Friday of Labor Day weekend in 1931, the beautiful Mystic Chutes was turned to ashes. The blaze was caused by a bolt of lightning about 7 am. The East Grand Rapids fire department, aided by the apparatus from Grand Rapids No. 11, managed to contain the fire enough to prevent the disaster from claiming more of the structures in the park. The Derby Racer suffered only scorching which was rapidly repaired. Once the conflagration began it was fueled by tar used to seal different parts of the tunnel.

With only $12,000 worth of insurance on the structure, the loss to James McElwee was great. Besides losing the amusement and funds generated by it, stored inside the building were 70 penny arcade machines that were also destroyed. In spite of this calamity the Labor Day celebration at Ramona went on as scheduled that year.

The tragedy didn't end with the obliteration of the Mystic Chutes. Three years later, a 16-year-old boy scout was killed when he and his buddies went climbing about the ruins. Instead of attending the closing services with the rest of the scouts at the jamboree across the road in the ballpark, these fellows stole away and went exploring. Despite posted warnings, the boys vaulted the fence that blocked off the ruins of the ride. The boy, who was quite heavy, climbed on the wheel and it started to move. He was crushed as a result. The mother brought a lawsuit against the Mystic Chute Company but to no avail as the owners were absolved of guilt in the incident.

Other Rides

The Merry-Go-Round in its final form came to Ramona Park in 1909, the Derby Racer in 1914 and the first of the Glidden miniature trains in 1922. These rides endured throughout the life of the park. Many other amusements came and went, replaced by those that were bigger and better and more in demand. One that would have lasted were it not for a fire in 1931 was the Mystic Chutes, a very successful and sought-after ride. It was not replaced. The people to whom credit belongs for bringing the best in amusements to the park, Austin McFadden, Louis DeLamarter and John and James McElwee, were on the lookout for the latest sensations to thrill the visitors in the coming season. It was their intention to present something new and exciting every year.

A High-Flying Failure

The miniature train at Ramona was a huge success, even in its early form of 1906. An attempt to provide a train-like ride in the treetops was begun in 1907. This ride never really got off the ground, so to speak. Mr. Albert J. Dutmer, a machinist for the railway company, was the inventor, and he tinkered with this contraption for quite some time. Its glorious description from the *GR Press* stated,

"[The railway] consists of a heavy cable suspended high in the air along which runs cars with a seating capacity of four or more persons. The cable is of steel and is an inch and one-eighth in diameter, the same size cable used in hauling the street cards of Grand Rapids in the old days of the cable railway. This cable is a quarter of a mile in length and extends from the new station on the west side of Ramona circle across the road to the park outside Ramona grounds. It gives a view of Reeds lake, then circles around to the west, re-crosses the road, re-enters the Ramona grounds at the northwest corner and comes back to the station, running high over the heads of persons on the grounds. Suspended from this cable are cars."

The building efforts were begun in April, 1907, it was placed in commission on the eleventh of July after several "adjustments" to mechanisms. The headline on August 9th, read, "***COASTS NO MORE Ramona's Aerial Attraction Goes Out of Business. Accident in Which Two Young Women Were Shaken Up Terminates Its Career at Resort.***" This did not end its career, nor Mr. Dutmer's, for he kept working on it. At one point the announcement was made that *"The aerial coaster was hailed by amusement men as a distinct 'find' in the attraction line."*

In 1908, attempts at making this device a viable amusement ride apparently were finally abandoned, for it was noted in mid-June that the park monkeys were *"performing tight wire stunts on the now disused cable upon which the aerial railroad formerly lurched its way. "*

READY ON SUNDAY

Ramona's Aerial Coaster Is Very Near Completion.

The Circle Swing

In 1905, the circle swing was introduced. Passengers rode in six airships that were suspended by cables from long yardarms stretching out from the top of a steel tower. This top revolved causing the airships to swing higher and higher until the riders felt the sensation of actually flying. One little lad was quoted, ***"Why, it's just like flying, in that swing, mamma, and it doesn't make you dizzy if you don't look down."***

Originally, this swing was located on the grounds in the place where the merry-go-round building eventually stood. Then, in 1912 it was moved to the shore of the lake, so that riders would actually swing out over the lake. This ride was removed by 1916.

Above, the circle swing perched on the shore, shown in 1914. In the background are, left, the cottages of Point Paulo, right, Consumers' Ice facilities.

Well-known postcard on the left shows the swings flying out over the water.

The Circle Swing in 1912, newly installed on the beach, snugged up to the children's playground. A corner of the Lakeside Club is visible lower right.

Rocket Swings

With a distinct resemblance to the Circle Swing, the Rocket Swings were introduced much later, and endured much longer.

Left,
rocket swing
in motion

Right,
operator view
of rocket
swing.

Other swinging devices, those in which the cars swung out on tethers while being spun in a circle, took several forms. Some of them were, airplane swing, rocket swing, and Ramona swing .

Venetian Swings, boats of gondola design, in brilliant colors. 1921

Photo from 1943 of another swing.

Various Airplane-Type Rides

Above, two views of the
Flying Skooter or Fly-O-Plane
installed for the 1947 season.

This whirling
airplane-
like ride was
located just
outside the
carousel
building, shown
in part on the
left.

High-flying ladies in 1947.

Visible under the plane is the armory building, center, and the front porch of the theater, right.

The Rolo-Plane
or
Loop-O-Plane

Invented in 1933, this device first came to Ramona Park in 1939. The introduction in the *GR Press* stated that customers would be, *"jousting with centrifugal force in the new Loop-O-Plane device."* In 1942, Billboard Magazine announced that at Ramona was a *"new style dual Loop-O-Plane."*

The Ferris Wheel

This May 1955 ad was from Billboard Magazine, a grim reminder that everything in the park had to go. There was a Ferris wheel in the park since 1924

FERRIS WHEEL—10 SEAT ADULT, PIPE wheel. Good running condition. Not junk. $1000 cash. H. Courtright, 2244 Wealthy, Grand Rapids, Mich.

At this time the Ferris wheel was located near the theater pavilion and lunch counter.

The Tilt-A-Whirl

These newsboys enjoy a ride on the Tilt-A-Whirl which was introduced into the park in 1943.

View of the undulating platform on which the Tilt-A-Whirl cars ran. Visible on the right is the power source.

The Whip

Installed in 1920, the whip was another ride which continued to the end. It consisted of twelve cars, each designed to accommodate 2 passengers. The cars were attached by an arm and strong spring to a horizontal wheel in the center which was turned by an electric motor. The cars ran on a steel-plated elliptical platform, and when the cars made the turns, they were 'whipped' around the circle. It was described as being a *"snappy, jerky, zippy"* ride, and reminiscent of the kids' game of Crack-the-Whip. This, like so many other "diversions," was in operation at Coney Island and other prominent parks around the country. In 1947, the ride was upgraded with more modern "cars."

GR Herald newsies on the whip in 1941.

View of the whip apparatus showing the carousel building in the background.

The Skooter

The ride known as, "The Skooter," or Bumper Cars, was introduced in 1924 and this popular ride existed in the park to its last days. The cost to construct the amusement was $20,000.

The idea for this apparatus came about in 1922 when the concept model was tested. Lusse Manufacturing started making bumper cars in Philadelphia in 1923. Prior to that, the company was a small machine shop, producing cigar boxes, beer bottle washing machines and carousel machinery.

Each car could carry two people and it was operated by a quarter-horse electric motor, controlled by the driver. Current traveled through a shock-proof bamboo trolley pole which stayed in contact with the electrified ceiling. Surrounding the car was a large, solid rubber bumper. The inner wall of the building was protected by a spring guard rail. The floor of the building measured 50 feet by 100 feet, offering plenty of room to get a head start before ramming into another vehicle. Between bumping into other cars or the outside rail, a great deal of action could be attained. This was described as "human billiards."

While there was no licensing requirement to driving a bumper car, there was a minimum height that a driver had to reach. Apparently the management felt it was necessary to be tall enough that a person's foot could reach that "gas" pedal. Those entering this ride were admonished to ***step on the gas and keep to the right.***

In 1941, the *GR Press* newsboys try their hands and feet at the driving game.

The Skooter building was located near the train station. Behind it the aeroplane swing ride is just visible

229

Crowds of people are gathered at the edge of the wooden
boat ride; the Skooter building is behind them.

The Caterpillar

In 1923, another McElwee ride was added that had the descriptive name of "The Caterpillar." It was called an entertaining experience for grown ups and kiddies. The "cars" were connected end-to-end and traveled train-like over a circular, undulating track. Once underway, a green canopy would slowly begin to surround the cars until they were fully encapsulated at maximum velocity. The covered cars resembled the long, green worm of the same name. This ride was advertised for sale in Billboard Magazine in 1947.

The Pretzel

The ride called, "The Pretzel," endures in the memories of park visitors as "the scary place" or "the spook house." There were spooky parts to the Fun House, but the whole Pretzel was purposely designed for fright. The building was just south of the French-fry stand and rifle range. To the west of that building was the Tilt-A-Whirl, and southwest was the Whip. The front of the building, facing north, was longer than it was deep, and was basically a porch that ran the length of the building, with an oversized hand rail and a stairway near the center. The name of the ride was derived from the shape of the track inside, twisting and turning in all directions and back again.

Riders were settled into cars that had a bar to grab, probably for aiding the riders' orientation in the dark more than for safety. On the front of the car was a bumper, and when the car was released to the control of the device that moved it forward on tracks, that bumper would literally open the doors of the building with a bang. The doors were spring-loaded, and slammed shut as soon as the car cleared them. At some point the car was pulled through a curtain of stringy streamers that hung down and were drawn across the passengers.

Once inside the rider was engulfed in total darkness, broken only intermittently by flashing lights or illumined creatures. According to Hap Hecker,

"The car would jerk from left to right and back again, and follow the pretzel-ish series of tracks. Any time you approached a wall, there was likely a great surprise, like a built-up closet with no door and a ghastly-looking creature staring right at you as the purple light flashed on momentarily, just enough to see but not see the scary object, and the car rattled on, jerking your head as it made the wild turns. The only noise was the car on the track. There were a few bright lights, to flash instantaneously, dim lights, morbid green lights to illumine a haunted face,

but mostly just plain darkness. For those young couples having been there quite a bit, it really was not a big deal, not that scary, but a good place to neck. Once having exited the wood doors, the car coasted to a stop, rounded the right turn, and lined up with all the other cars waiting there for the next riders."

Mr. Hecker worked in the park, and when questioned about any human "assistance" in the spook house, he replied,

"It was probably not approved but if the ride operator knew you, he might let a park employee or two go in - as live ghosts - and have a little fun. This did not happen much, and not often, and we were usually reminded, 'make sure you behave yourselves.' And we did. Once we were used to the dark, we could just make out the cars, where they were, and we stayed out of their way. Then we might tap a person on the back, or top of the head, just to hear them scream. All in good fun. But if one of us did misbehave, he would likely have been fired - on the spot. I never did see the place with lights turned on, so have no idea how it really looked."

Jim and Doug Budzynski, emerging.

The Motor-Drome

These Billboard Magazine ads tell the story of the "drome" at Ramona in 1947. It was a spectator amusement with professionals exhibiting their skills, riding motorcycles in a huge barrel-like structure. According to Jim Chrysler, employee at the park,

"The motorcycles were about 1935 Indian Scouts, the diameter of the drome was about 24 feet and was 14 feet high, there was about a three foot observation deck all around the wall, near the top of the wall there was a cable stretched to protect the patrons and the riders, stairs were on both sides of the attraction. The only accident that I know of was when one of the riders had the brake rod come loose of the pedal and jam into the wall, throwing the rider and bike into the center. I still remember the chant we used to entice customers to come in and watch: 'Hey folks it's those motorcycle maniacs, racing, riding, slipping, sliding, dipping diving, climbing board walls that are straight up and down. You don't want to miss it, it's a thrill a minute here at thrill arena.'"

231

Above, a 1944 photo of an area on the midway shows park benches, the carousel, the curved roof of Ramona Gardens, the Ferris wheel and the train station. Peeking over the top of the station roof is the Rolo-Plane.

Right, a set of complimentary tickets, issued in 1931, the last year that the Mystic Chutes existed.

Ramona Park was for everyone. Little kids, teenagers, young singles, parents and grandparents all enjoyed going to the park, albeit for different reasons. It was a great place to "pick up chicks" and a great place to forget the troubles of the day. For the little ones, it had a different allure than for their grandparents, who might even have met there in days of yore. From the very beginning of the theater in 1897 right up until the theater was demolished, the Railroad company officials brought entertainment to the boards that was appropriate for all members of the family. The same principle was followed with the concessions and rides that were engaged. Consideration for the family reigned. But, beyond that, for the children there were special days, special rides and playgrounds.

SPECIAL DAYS

CHILDREN'S OWN DAY!
RAMONA Will Give Them a Happy Time SATURDAY

Balloon Ascension, Band Concert, Monkies, Ponies. Dozens of Attractions. Opening of Miniature Railway.

DON'T LET THE LITTLE ONES MISS THE FUN!

Even though the day-to-day offerings of the park always appealed to the youngsters, much effort was made to offer events and attractions that were especially tailored for the little ones. An early example was Children's Day. In June, 1906, the park held a special event just for children. The occasion advertised above was the formal opening of the new miniature railroad as well as the first time the new bandstand was used. The day drew so many little ones that it was proposed to repeat it during the summer.

A bigger and better special day for children was held in August that year. Besides a performance of Watson's Farmyard Circus in the theater, a toy hunt was to be added. The plan was to write the names of toys on tags, then hide the tags about the midway area. Any child finding a tag would be given the named toy. This might have been a good idea, but the plans had to be changed at the last minute.

Ramona Park Special
Next SATURDAY, Aug. 18,
CHILDREN'S DAY.

Toy Hunt on Ramona Circle
Come Early, Children, and Bring Your Mamas.

"Even electrical storms and drenching rains could not spoil the toy hunt at Ramona on Saturday. The weather prevented the original plans being carried out in full, but a shift was made that caused the distribution of the toys just the same. Tags marked with the names of different toys were hidden at various parts of the grounds, and the hunt was scheduled to begin immediately after the performance in the theater. The terrific rain that came up suddenly caused a hurried change, however. Most of the tags were collected and placed in bags. All the children were called into the theater and as they passed out each was given a bag, some bags being empty and some containing tags. The child that drew a tag received the toy called for, and for a time the liveliest kind of a business was done by the toy shop."

To top the previous Children's Day event, the park officials planned to give free pets to the children at a mid-September 1906 gala. In May, two little ponies were put on exhibit in the park with the intention of giving them away at the end of the season. Children visiting through the summer would receive a ticket with a number, and a drawing was to be held on the big day. This idea was expanded until the give-away was not just the two ponies but various other pets as well. One can only imagine the surprise on a mother's face when little Junior or little Susie brought home two ponies, or a monkey, or a goat, not to mention white mice.

Added to the activities of the Children's Days of 1906 were the doll and teddy bear contests held in 1907. The Ramona Theater Orchestra led a parade through the park, followed by dolls and carriages and teddy bears. They marched twice around the Circle and then were judged. The winning doll carriage was adorned with a mass of pink rosebuds, and the young lass with it carried a pink rosebud parasol. As for the winning Teddy bear, it was dressed in a rough rider suit. This was most appropriate because in 1907, the "Teddy Bear" was a new toy, named for President Roosevelt.

The Later Kiddies' Days

The early annual events for children took place for only three years. Special Kiddies' Days were revived in 1926, and by this time they were attended by thousands of youngsters. Local merchants, manufacturers, banks and citizens contributed "souvenirs" that were given away to every child, and rides were reduced by half for the day. The lucky ones whose ticket numbers were called received some choice prizes. Many children were accompanied by parents, adding numbers to the crowds. The event in 1928, when some 70,000 people attended, was even preserved on silent movie film.

Above, entryway for the Kiddies' Day event in 1927.

Left, the crowds coming and going on the south side of the Derby Racer

234

Right, as a precaution, first aid stations were set up in case of small emergencies, and to care for the occasional lost child.

Below, a glimpse of the crowds moving around to the next place of amusement.

Left, note the towers of the Derby Racer, and the arched roof of Ramona Gardens. Barely discernible is the track for the miniature train.

The children had plenty to eat. Some opted to exist on cotton candy and Cracker Jacks, or participate in pie or banana eating contests. Others took advantage of special prices at the park lunch stands. Still others came with parents who brought a basket picnic.

235

Fourth Annual Kiddies Day

Ramona Park, Grand Rapids

Thursday, August 16, 1928

No 27043

To Be Given Away Free

This Ticket is Good for Drawing on Whippet Car, Pony, 20 Special Bicycles, 11 Miniature Automobiles, Radio Sets and other Big Feature Presents.

HALF FARE ON ALL RIDES FOR EVERYBODY THIS DATE ONLY

Bring This Ticket

to Ramona Park Aug. 16. It must be presented at Drawing — Kiddies During Day and Everybody at Night. **FREE SOUVENIRS** for every Child

Ticket to the give-away raffle for Kiddies.

Winner had to be present when the number was called in order to claim the prize.

Right, a view of the prize board shows the things that were donated for give-away. Number 76 is particularly notable. Winning numbers were drawn at various times through the day. Some years the festivities didn't end until long after dark.

Below, the crowd anxiously awaits the next prize drawing.

Above, so great were the crowds that special details of policemen were engaged to keep order.

Left, little gal riding one of the ponies that was to be given away.

Right, headline for the 1929 event.

CHILDREN FROLIC AT RAMONA PARK

Third Annual Kiddies Day Reported Largest Thus Far Held.

GIVE 300,000 SOUVENIRS

This close-up view shows the eager faces of the "kiddies" and the occasional adult.

Note the clothing, especially the hats.

These young ladies,
dressed in their finery
for the occasion,
pause to rest ...
among their souvenirs

Imagine the efforts required
to clean up after the event in
order to ready the grounds
for the next day's crowd.

In 1928, the kiddies would have
been able to visit the "Hawaiian
Hut" for their first experience
in learning how to play the "uke."

The newspaper ad states:
"At the Hawaiian Hut you can learn to
play those lilting, haunting Hawaiian
airs in a few short weeks.
Instruction is given daily."

The railway company also provided a day of joy for individuals who were in unfortunate circumstances. Before the amusement park existed, the company often treated youngsters from the Children's Home to a picnic and ride on one of the steamers. In 1892 it was reported that some of the youngsters had their first taste of ice cream at the lake. Events were also held for orphans and children who were crippled or in rehabilitation. In the early 1900s, the Association for the Blind held an annual picnic, and some years it was at Ramona.

Loading the children in a taxi to be taken back to their facility. Of particular note is the electrical box on the post behind the man holding the car door open.

Children's Day for fifty children from the Butterworth Orthopedic Clinic included a ride on the steamer, "Ramona."

Equipped Playgrounds

The Playgrounds

All sorts of amusement devices for making the little folk happy.

241. Playgrounds at Reeds Lake, Grand Rapids, Mich.

View of the beach area playground from the steamer dock. Also visible are Miller's boats at the water's edge, the ball park upper left, merry-go-round building behind trees and the theater upper right.

Simple playground equipment such as swings, slides and see-saws were always great fun for little tykes. Various places in the park served as picnic areas over the years and there was usually some sort of playground equipment located nearby. However, in 1909, park manager Louis J. DeLamarter put his own dream in motion and created a special play area for the wee ones. Located on the beach formerly taken up by the Miller's Landing resort, just south of the park steamer landing, this new place was considered to be ideal for the purpose.

Rescued from the Human Laundry of the year before, the big slide was moved to this beach playground. There were four slides altogether, including one mounted on the side of the hill. A long row of swings was provided. These swings were low and intended primarily for the small children. There were also regular teeter-totters.

Parents could leave their tots at the play-ground, confident of their safety because of a full-time guard hired to watch over the little ones along with a person with "kindergartner training." The adults could sit on seats that were provided for observing the mirthful activities.

The formerly grassy area was turned into a beach and a section in the lake was designated and set apart as a wading pool. Another important feature was a large sandbox, covered with a canopy, and filled with genuine Lake Michigan sand.

In 1912, this area was enlarged by building a wall out into the lake and filling the interior with sand from dredging the lake using a "sandsucker," shown at right.

Prior to opening in 1910, this *GR Press* announcement was made,

"The children's playgrounds will be added to. The new equipment will include more boats in which the youngsters can paddle about in the inclosed shallow wading beach at the edge of the lake, and a real street car on which they can play motorman, conductor and passengers. This street car will be painted like the regulation cars and will be fitted out with brakes, electric controller, bells, register and like equipment. The car will be stationary."

The street car was removed before the 1912 season, and burned.

6991. Reeds Lake, Grand Rapids, Mich.

View of Lake Avenue (Lakeside) showing the merry-go-round building, theater and Lakeside Club. Note the streetcar on the grass.

"A unique feature is the giant rocker ['rolling wave']. This is a big rocking contrivance that will hold 25 or 30 children at a time and give them all a taste of life on the ocean wave. They are securely inclosed so that they cannot rock themselves out."

The man with his family in the photo above is Henry H. Tinkham, one-time member of the staff of the Grand Rapids Herald, Post and Press.

To the right, a view of the swings on the beach playground,

The Major A. B. Watson steamer awaits at the dock in the background.

241

KIDDIE RIDES

Fun and Thrill Rides Galore
KIDDIE LAND
NEW BABY WHIP • KIDDIE FERRIS WHEEL
KIDDIE AUTOS • REAL MIDGET AUTO RACES

MINIATURE RAILWAY
MERRY-GO-ROUND
HOUSE OF FUN & MYSTERY
SKOOTERS • ROLL O' PLANES
GIANT FERRIS WHEEL
TILT-A-WHIRL

Ramona's Famous
ROLLER COASTER
85 FOOT DIP

The merry-go-round, of course, had great appeal for children and grown-ups of all ages. The same was true of the miniature train. Pony rides were around almost as long as the park. In 1942, midget autos were introduced. There were also miniature boats that were actually propelled by machinery underwater, the water being just for the illusion.

In 1945, in addition to the regular Ramona favorite riding devices, the park created a complete Kiddie Land, including a baby whip, kiddie Ferris wheel, kiddie autos and real honest to goodness midget auto racers. Prior to this, other rides were available that were child-sized, but not necessarily clustered.

Jim Chrysler worked at Kiddie Land when it first opened. He was very young at the time, but as he points out, men were not available for hire during the war. The pictures below belong to him. His story is in the captions.

"When I was eleven years old, I don't remember just how I got the job, possibly because I was a neighbor of the Barr family and Fred Barr was the park manager then, but I was a ride operator for Kiddieland at Ramona Park. I also sold tickets at 14 cents each ride."

Jim is the tall young man dressed in white, standing between the two rides.

"I was paid $10.00 a week, of which I received a check for $9.90 after FICA was taken out. The owners of the rides were Ernest Bates with Lou DeLamarter Jr. (as a silent partner).

This picture was taken from a different angle showing the pavilion in the background where Fred's office was located and the Marcus shows took place."

Boat rides in a canal, and in a tank.

The Miniature Train.

Long-time favorite, the carousel.

The mini version of the Whip. The kiddie Ferris wheel just visible, far right.

Above and right: Kiddie auto rides at different times, and located in different places in the park. On the right, Nancy Nichoson (Myers) "steers" her truck around the circle.

Below, the newspaper caption read:
"Take 'Sample Ride' in New Ramona Concession"

"They couldn't wait for the opening on Saturday of the rides at Ramona Park, so these children of Fred Barr, manager of the park, enjoyed a 'preview' of one of the new rides Tuesday. Here, JIMMY, 5; COLLEEN, 3, and HANNAH, 2, right, try out the kiddies midget automobiles, a new attraction this season at Ramona. The park also will have a ferris wheel, dual loop-a-plane and streamlined skooter cars as new attractions."

GR Press, May, 1942

Two different plane rides. On the right, Nancy Nichoson (Myers) and friend Arlene House, who is holding a Shirley Temple picture on her lap.

Below, the "modern" kiddie airplane ride.

Ramona Park's Newest Ride Sensation!

SILVER STREAK

12 — Streamlined Cars — 12

Mile-a-Minute Fun
For Young or Old

"Ramona Park's opening Saturday will give park patrons their first chance at a new, fast ride—a streamlined version of the merry-go-round. In the photo FRED HOLLINGSWORTH, JR., son of the ride manager, BONNIE BARR and HER brother JIMMY, children of the park manager, Freddie Barr, get a preview of the thrills the new ride offers."

GR Press, May 23, 1941

PONY RIDES

Pony rides were popular for a great many years, beginning in 1913, and lasting until the final days of the park. They varied from riding in carts behind ponies to riding on the back of a pony led around the ring, and from Shetlands to burros. There were even goat carts. The pony track was moved to various parts of the park, depending on where other attractions needed to be placed.

One year horses were brought in as well, and instruction was offered to the ladies. *"Riding habits will be provided for the women riders and as soon as the riders become proficient, horses may be rented for rides outside the grounds and for the timid ones, escorts will be provided."* The year 1915 was when the Wild West show performed all summer in the area near the roller coaster, and instruction came from one of the performers.

Ramona Pony Livery

A ride on a real live pony is justly due every boy and girl, and at Ramona Pony Livery this may be enjoyed in safety and under personal direction of Miss Ada Summerville, champion horsewoman of the world.   1915

Above, Paula Worden (Naujalis) atop a burro, in one of the last years of the park. Notice the lake in the background along with the boat livery on the shore behind the Lakeside Tavern

NEW PONY TRACK IS INSTALLED ON CIRCLE

A new pony track has been installed at Ramona under the management of Glenn McCarthy of Grand Rapids. A better grade of ponies than in former years has been obtained.

The pony track always has proved a popular amusement features with the children, and this year it is expected to prove more popular than ever before. The new ponies are gentle, and careful attendants are on the job daily to make the rides more enjoyable than in past seasons.

—1927

The "ponies" or burros waiting to carry their precious burdens around the ring. The little girl reaches in to touch the smiling animal.

In 1941, the Ramona ponies made the news when they went out on the town. The GR Press reported:

Ponies Trek Homeward After a Night Out

"*Their unauthorized leave of absence, these nine Shetland ponies are shown trekking back to their Ramona park corral after a night spent grazing in the Breton-Sunnyside area. The ponies wandered out of their stables when someone opened the door after the park closed Sunday night. Riding the lead pony is Edwin A. Courtney of Bluffton, IN, the owner. At the rear is Albert DeBoer, of Breton, who helped round up the fugitives Monday. The three other ponies were returned to the park later in the day.*

"*The ponies, owned by Edwin Courtney, who conducts a juvenile livery at the park, were corralled in their stables Sunday night as usual, but early morning motorists southeast of the city blinked their eyes when they saw the highway cluttered with the midget animals.*

"*East Grand Rapids police were notified and Williams, Donahue and Winks, 'armed' with ropes, set out on the roundup. Most of the ponies were found in the vicinity of Breton and Sunnyside Dr. three of them having nosed their way into an oversized chicken coop. 'Someone opened the gate,' was the only explanation Courtney could offer as to how the ponies got loose.*"

Park manager, Danny Boon, jokes around with the goat cart, one of the rides offered to children at Ramona in 1922.

Children posing for a picture in a Ramona goat cart.

THE DAYS OF PONY RIDES

To this day, the leather-smell of bridles and saddles, the feel of straw and hay and the pungent aroma of a stables immediately transport me back to 1949. I was only ten years of age and had my first job—leading "Little Silver" around the circular corral at Ramona Park.

Growing up in Madison Square, the best thing that could happen to me was to be taken to Ramona, and early that summer, my big brother and I boarded the Madison Bus to downtown Grand Rapids where we transferred to the Wealthy Street Bus whose terminus was Ramona Park in East Grand Rapids.

As soon as the bus door opened, you could hear the clickety clack of the roller coaster ascending its cross-beamed mountain. The sounds decrescendoed as it slowly reached it peak. For a moment, near silence while the front cars peered carefully down the 85 foot drop, then the screams of delight while, it seemed, the coaster took flight.

I couldn't wait.

I don't know where I got the idea or the nerve, but I inquired about a job leading the ponies around the ring; and much to my surprise, I was hired on the spot and started work the next week. My bosses were a pair of brothers, Junior and Sonny.

Though skeptical, my mother packed me a lunch and gave me the needed 20 cents for bus fare, 10 cents each way. It was only when I became a father myself and my children grew to 10 years of age that I was able to understand my mother's angst about my working at an amusement park. I had to leave our house at 125 Hall Street S.W. around 11:00 am and walk to Division Avenue to catch the Division Bus to downtown where I would transfer to the Wealthy Street Bus.

When I became an adult, I could not imagine allowing my 10 year old child taking a bus all alone and traveling the city like that even during the daytime, but the ride back home at night was even more harrowing. I worked until the park closed – I think at 11:00 p.m. I caught the last Wealthy Street Bus that left the park and got me downtown where I transferred to the last Division Avenue Bus back to Hall Street. By then it was nearly midnight, and I remember running the entire distance from Division Avenue to the door to our house.

After a few weeks, one of my brothers started working with the ponies, too, and as I look back on it, my mother probably suggested that.

Before the summer was over, three or four other boys from our neighborhood also got jobs at the stables, and we would all go to the park as early in the morning as we could in order to play with the ponies while they were pasturing alongside and beneath the roller coaster. We could ride the ponies bareback and play cowboys and Indians in a way that other kids could only dream. I can still see the ponies: Silver, Little Silver, Blackie the shortest and fattest of them all and Wendy, the largest.

By noon, we had to get to work brushing the ponies, feeding them, cleaning them, getting them saddled and ready for their day's work.

Walking around a circular corral for ten hours was tiring, even for a ten year old, but it was a fun kind of tired.

There were many "fringe benefits" to working in the park. I got to know the vendors and the people who ran all the rides, and they were generous to give free rides to the "pony kids." Some of the rides lost their thrill, so, in the case of the roller coaster, we rode standing up frontwards, then standing up backwards. We did the same with the slides in the fun house. There was no such thing as "risk management" or "safe from harm" in those days, and you know what, we survived very well.

Dennis Phillips

This from B.J. Muir Crosby, lifetime equestrian, who grew up in East Grand Rapids:

"As far back as I can remember I was interested in horses. When I was about 4 years old I asked for a horse for my birthday. My parents reminded me that the family had no place to keep it. So, at age 6 or 7, I went to Ramona Park, which was close by, to ride the ponies. As soon as I got on the pony, I started kicking my feet to urge it on to a gallop. That was the way it was done in the movies. But, I had to just ride it slowly around in a circle. At that time, the pony track was on the north side of the roller coaster, the little train went by very close to the pony track.

Picture shows a glimpse of the pony track as it was in 1947.
The dancer, Patricia McPhilamy, is posing on the pony for a publicity shot for a Baby Welfare Guild event.

248

Events

Visiting Ramona Park turned any day into a special day. But there were also many special events for everyone to enjoy.

**Balloons
Picnics
Holidays
Other Events**

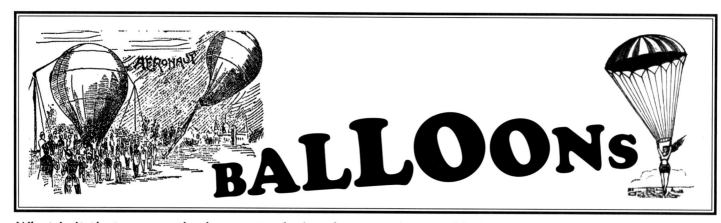

BALLOONS

What is it that causes the human to desire the experience of being snatched from the arms of terra firma into nebulous regions of the firmament? Once borne aloft, this human must then yield to the power of gravity and plummet back to the level from whence he came. Just as curious is the question of what causes the human to want to witness this spectacle. From the very early years of resortdom at Reeds Lake, balloonatics have plied their trade before thousands of viewers. This was always a two-part affair, consisting of a balloon ascension and parachute drop. Such thrill-seeking, death-defying events continued until Ramona Park plummeted into obscurity. They varied in presentation and method, but they always created the excitement of the unknown.

How it All Began

The idea of an object being carried aloft by heat came from the observance of bits of paper and ash rising into the air above a bonfire. The Montgolfier brothers thought If the heated air were captured in a vessel, it might also rise. They were successful in causing a small sack of taffeta cloth to rise to the ceiling after being filled with hot air. Being in the paper manufacturing business gave them materials to work with, namely, paper and fabric.

The first large-scale balloon flight was conducted in France in June of 1783. The large bag was made of cloth, lined with paper coated with alum as fireproofing and held together with a multitude of buttons. Since they thought smoke was the source of lift, they built a fire from objects that caused great clouds of smoke.

This balloon rose up to about 1,000 meters and "flew" about 2 kilometers. The next test a couple of months later was with a larger balloon carrying a basket with three animals. The beast and birds arrived back on earth unharmed.

In October, 1783, the Pennsylvania Packet carried these words:

"The messieurs Montgolfier, who are said to be very enterprising geniuses, have let fly, at Anonay, a house of 36 feet in length, 26 in breadth and height. It is true the house was built of cloth, and covered with paper. But the means they employed is new, if it is, as we are assured, the simple action of smoke."

In November that year, two men were borne up to a height of 900 meters and landed safely, 10 kilometers away.

Balloon being inflated at Manhattan Beach about 1888.

Since great crowds of people flocked to balloon ascensions, the resorts at Reeds Lake would schedule these events to draw out potential business. While admission was not charged, as long as people were there, they sought other ways to spend their money. The lake was a good place for balloonists to conduct their exhibitions because of the potential of landing in the lake or on the shore.

Leland Park was on the southeast shore of the lake. This ascension in 1899 was scheduled for two weeks prior to the opening of the Ramona Theater which advertised a famous balloonist in "Kid" Hanner.

Early Balloonists

The balloonists, also known as aeronauts, traveled around the country to pursue their careers, much as did the vaudevillians of the times. The males adopted distinguished monikers like, "professor" or "daredevil," and the women used "madam," "mademoiselle" or "lady." They also made outrageous claims in their publicity like, "the most intrepid and daring" or "most difficult feats ever performed." In census records these people listed their occupation as aeronaut.

While some of the performers at Reeds Lake and Ramona Park were visitors, coming here by contract, some lived in the area, even in East Grand Rapids. The early ones referenced in this section are:

- "Prof." WW Jones, early 1890s
- The Meixell family, Delbert, Mme (Etta) and son, Grant, 1900 - 1909
- Ralph W. Bottriell, 1906, 1907
- Henry A. Phelps , 1908 thru 1922, left G.R., returned 1929 – eventually had his own company, "The American Balloon Company"

Balloonists needed a whole crew to assist in these ascensions, and sometimes those aides would become aeronauts themselves. Besides making flights of their own, some balloonists held schools for young, interested potential fliers. One neophyte, for example, was Bert Fyke who worked at Ramona as a soda water dispenser. After watching these events, he became a student and eventually "flew." Del Meixell stated in 1907, *"I have put many a boy in the balloon business, running a regular balloon school. I have made a number of balloon inventions, such as the gasoline inflater, the bunched up parachute and the apparatus that holds the balloon down while it is being filled. My latest invention is a light life preserver."*

Regarding the professional balloonist, this comment was made by Prof. WW Jones in 1892: *"The balloon ascension profession is on the wane. Six or eight years ago there were not more than twenty aeronauts in the United States and they were in great demand for all large out-door events, like fairs, reunions and legal holidays. The country is now filled with balloonists."*

Regarding remuneration, Prof. Jones related, *"This balloon business is never tiresome and it takes you about the country and you see everything. I make $40 a week right along and only work one afternoon each week, and I don't know but I have about as good a time as any of the rest of you."*

In 1901, Prof. Meixell received $150 for two ascensions at a Muskegon event.

In 1905, the Aero Club of America was formed to further the cause of aviation in this country. While the aeroplane was in its infancy, hot-air and gas ballooning had a growing following. Some balloonists were issued pilot's licenses by this group. The organization also kept the official records for the balloon industry – highest flight, largest balloon, etc. In 1922 the National Aeronautics Association was born out of this group.

The Equipment

The big bag was also known as "the envelope." Constructed of various kinds of fabric and of varying sizes, they were primarily of the same shape. The usual cloth used was "sheeting" or canvas or sail cloth. This was far less expensive than the preferred silk, but much heavier.

An example of the formula for construction of a balloon forty feet high: *Twenty four strips of fabric, each fifty-six feet long and four feet nine inches across at a point five feet above the center of the strip, narrowing to one foot six inches at the bottom. This would produce a pear-shaped balloon with a ten-foot hole in the bottom. An envelope this size could lift about 250 pounds total, human and equipment, to a height of 2,000 feet.*

A forty-foot balloon was actually quite small. Since the bigger balloons could sustain flight longer it gave the acrobatic performer more time for stunts. Balloons over 100 foot high were being used as early as 1901.

Regarding balloon construction, Prof Jones said: *"Professional aeronauts, who have made money, usually employ sail-makers and build their own balloons."*

To inflate the balloon in the early days, a fire was started with kindling in a simple trench in the ground, and fed with some sort of fuel to provide a very hot fire. The smoke and hot air rose up into the envelope, inflating it. Even in the early 1900s some crews used inflating devices which generated hot air from gasoline.

To prevent premature lift-off, the burgeoning balloon was secured to stakes with ropes. Once it was deemed fully inflated, the balloon was released from its bonds.

The balloon had no source of heat to sustain flight once it left earth, so the envelope would eventually cease to rise when the air inside had cooled off sufficiently. The bigger the balloon, the higher it could go. When it reached the point when it started to fall, the rider would disconnect.

With the release of this much weight, the balloon would start to rise again and continue its journey until depleted of its hot air. Sometimes a heavy "tipping-bag" was attached to the top of the balloon so it would invert when the human separated, and it would lose its air sooner and not float so far away from where the pilot landed.

Another essential piece of equipment was the parachute. This was not the apparatus known by the modern world, contained in a back-pack and released with a rip-cord. This was a very simple device, made of the same material as the balloon. Multiple ropes or lines about twenty feet long were attached to a steel ring from which the trapeze hung, the other end attached to the balloon. When the balloon was cut loose from moorings which held it in place during the filling, the whole affair jerked upward with the balloonist the last to rise off the ground. Later, the rope holding the parachute to the balloon had to be cut in order for the parachute to be released. This was sometimes done by the balloonist pulling a sliding knife operated by a rope.

If something went wrong with this plan, the parachute not releasing for example, it was possible for the aeronaut to simply ride the balloon down. But this was not preferred as there was no control over when or where the balloon landed. Depending on wind currents, this could be a considerable distance away.

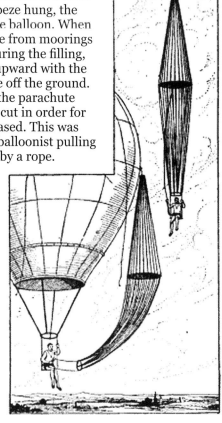

Two methods of attaching the parachute, as shown in Popular Mechanics in 1910

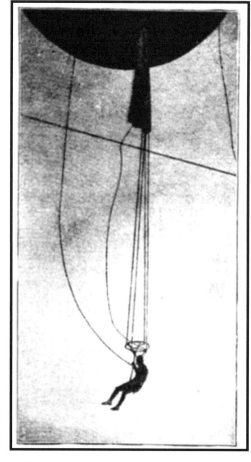

Balloonist getting ready to cut the parachute loose

With no basket or gondola attached to the balloon, the aeronaut had to grab onto something for the ride up. Usually it was a bar known as the trapeze, and usually the rider would perform acrobatic stunts on the bar during the ascension. Then, in the process of descending, more acrobatic feats were sometimes performed while the balloonist was suspended from the parachute.

In the 1892 interview, Prof. Jones stated,

"One curious fact about ballooning, is that you never feel a breeze after you leave the ground. These sensations begin at the moment the aeronaut seizes the bar of the trapeze and is jerked from the earth. Grasping the bar the sensation is like that of being seated in a swing. For the first 100 feet there is a realization of ascent, objects below appear smaller and smaller, until they gradually fade from view and the earth appears flat and the sounds below die away in a murmur and it is then that the balloon seems stationary and the earth falling away from view."

Variations on a Theme

Balloonists were always trying to come up with new exploits to attract people and thrill crowds. One such trick was to employ double or triple parachutes. The 1909 description of the latter follows:

"The parachute is a new contrivance of the three-story kind, and drops with it are expected to prove unusually thrilling. They are red, white and blue in color and the effect is said to be spectacular when two of them are dropping to the earth at the same time with their human burdens."

Needless to say, this was an extremely dangerous stunt, not something that could be readily practiced. With three parachutes that needed to function without a hitch, there was more opportunity for failure.

An unfortunate stunt performed by a few balloonatics during the early years was taking animals up with them and then releasing them in their own parachute. In 1891, Profs. McEwen and Hunter performed this act at Reeds Lake with the 165 pound boar hound belonging to Charles Godfroy. People flocked to the lake to see this, even the ones who didn't believe it would actually happen. After landing in the lake, the balloonist and dog were pulled aboard the launch Sport which was waiting. It was reported that,

"The excitement was intense. Women screamed and some turned faint. The trombone player of the band was so excited that he dropped his instrument out of the bandstand and never missed it till he attempted to play. The crowd welcomed the balloonist and dog with hand clapping and shouts on their safe return."

Reeds Lake—in the Evening
Sensational Searchlight Balloon Ascension and Parachute Drop

Another interesting type of balloon ascent was done after dark. In order for the crowd to view the proceedings, the searchlight, perched atop the Ramona Theater, was trained on the balloon and parachute. To add spectacle to this, sometimes confetti was released as well. Another stunt performed after dark was the release of fireworks from the balloon. One year at the meat cutters picnic, four "fire" balloons 5 feet wide and 20 feet high were released and watched until the flickering, twinkling lights were lost among the stars.

One of the most bizarre variations was in 1892, the plan for a couple to be married aloft. A contract was signed with Warren Swetland of the Railroad Pavilion, that stated, *"...Mr. Deer and lady to be publicly joined in marriage while on the trapeze bar and to ascend together with the balloon to a height of fifteen hundred feet from the earth (the marriage and the height of the trip to be treated as of the essence of the contract)."* Sadly, Mr. Deer backed out of the contract prior to publicity of the event becoming widespread. The newspaper announcement said nothing about having enlisted the services of a minister.

Also in the realm of the bizarre would have to be the combination of the cannon shot and balloon ascension. In this stunt, the balloonist is encased in a cannon on the ascent, and then shot from the cannon with the parachute, for the descent. Prof. Delbert Meixell of East Grand Rapids was one of the first to perform this in the Reeds Lake area. The *GR Press* in August, 1900, stated,

"The balloon rose at about 6 o'clock. Attached to it was a large iron cannon. There was no sign of the aeronaut. When the balloon had gone up to a great height there was a puff of smoke from the cannon, followed by a dull boom, the big gun tipped its muzzle downward and professor Meixell shot out. He fell rapidly for a considerable distance, and then the parachute opened and he floated safely to the ground. The ascension was decidedly more thrilling than the ordinary parachute exhibition. The cannon ascension is considered more dangerous than the usual type of ballooning and it is said that but three men have essayed it."

Unfortunately, this stunt was attempted the next year in Muskegon by one of Prof. Meixell's crew and it ended in tragedy. The boy was apparently too heavy for the braces supporting the cannon and he fell to his death from a great height without the parachute.

One of the variations on the simple ascension and drop routine was the balloon race. It wasn't a matter of distance covered, or reaching a destination first. The winner of this kind of race was either the balloon that rose the highest before ceasing its ascent, or the balloonist who held on longest before cutting loose for the descent. Races were also held between three or even four balloons.

The first such race held at Ramona was in September 1906. Members of the Meixell family living in East Grand Rapids, a father, mother and foster son, were all in the business. Balloonists hired crews of helpers, some of whom learned the trade as well. This was the case with Ralph Bottriell, on his own by 1906, who challenged his former mentor Meixell to such a race. Their balloons were comparable in size, about 60 feet tall.

When the day of the race came along, at the last minute, Del Meixell decided to use his son Grant, age 13, to man his balloon. Seeing this, Bottriell determined to send up Abe Collins, one of his crew who was of comparable size and age. Neither boy had flown before, so they were evenly matched in that respect.

Both balloons went almost straight up for a considerable distance and then drifted over the lake. The blunt-headed Bottriel balloon reached its full flight first and began to drop. The Meixell balloon went beyond, and just when it had apparently reached its highest point young Grant cut loose his parachute. Collins waited some time later and then let go. Both parachutes opened prettily. Collins descended more rapidly and landed on the shore near the old Leland park. Young Meixell landed in the lake half-way between Leland park and Manhattan. Both were picked up by a large steamboat. Young Meixell was given an ovation when he landed, a huge mob surging around him.

As a side note to this race story, Mr. Ralph Bottriell, who was a bell boy in the Sweets Hotel in 1900, took to the aeronautical profession in a serious way. Not only did he perform in these events, he made a career of parachutes. He enlisted in the army and on May 19, 1919, he tested the first backpack-style, free-fall parachute. In 1929 US Army Sgt. R. W. Bottriell held the world's record for parachute jumps with 500. At that number, Bottriell stopped parachuting to become a full time ground instructor. Bottriell eventually became chief parachute instructor at Kelly Field in Texas and earned the Distinguished Flying Cross in 1933 for service as an experimental parachute tester.

1919. Balloon Race, Reeds Lake, Grand Rapids, Mich.

Note the multitudes of people gathered for this spectacle, positioning themselves wherever space could be found. This event most likely took place at the Labor Day celebration of 1908. Visible on the shore is the back of the Phoenix Club which opened in 1907, and between the balloons is the Lake View Hotel which burned early in 1909.

Dangers, Hazards and Tragedies

The story of ballooning at Reeds Lake and Ramona Park would not be complete without mentioning the dangers, hazards and tragedies that could and did occur. It is always difficult for people to understand what drives the daredevil, what motivates the adventurous, to tempt fate for the sake of an audience. It is interesting to read what was said by the balloonists themselves on the subject of danger.

In 1892, Prof. WW Jones said: *"It is not such a trick as you might suppose to go up in a balloon. I do not think that balloon riding is much more perilous than riding on a railroad train or going on and off an electric car with a double track in the street. I believe that when our time comes, we will have to go, but not any sooner.*

"The greatest worry to me is always before the balloon starts, for the slightest mistake is liable to make serious trouble. When the balloon is fairly away from the earth, I am always relieved when I find everything is all right, and then as I sail along, I begin to wonder just where I am going to light. To land in the right spot is the science of the business."

From Del Meixell in 1907, *"There's not such a great risk in ballooning. As far as danger goes, I'd rather be an aeronaut than a motorman on a street car. I think the aeronaut is the safer. The greatest danger in ballooning is experienced when leaving the ground. As a rule there is no danger when one gets up above the trees, buildings and telegraph wires. Most accidents are due to the inexperience of those in charge."*

In 1909, Prof. Henry A. Phelps, by that time known as a truly reckless member of the profession, adds his opinion: *"I feel just as safe 5,000 feet up in the air as I do on solid earth. In fact, I never consider my profession as leading me into danger, except when I apply for life insurance. Then I know it must be, for no company will accept the risk. I have lots of fun with insurance agents when they come to write me up for a policy."*

One obvious danger was that of a failure of the parachute to open. This usually led to death or great harm coming to the balloonist upon landing. If the parachute didn't release, it was possible to ride the balloon down, but at greater risk than with a parachute. Some did survive this calamity. This is addressed by Ralph Bottriell in 1907, when he stated,

"I have had only two narrow escapes. One was last summer on Japanese night at Ramona. When I cut the parachute loose it got tangled in the cable of the machine used to hold the balloon while being inflated. I heard the parachute tear and then it caught firmly on the cable. It was dark and I could not see the trouble. I expected every minute the parachute would tear loose and then it would have been all up with me with a torn parachute. However, I rode the balloon safely until it came down.

"The third ascension I ever made I did the cannon trick at Albion and got tangled in the parachute ropes. I fell 1,000 feet before the parachute opened."

Even when the balloonist began the descent with a successfully opened parachute, there were still all sorts of hazards to be met on the way down. One of the worst was high tension wires. As with telegraph or telephone wires, there was the danger of being hung, but wires teeming with electricity could and did kill people who touched them. This was the case with the wife of Prof. Meixell. For the Fourth of July celebration in Lowell in 1909, she was blown into high tension wires. She received the jolt of the electricity and then fell to the ground. A few days later she died of her injuries. After her accident, and before she perished, her son, Grant, experienced the same malady at Jenison Park in Holland. He was fortunate, however, for he did not come into contact with the high tension wires, and a crew was able to catch him when he dropped to earth. This boy had already escaped certain permanent injury when he landed on and crashed through the glass roof of the greenhouse situated just a couple blocks from Reeds Lake. After the death of Mrs. Meixell, the husband and son retired from the profession.

Besides problems with the parachute, there were also cases of problems with the envelope. If the seams weren't checked regularly, they could spring a leak causing the balloon to start dropping too quickly for the rider's parachute to open. Then there was always the humorous possibility that the balloon could escape its bonds and go off by itself to unknown regions. Without the weight of the passenger, it could fly alone much higher and farther.

Since some sort of fire was involved in the inflation process, whether open pit fire or gasoline inflator, any number of items could go up in flames. With so many ropes attached to the balloon and parachute, keeping them from becoming singed or partially burned was a challenge. If a fire was discovered before takeoff, the flight could be aborted. But, once the rider was in the air, he had to deal with difficulties on the spot. One time, the inflator itself got tangled in the ropes and started to rise with the balloon. The machine broke away and exploded as it started to fall. This could have presented great danger to the crowds below, but in this case they were lucky. Another similar occurrence when the inflator became snagged in the lines and rose with the balloon, the aeronaut managed to hold on to the burning machine until the whole affair was over the water where he cut it loose to be extinguished as it fell in.

Another fire tragedy was averted in 1892 during a fire-pit inflation on the shore of the lake, when one of the crew persons was feeding the fire with kerosene, and spilled some on his clothing which immediately ignited. Although he was instantly engulfed in flames, he managed to run into the lake and quell the blaze before he was seriously burned.

Later Balloonists

Noted aeronauts of earlier times are listed near the beginning of this section. The names and faces changed over the years but the feats were essentially the same with a few variations added. Mention is made here of some of the more remembered performers.

Milo Webster, known as "Daredevil" Milo, was performing in 1922. At that time one of the best stunts in his repertoire was to ascend in a straightjacket from which he extricated himself on the descent. His next appearance of note was in 1926, dropping from an aeroplane into the athletic park field.

Ted Sweet gained fame as the only one-legged balloonist and parachute jumper in the United States. He performed at Ramona from 1931 to 1934.

In 1935 **Howard "Skyrocket" Hull** made his own distinction. *"An ascension into the atmosphere hanging by his heels on the balloon trapeze will be an added thrill provided by Howard (Skyrocket) Hull when he makes his double parachute drop from a balloon at Ramona park Sunday. At 2,000 feet he will perform a loop and other stunts on the trapeze before cutting away with his two parachutes, on which he does some fancy swinging."*

Also in 1935 performances were seen by the "Human Bat." Mr. **Merton E. Coleman** used a bat-wing suit that allowed him to fall or glide 2,000 feet before opening his parachute.

In the late 1930s and early 1940s a familiar face at Ramona was balloonist **Pee Wee Brown**. His act was called the "Leap for Life." He made his own balloon and parachute and in his short aeronautical career, made more than 1,000 trips into the atmosphere.

Merton E Coleman
"The Human Bat"

He was one aeronaut who retired from the work instead of meeting a tragic end. He had a few incidents in his long career, but nothing life threatening. Some were thrilling, to be sure, like landing on the Derby Racer tracks. Another unusual landing was recorded in the *GR Press* in May, 1938.

When the wind shifted suddenly, the balloon would come down in an unexpected place - like Fisk Lake. The little gal in the photo to the right was 10-year-old Nancy "Pete" Thompson who lived on the lake. Pee Wee had experienced a normal launch at Ramona Park, but the wind carried him in the wrong direction. He cut himself loose and was coming down in the middle of Fisk Lake. He hollered, and Pete heard the call. Although she was an accomplished swimmer and could handle the boat, she wasn't allowed to go out alone. So she summoned the maid to sit in the back of the rescue boat while she went out on her mission. That was the story that made the paper.

Meanwhile, another young person who lived in the neighborhood also heard the pleas for help, Master Hamilton Berry. In his words, *"One day I heard a voice calling 'HELP, HELP, I can't swim!!!' I looked up to see him drifting into Fisk lake. The neighbor boys and I ran to get our boat to rescue him, but 'Peter' Thompson got to him first as she lived on the lake shore. All we got was to pull the greasy old bag out as it had followed him into the water."* The boys were unsung heroes, not even making the story in the paper!

"Pete" Thompson, rescuer

While a pole-sitter doesn't qualify as an aeronaut, the performer is, for a time, quite up in the air. One such daredevil came to Ramona Park toward the end of July in 1946. "Mad" Marshall Jacobs scheduled himself for a 41-day stunt which was to end on Labor Day. His 308-foot pole was trucked from Coshocton, Ohio, and set up in the park for his spectacle. When he was 22 days into the period, he called it quits. His reason was that he had demanded a telephone to be installed on the pole so he could phone his new bride, but he was refused. Although manager Fred Barr was cited as being at fault, the truth was that the telephone company had more orders than they could fill at the time, and it didn't consider Mad Marshall's need as "essential."

Balloon Ascensions in the 1950s

The balloonist at Ramona Park in the early 1950s was Col. Frank L. Heistand. As the Billboard magazine ad, left, indicates, he was still using the old technique to inflate the balloon.

The following information on Col. Heistand came from Mr. Warren "Hap" Hecker, who on many occasions assisted the Colonel in these events.

Upon his arrival in town, driving the one-ton truck which hauled the balloon, equipment and house trailer, the Colonel located a spot to set up shop and housekeeping in the field behind the Derby Racer. This was his home and the place where the balloon was kept on a pallet and covered by a tarp while it waited.

Part of his equipment was a sewing machine which he set up under a tree with a yard light on it. This he used for repairs, patches for the parachute or balloon, or for reattaching ropes.

Col. Heistand, with his pet raccoon.

On the right is the scene of the action, at the end of the summer. This was the former location of the theater which enjoyed its last season in 1949. The western sky is back of the buildings, the lake behind the viewer.

The 55-gallon drum in the photo, right, was the "stack" and the stakes to which the growing balloon was tethered can also be seen. The balloon was placed directly over this stack. Not visible is the trench, covered over for safety at this time. It was about 2-3 feet wide and deep, the top covered with a sheet of tin, then another foot of dirt.

This is the beginning of the set-up, unfolding the balloon like a giant tent. There were two tall elm trees situated the right distance apart and into which large pulleys were fastened. The top of the balloon was attached to a rope strung through the pulleys. This held the balloon in place during inflation.

The fire was started with kindling in the pit well ahead of the scheduled departure time so it would be at just the right stage for the big event. The blowing up of the balloon was actually part of the entertainment as people enjoyed watching the whole procedure.

Col. Heistand made his own parachute and he supervised the preparation of it before the flight. Helping in this all-important task is assistant Hap Hecker. The nylon ropes, 15-20 feet long, are shown on the left. These were fastened to points around the chute and on the opposite end, a ring. This was similar to laying out and folding a sailboat sail. Starting at the top, the longitudinal bunch of material was also folded very neatly with accordion folds, and bits of newspaper were placed between each fold until all the material was gathered into a neat package about 2 ft. square. The wad of nylon lines was folded almost the same way, and worked into the package of chute material. The ring was placed on the top of the bundle and lashed with the rope that would later be cut in order to free the package. The weight of a man sitting in the sling under the round ring pulled all the package into a full out mass which then filled with air.

The balloon was stretched out over the stack and the enclosed part of the fire pit.

The aeronaut dons the sooty coveralls that protected his clothes while dealing with the fire.

Inside the balloon were heavy ropes that connected half-full sandbags to iron stakes in the ground. These held the sides of the collapsed balloon away from the hot stack. They had to be adjusted as the shape of the balloon changed. An opening in the side of the balloon allowed crew members to enter the inner sanctum and change the position of the sandbags.

The raging fire can be seen along with the bricks lining the fire pit. Wood for kindling and sustaining a blaze is stacked up as well. The Colonel is seen building up the fire.

Note the tin cup in the hand of the Colonel. It would appear as though he was about to have a last cup of coffee before taking off.

Not coffee! The cup contained gasoline or kerosene for that last great blast of hot air.

The fully inflated globe is ready for takeoff. The Colonel had removed the fire suit, climbed onto the sling, and grabbed the parachute. He cut the last of the lines securing the balloon with a linoleum knife held at the ready on a lanyard.

Up, up and away. At some point when the balloon reached sufficient height, and hopefully still within view of the great crowds, the parachute was freed from the balloon. The moment the chute filled with air, the big white puff in the sky slowly dropped toward the earth - or lake. Because Col. Heistand was not a swimmer, before climbing into the harness, he would go down to the ship Ramona, and retrieve a life jacket. If he fell into the lake, he was picked up by a boat standing by.

And, of course, the balloon had to be retrieved also. It could land in a nearby yard or many blocks away, depending on the wind and the height it reached before losing its load. The Colonel's crew would closely follow its path, then venture out to bring it back. At times, a reward was offered to spectators who retrieved the balloon.

2 Chutists Die As Balloon Falls in River

PARKERSBURG, W. Va., Aug. 24 (UP)—Two parachutists drowned near the Wood County Fair today when their balloon dropped into the Ohio River as thousands of fairground spectators watched.

The balloon, which was to have made an ascent of 3000 feet before the two took their plunge over the fairgrounds, suddenly ceased to rise, drifted slowly toward midstream, and then crashed into the water.

One policeman said the two men, strapped in separate harnesses, dangled helplessly from the balloon and struggled to navigate it to dry land.

This article from the San Diego Union, August 25, 1952, doesn't mention names, but this was what happened to the Colonel and a fellow performer. He must have gone to this show right after performing at Ramona. He wasn't wearing a life jacket, this time.

Life is a Picnic

From the earliest days when people from the city ventured out to Reeds Lake, to the last days of Ramona Park, picnics were a source of enjoyment for everyone from small families to thousands of members of an organization. A picnic could be an all-day affair. The picnics of yesteryear offered much more than just a meal. There were games for everyone, music to kick back and enjoy, and dancing until the wee hours of the morning. And, in those early years, everything folks needed for a picnic had to be toted with them. They came first by horse and buggy or omnibus, then the street railway, electric street car, then buses and private cars. Many places around the lake had picnic facilities, but this story is about those held on the street railway property.

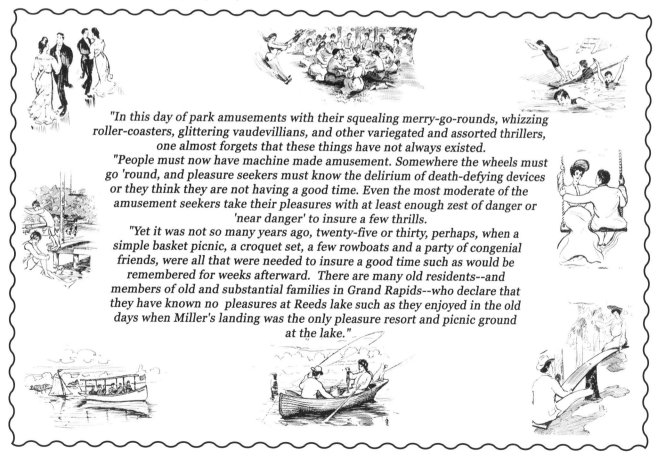

"In this day of park amusements with their squealing merry-go-rounds, whizzing roller-coasters, glittering vaudevillians, and other variegated and assorted thrillers, one almost forgets that these things have not always existed.

"People must now have machine made amusement. Somewhere the wheels must go 'round, and pleasure seekers must know the delirium of death-defying devices or they think they are not having a good time. Even the most moderate of the amusement seekers take their pleasures with at least enough zest of danger or 'near danger' to insure a few thrills.

"Yet it was not so many years ago, twenty-five or thirty, perhaps, when a simple basket picnic, a croquet set, a few rowboats and a party of congenial friends, were all that were needed to insure a good time such as would be remembered for weeks afterward. There are many old residents--and members of old and substantial families in Grand Rapids--who declare that they have known no pleasures at Reeds lake such as they enjoyed in the old days when Miller's landing was the only pleasure resort and picnic ground at the lake."

Conceivably, these words could have been written in the 1940s or 1950s, or at least when 'modern' entertainment ruled and life was getting complicated. But, not so. This reminiscence was printed in the *GR Press* in 1907!

It was 1882 when the railway opened its first pavilion on property that it had purchased in late 1881. Since they owned the property, the company had a say in the conduct of people who frequented the picnic grounds and building. It was necessary to place restrictions on people in order for it to become a place for families to gather because, by this time, there were many saloons around the lake that attracted rowdies. The pavilion offered a place for people to duck inside when the weather was un-picnic-like, or the sun beat down too harshly. The inside was also opened up for dancing in the evenings. The pavilion offered food and tableware for people if they chose not to bring their own.

In 1897, the third pavilion on the premises was built mainly as a theater. There were facilities around the grounds where people could enjoy their meals outdoors on tables in the shade, and, on occasion when a very large gathering was scheduled, they were allowed inside in a bad storm.

The grove to the north of the pavilion, in 1899, had tables, benches, and swings, and the old steam merry-go-round for the children.

The grounds to the south of Ramona Athletic Park served as a picnic area for a few years. In the spring of 1905, the *GR Press* stated,

"Improvements being made there will convert that into one of the prettiest parks imaginable. Mr. Hanchett is determined to make it attractive for Sunday school picnics. A large kitchen has been built and supplied with a range, dishes, etc. and benches, swings and tables will be erected in time for the benefit of picnickers."

Below, the park in 1907. The arrow shows the location of the Hanchett picnic grounds. Lake became Lakeside, Clinton became Lake Drive.

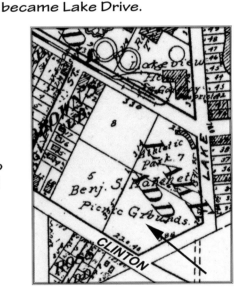

Left, front porch of the first pavilion, a place to relax, cool off and gaze out at the waters of Reeds Lake

Families came to Ramona for picnics and organizations held huge picnics on the Ramona grounds. Not only were the facilities for the meal outstanding but there was so much for people to do before and after eating. Some of the groups that came to the park annually were:

The Meat Cutters, Butchers, and Grocers
 - they closed their stores for the day
Employees of the Street Railway Company and
 the Pere Marquette
The I.O.O.F., Rebekahs and Maccabees
The "Old Residents" or "Old Settlers" Association
Wholesale Dealers' Association, Merchants Week
Boy Scouts and Girl Scouts

Other frequent visitors:

Reunions for family associations
 and school classes
Wurzburgs, Herpolsheimers and
 Steketees employees
The various lodges and temple
 groups associated with
 Masons and Eastern Star
The Grand Rapids Association
 for the Blind
Neighborhood associations
Residents of other towns like
 Middleville, Greenville and
 Lakeview

Over the years, the picnic area was moved around to best accommodate both the picnickers and the growing number of amusements on the grounds. The area north of Ramona Park, across Barnard Ave was purchased by the park for this reason, and small shelters were built. Also at one point, for the sake of convenience, a cook house was provided with hot plate gas stoves. Another place that was set up for picnics was the far west side of property along the fence. A pavilion was also provided here. In the first three decades of the 20th century, Manhattan Beach was also known for its picnic facilities, which drew people away from the railroad property,

The area on the beach occupied by the O-Wash-Ta-Nong Club before 1918 was also used for picnics after the club burned down. The tennis and handball courts survived, so they were available along with playground equipment. Another area that served as picnic grounds in the 1920s was the old Huber Summer Gardens property on the extreme northwest corner of the Ramona block, The Huber pavilion, briefly the Rendezvous Club, was available in case of rain. This area also had equipment for outdoor sport and play. By this time it was necessary to provide parking space for the growing number of privately owned automobiles. In the 1940s, picnickers had the use of outdoor fireplaces or "roasting stoves."

The arrow shows the picnic grounds to the north of the park. Aerial view is from Ramona Park's last days. By this time, the theater is gone.

Picnic Food

1902 advertisement

Surprisingly, the ad above from 1898 mentions paper plates and potato chips. There was a huge potato chip factory in Lynn, Mass. by 1878, and paper plates were around in the 1880s.

263

View of a 1909 picnic. Note items on the table like newspapers and a jar, iced tea or moonshine?

When you pack the picnic basket!

Libby's

Unsweetened Evaporated **Milk**

The can with the blue and white pyramid label

Rich and creamy for your coffee

"Let your grocer be your milkman"

1922 - No worries about this beverage spoiling without refrigeration

The Picnic You'll Enjoy

For an out-of-door lunch anywhere, don't neglect to take a supply of Silver Foam or Export.

You never know what the water supply may be, and what would the picnic be without either of these fine beers?

Order from your dealer, or order from the Bottling Plant direct.

Grand Rapids Brewing Co. GRAND RAPIDS, MICH.

BOTH 'PHONES
Bell M. 340
Cits. 5340

Speaking of beverage, even the Grand Rapids Brewing Company jumped on the picnic band-wagon - 1911.

ROAST ALL NIGHT

Whole Ox Will Bo Put on Fire at Ramona Tomorrow Night.

In the circle is a large pit, in which a whole ox is to be roasted for the barbecue on Saturday afternoon and evening. The ox will be put on the huge split tomorrow evening and will be roasted all night over the coals of a fire that will be started some time previously. The serving of the ox will begin about 5 o'clock Saturday afternoon and continue throughout the evening.

GR Press, August, 1907

264

Picnic Fashions

A *GR Press* ad from 1916 shows the latest in picnic fashion and describes the very best of picnic accoutrements.

An actual picnic party at Ramona Park showing what the local society ladies wore to a picnic in 1916

A Fourth of July Picnic

265

Picnic Fun

Lollygagging on the lawn

Croquet

Listening to live band music

Fat Men's Race

Contests:

Fat man's race
Sack race
Three-Legged race
Wheelbarrow race – contestants wheeled the barrow with a rider
Blindfold race
Tug of war
Dog Race – getting down on all fours to "run"
Hop, Skip and Jump ???
Egg race – carrying an egg on a spoon
Smoking race – each contestant to smoke pipe, must be lighted at end
Ladies' Soap race ???

Organized games were as much a part of a picnic as the food. On the day following the picnic, newspapers would publish the names of the winners who generally received cash prizes. Would someone feel proud of being mentioned for winning the fat man's race? Other than prizes, hardly any expense was required in preparation for the fun. In addition to the ubiquitous baseball games, there were sports of various types, some resembling field games at a modern-day track meet. Races of all sorts were the most prevalent.

Sack Race

266

View of the picnic grounds in 1930 on the occasion of the
annual Kiddies' Day event.

Elks to Show 2,500 Children
Mid-Summer Santa Claus

Below, a publicity shot taken on the
porch of the Ramona Theater, for one of
the Elks events at Ramona Park.

In 1929, this headline announced
the annual Elks Club picnic at
Ramona for the *"Young army of tots
without usual privileges."*

The children assembled at the
Elks temple downtown and were
transported by "trolley" to Ramona.
There was a pageant staged in the
ballpark, hundreds of races with
prizes for winners, pie-eating and
watermelon contests, and a *"girls'
money hunt in a vat of flour."* Then
the picnic of pop and hotdogs was
enjoyed by all.

"48" ELKS MARDI GRAS "48"
RAMONA PARK
September 10 to 16, Inclusive
*The Biggest, Grandest, Most Stupendous
Affair Grand Rapids Has Ever Seen*
"48" Ramona Park—Sept. 10 to 16, Inclusive "48"

GR Press ad for special
Elks event in 1922

Boys, Look!
PRESS
NEWSBOYS'
PICNIC

AT RAMONA PARK,
REEDS LAKE

One of the groups that came back to Ramona Park year after year was the Grand Rapids Press newsboys. In 1894, the First Annual Newsboys Picnic was held at Reeds Lake as a special reward for the boys who sold and distributed the papers. This was before Ramona Park existed, but the railway company was still the host of the event. It was a new idea and a notice was posted in the paper to the parents of the carriers, encouraging them to allow their sons to participate in the "safe and delightful" afternoon. They were encouraged to bring a lunch, and even two lunches to share with a less fortunate boy.

Much planning went into this affair, but the day before it was to take place, it was postponed. The announcement in the Press stated, *"Postponed until strike troubles abate. Newsboys making too much money to take a day's pleasure; citizens must have the news."* This was a reference to the great railroad strike that began with the Pullman Company.

On the actual day of the picnic, one week later, the city went all out for the boys. The youngsters were given badges as tickets to the park, and then the day began with a parade which started at the Press offices, Pearl at the bridge. First in the lineup for the parade was the police escort followed by the newly formed Newsboys' Band. Then came the newsboys themselves, organized by substations. They marched up Pearl to Division, down Monroe to Canal, over Bridge to Scribner to meet their ride. It took fourteen cars of a special train to carry them to the lake. Along the way they were greeted by citizens.

The crowd at the lake was *"over 850 voracious and vociferous boys,"* who listened to speeches, ate their lunches which were brought out by dray, and played games. The day finished for them with a cruise on the steamer, *Hazel A.* Even though it was a great success, the next ten annual picnics were held in Muskegon.

In March of 1894, the first Press Newsboys' Band was formed. It was scheduled to make its debut in the Reeds Lake pavilion the day of the picnic. Even though the picnic was postponed, the band played on...

Commissary Department Busy.	
To make this possible the following total of grub was necessary:	
Special cookies	7,000
Hot frankfurters	1,400
Parker House rolls	1,400
Cupcakes	1,400
Cinnamon rolls	1,400
Pickles	1,400
Ice cream cones	1,400
Bananas	1,400
Total	16,800

For the first picnic in 1894, the boys were asked to bring their own lunches. In subsequent years, the park furnished the eats. Note (above) what was served to the boys in 1914.

When the Press Newsboys' Picnics returned to Reeds Lake in 1905, they had a different reception than in 1894. The boys were given tickets to the individual rides and concessions and were turned loose to do as they wished. The above photos were from two different eras, the left in the 1920s, the right in 1950; both are about exchanging tickets.

Youngsters are waiting for their boat ride.

The first group of news-
boys had an excursion on
the *Hazel A.*
This photo shows the
crowd on the *Ramona*, so
it had to have been taken
after 1922.

How many people could fit
on this boat at one time?
The newsboys tried to
find the answer to that
question.

Three views from the
1920s, the boys
enjoying their food.

Note the tough guy
smoking his hot-dog in
the photo to the left.

270

Not only did the newsboys of the *GR Press* have a day at
Ramona, so did the *GR Herald* Newsies.
These pictures were taken at their event in 1950.

The Nehi

The Hotdogs

The Ice Cream

"Drinking" Buddies

Ramona Park was the place to go for the major summer holidays. Before the days of the amusement park, people congregated at Reeds Lake to celebrate all manner of events. Holidays were peak times of attendance and the transportation companies always had to make special preparations to handle the crowds. On May 31, 1899, for example, the estimate was 10,000 persons in attendance, the major part of the crowd arriving at 2 o'clock in the afternoon. On that day, it was also estimated that *"over 1,000 bicycles were stacked together under trees and along fences and against the pavilion."*

The annual opening day of Ramona Park nearly always occurred before Memorial Day so celebrations of that holiday at the lake were often anticlimactic. Management always arranged for special attractions in honor of the season openings, but on occasion there were also special events scheduled for Memorial Day. In 1909 such an event was described in the *GR Press* thus:

"Ramona is planning for one of the biggest Memorial day celebrations in its history Monday. The fifteen mile bicycle road race, which will start and end in front of the pavilion, of course is one of the big features, but there will be plenty of others to keep the crowd busy. Mme. Meixell will make another dash for the clouds in a balloon. She will ascend from the shores of the lake late in the afternoon and make the usual parachute drop."

Special balloon ascensions were not an infrequent Memorial Day event. In 1916, the aeronaut Henry A. Phelps made a usual ascension, but on the descent he provided an extra sensation by waiting too late to cut loose and he hit the ground a little too hard. He recovered a while later to jump again. That same day Bud Morriss did an exhibition in his Benoist Hydro-Aeroplane for the purpose of demonstrating the use of the vehicle in wartime by hovering over the steamers and cottages. His landing on the lake was less than spectacular since it was hampered by a profusion of rowboats. Daredevil Milo thrilled crowds in

1922 by performing a straight jacket escape on his descent.

Often special shows were scheduled for the theater in honor of this day and often they experienced record crowds as a result. In 1942, a two day celebration was scheduled. Included in the festivities were a hill-billy musical performance held on a special outdoor stage erected in the center of the park. Also Blinky the Clown and Kiddies Funster were on the docket, as well as balloonist "Pee Wee Brown" doing his thrilling "Leap for Life."

By far the most grand celebratory event of the year was the Fourth of July. The biggest crowds were expected and received and the biggest attractions were presented. For many years the *GR Press* printed a full-page on June 30th or July 1st, advertising not only the festivities of the celebration but all of the attractions that were available around the lake.

When evening arrived, after the final theater performance, people who stayed at the park were treated to spectacular pyrotechnic displays. These heavenly illuminations were not merely the firing of Roman candles or aerial fountains into the dark skies, they were works of art. In 1909, for example, the display was advertised to last about an hour, culminating with "Niagara Falls in Fire" itself of ten minutes duration.

The Independence Day celebration in 1913 was headlined as "Old Fashioned Time for Fourth of July." This included a balloon ascension, races, contests and games and particular attention to the fireworks. This display took five days to prepare as the fireworks were mounted on floats and barges anchored out in the lake. One of the features was

the figures of Mutt and Jeff outlined in fire and *"poor little Jeff met his usual finish."* In this display also were "Roosevelt in Africa" showing the colonel on his hunt surrounded by wild animals, a "tempest wheel" throwing a circle of sparks for sixty feet and "floating swans" outlined in fire that glided over the surface of the lake. It was finished off with a huge American flag in fire. In 1919, appropriately, a display was arranged to demonstrate *"rockets that were used to direct artillery fire and various types of fiery signals employed in conflict will be used during the exhibition, which will be conducted by Grand Rapids army recruiting officers as a part of the campaign for recruits."*

There was a profusion of parades, both in the heart of the big city and at the lake. Local bands, marching organizations, floats, horses, automobiles, carriages and the like processed past thousands of spectators lining the streets. After the parade, people dispersed to go to a number of parks, Ramona generally being the most widely visited.

Children's parade at Ramona. The sign says, "Celebrate the 4th at Ramona." Huber's Summer Garden is in the background. Photo was likely taken on the old Barnard Street north of the park grounds proper.

273

While this 4th of July parade in the photo was not at Ramona, it shows a city parade which may have culminated with participants motoring out to Ramona for the rest of the day.

SPEND THE FOURTH AT RAMONA
A REAL OLD FASHIONED CELEBRATION

People celebrated differently as the century wore on. In those "good old days" people were entertained with games and contests. Later on the rides were the biggest attraction. Ramona Gardens began to have Dawn Dances that lasted all night prior to the 4th in the late 1930s and early 1940s.

Giant Fireworks Display

Sack Races, Potato Race   Banana Eating Contest
Three-Legged Race   Ladies' Nail Driving Contest
Pie Eating Contest   Ladies' Wood Sawing Contest

1912

OLD-FASHIONED
CONTESTS
PRIZES FOR WINNERS
"HEINIE" LIGHTNER IN CHARGE
FROM 11 A. M. TO 12 NOON

Special Cash Prizes in Gold
1—FOR LONGEST DISTANCE DRIVEN!
2—FOR BIGGEST FAMILY IN ATTENDANCE!
3—FOR OLDEST AUTO, YES, ANY MAKE!
4—FOR OLDEST PERSON ATTENDING!

BIG FAMILY PICNIC
IN COOL SHADY GROVE
FREE
ACCOMMODATIONS
BRING THE FAMILY!
ENJOY THE DAY!

1929

FUN FOR ALL!
PIE EATING!   WATERMELON!   GREASED POLE and Other Contests!
CASH PRIZES TO THE WINNERS!

1935

GIGANTIC
GORGEOUS **FIREWORKS** BREATH-TAKING DISPLAY
BIGGER, BRIGHTER THAN EVER BEFORE!
LATEST AERIAL SPECIALTIES AND SET PIECES!

BIG BALLOON ASCENSION
AND "LEAP-FOR-LIFE" WITH   DARE-DEVIL "PEEWEE" BROWN

DANCE IN RAMONA GARDENS
BEAUTIFUL BALLROOM—SPLENDID FLOOR—FINE ORCHESTRA
DAWN DANCE—THURSDAY, JULY 3RD

1941

Celebrations of this holiday at Ramona through the life of the park underwent a metamorphosis of purpose. The same thing could be stated about the holiday in general all across the nation. These *GR Press* news article headings sum up the thrust of the early twentieth century Labor Day celebrations in Grand Rapids. There were huge parades in the downtown streets and then recreation at Ramona Park. The participants were exclusively union members and their families. Those marching in the parades did so with great pride in their respective trades. Besides those who marched, there were floats representing the various unions. In 1910, for example, the parade was said to be three miles in length and included many of the sixty-two Grand Rapids unions and those from other cities.

Ads from the *GR Herald* from 1940, left and 1941, right

The time spent at Ramona Park was for picnicking, play and participation in sports events. There were baseball games between rival union teams in the Ramona Athletic Field and various contests for amateurs with significant prizes for the victors. Sometimes the crowds heard speakers in the theater or the picnic grove. The most notable of these was Clarence Darrow in 1916. He appeared because the scheduled speaker, Mother Jones, had become ill.

There were no parades from 1914 through 1918, the war being referenced as the reason. However, when the 1919 pageant was staged, it added the dimension of the returning veterans to the celebration theme. In 1922, the Trades and Labor Council, which oversaw the events, ceased the parades once more. Not only that, the venue for the post-parade celebration was moved away from Ramona Park to the West Michigan State Fairgrounds.

Since Labor Day came at the end of the summer, it also usually marked the end of the amusement park season. Thus, the holiday often turned into a three-day event for the general public at Ramona, a last hurrah. The offerings changed as well to spectacles similar to the Fourth of July, that being grandiose displays of fireworks and parachute jumps. In 1925 it was actually a five day Mardi Gras Carnival at the end of which a Chevrolet Coach was given away.

275

JAPANESE FETES

In the early part of the twentieth century, people were enthralled with all things Japanese. From the year 1906 through 1914, they came in droves to the celebration of the Japanese Fetes at Ramona Park. The whole park was transformed into a fairyland. As the years progressed, so did the extent of the preparations, decorations and entertainment. The introduction each year boasted, *"better than the year before,"* and each year it lived up to that proclamation. Similar events referred to as "Venetian" and "Fairyland" were also held.

The Fetes consisted of two nights during the week, consecutive if no rain, when the whole park was festooned with Japanese decorations and special attractions which culminated in fireworks and balloon ascensions. In 1906, lanterns were hung in profusion throughout the Circle, and candles inside them were lit beginning at sundown. Not just dozens but some 5,000 of them! Not only the theater and midway, but the figure-eight, Palace of Mirth and Old Mill and other amusements were thus adorned. And not just Ramona Park, but resorts around the lake, even the steamships, joined in the festivities by wearing colored lights and lanterns. Park employees and some of the attendees donned Japanese kimonos to become part of the panorama.

In addition to lights and lanterns, thousands of feet of crepe paper transformed buildings into pagodas, inside and out. One year, yards of bamboo transformed the theater entrance into a Japanese temple. Another time, massive amounts of fragrant hemlock boughs converted the inside of the dancing pavilion into a Japanese lawn party. Other items used in decoration were rushes, chrysanthemums, cherry blossoms and flags.

In 1909, all the lanterns were changed over from candle power to electricity. Because of this, not only did the occasional burning lanterns cease to fall on visitors, but the whole park could be lit at one time with the flip of a switch. Besides the fire danger, one problem with lighting thousands of candles was that the first ones to be lit, burned down by the time the process reached the last of the lanterns!

Postcard showing lanterns and lights decorating the theater and walkways.

The upper view shows the lit-up figure-eight; below, lights and the searchlight.

For this event each year, it took a small army of carpenters and electricians, sometimes working around the clock, to string the lights and build the special displays. Some of the more unusual structures included a revolving electrical windmill high up on a tower which spun like a fire wheel with varicolored lights; a Japanese junk mounted on a pagoda-like framework, built over a large flower bed; a Japanese village which included an open pagoda with Geisha girls dancing and singing. Even an occasional jinrikisha drawn by Japanese boys was seen carrying little Japanese girls.

The fireworks displays, provided by the Japanese and headed up by professional Jack Campbell out of Chicago, surpassed even those provided during the Fourth of July celebrations. In 1913, for example, it was stated that, ***"A fireworks factory has been established in the Ramona picnic grove and a force of experts are at work under the direction of Jack Campbell."*** The usual program of skyrockets, pinwheels and Roman candles was just the beginning for such elaborate displays as the "Japanese Maple Tree," a tree that revolved and opened turning into springs of sparks with the leaves afire. Other displays were named,

"The Fountain of Light,"
"The Walking Elephant,"
"The Blazing Sun,"
"Roosevelt in Africa."

Also depicted were a fiery Japanese pagoda, a huge colored fan, and a see-saw.

Daylight fireworks included large bombs hurled high in the air exploding not with showers of stars and sparks, but releasing various fantastic objects such as dogs, pigs, dragons and other animals floating about in the air.

Japanese Fete decorations inside one of the rides, possibly The Old Mill?

Night scene in 1908: The Japanese junk off to the right; the streetcar loop just beyond that; the merry-go-round and refreshment stand; Godfroy's Theater behind the carousel; the Ramona Athletic Field; Ten-Cate Hotel across from the ballpark; the Masonic Home in the distance.

Balloon ascensions, although special, were not so uncommon at Ramona. However, those executed during the Japanese Fetes were done at night. The aeronauts were illuminated by the searchlight, sometimes carrying colored flares, sometimes releasing confetti which sparkled in the beams as the parachute brought its precious cargo safely to earth.

In 1913 it was estimated that 25,000 persons had made the trip out to the lake in one evening for the event. Manager DeLamarter, the brainpower behind the events, estimated also that it was the largest crowd ever concentrated at one time on the grounds. Some 20,000 of those people had come by street car. The next year, 1914, it was announced that there would no longer be any Japanese nights. The repercussions from such a declaration were so strong that Ramona management relented and put on the biggest spread ever. The reluctance to do so was borne of the fact that so much money was spent on the adornments that the receipts didn't cover the expenses. This was the last year for the event, however.

Left, close-up of the Japanese Junk, and stand, girls aboard, and gardens beneath.

No. 162 Japanese Night at Reed's Lake, Grand Rapids, Mich.

People have puzzled over this familiar postcard, titled, **"Japanese Night at Reed's Lake, Grand Rapids, Mich."** The people in the picture do not appear to be Japanese, nor does the decor of the horses or the object being drawn by them. But the story behind the card explains the mystery.

On June 10, 1909, there was a Civic Pageant in downtown Grand Rapids, sponsored by the Grand Rapids Advertisers' Club. The event was a parade with floats created by local businesses, and also automobiles and carriages. It was held during the fourth annual Merchants' Week. The floats were termed *"florally decorated equipages"* on the nature of those seen at Mardi Gras in New Orleans.

What did all that have to do with the postcard? The float entered into the pageant by the street railway company was awarded the big prize for beauty in the industrial class and the postcard shows that float. It was designed by Louis J. DeLamarter, and was deemed, *"the most beautiful float ever seen in this city."* On it were seven girls in Japanese costume seated in a large gondola drawn by a swan, on mirrors arranged to give a realistic water effect. *"Along the side of the float was pictured 'Ramona' in red flowers, also the dates of the Japanese night festivities. The float was drawn by eight horses, with six Negro grooms."*

To be precise, the float shown in the postcard was not actually the same one that won in the pageant. The picture was taken on August 18 or 19 at the Japanese Fete at Ramona, the civic event was in June. The whole float was reproduced in every detail, including the horses and grooms.

Postcard of the actual float in the downtown pageant.

Ramona Float, Grand Rapids, Mich.

Scouts

Scouts were among the special groups which regularly enjoyed the delights of Ramona Park. The Girl Scout organization in America was born in March of 1912, and in 1915, the first event took place at Ramona for both the Boy Scouts and Girl Scouts of the area. As with other groups, the railway company and park management were very generous in providing the youngsters with a grand experience.

Scouts' Spring Reunion

Boy and Girl Scouts in their First Annual Spring Reunion including a downtown "hike," a basket picnic, a visit to all Ramona's concessions, and an entertainment by the Scouts in Ramona Theater, which will be free to all. "The Scouts are to be reckoned with—this spring reunion will be a tremendous success."

HUNDREDS ROMP OUT AT RAMONA

Boy and Girl Scouts Help to Usher in the 1915 Opening

The 1915 event was billed as *"the first joint mass meeting of the Girl and Boy Scouts of this city."* Festivities began at the West Side Car Barns where the male troops gathered. They marched in a parade led by the Boy Scout Drum and Bugle Corps, to Fulton Street Park where they were joined by the Girl Scouts. Six special street cars took the crowd to Ramona to enjoy the rest of the day.

Their amusement park adventure began with free time to roam about, which included a ride on the steamer. The lunches they each brought were consumed in the picnic grounds, followed by performances in the theater in which they took part.

In 1916, the city of Grand Rapids was host to the world famous Columbia Park Boys' Club from San Francisco, which joined in the scout parade downtown. At Ramona, the visiting club gave a public demonstration in the theater of *"marches, tumbling, folk dancing, dress parade and spectacular feats."*

The last joint rally and visit to Ramona occurred again in 1917. In 1920 just the Boy Scouts were invited to frolic as guests of Manager DeLamarter at Ramona's annual opening day.

Attractive Group of Girl Scouts

The girl scouts of Sigsbee call themselves "Daffodils," and surely they are as charming as their name implies in their natty scout suits. There are 22 members, all uniformed. Mrs. C. S. Marshman is captain and Miss Dorothy Vincent lieutenant. This picture was taken at the big rally at Reed's lake.

1915

1916   Grand Rapids Girl Scouts

From 1927 to 1934, the Boy Scouts and Lions Club of Grand Rapids teamed up for festivities at the opening of Ramona Park. Each year a spring jamboree was held in the athletic park followed by recreation across the street. In 1927, it was stated that there were some 80 or 85 troops from Grand Rapids and western Michigan participating. Through the years this number grew.

The families of the scouts as well as the general public were treated to various exhibitions of scoutcraft, flag ceremonies, band concerts, parade and review as well as contests between the troops. A part of the festivities through these years was a huge picnic with food enough for the scouts and their families, served in the grove on dozens of tables decorated by the mothers. For the entertainment of the scouts and their parents, the Lions Club put on performances in the theater to raise money for Camp Lion.

Photo taken at the 1928 scout jamboree in Ramona Athletic Park

BOYS WHO GUIDED RAMONA THRONGS

The scouts were called on to assist the police force in handling the vast crowds that attended Kiddies' Days

GRAND RAPIDS ON PARADE

Ramona Gardens proved to be a successful setting for the **Grand Rapids on Parade** exposition, held in early September, 1946. This venture was sponsored by the Grand Rapids Junior Chamber of Commerce, designed to acquaint the townspeople with some of the local manufacturing companies. Upon visiting the exhibits, Charles O. Ransford, president of the Grand Rapids Senior Chamber, stated:

"I am astounded and immensely gratified by the excellent manner in which these products have been introduced to citizens of Grand Rapids, few of whom have any idea of the extent and variety of the City's industries. Next year it should include the products of every Grand Rapids manufacturer and should be staged in the Civic Auditorium."

PRIZES ★ ★ ★ PRIZES
"GRAND RAPIDS ON PARADE"
FREE: VAUDEVILLE ACTS
MUSIC
OVER 50 EXHIBITS
PRIZES EACH DAY
AT
RAMONA PARK SEPT. 5, 6, 7
SEE THE PRODUCTS MANUFACTURED IN GRAND RAPIDS and USED THROUGHOUT THE WORLD
10c Admission Charge to the Park
50 VALUABLE PRIZES EACH DAY
25 Prizes Each Afternoon   25 Prizes Each Evening
plus one **MAJOR PRIZE** each day
Such as a Radio, Shetland Pony, Lawn Mower, Kitchen Cabinet
ENTRANCE TO EXHIBITION BLDG. **FREE**
SPONSORED BY JUNIOR CHAMBER OF COMMERCE

Globe Displays Underwear Products

Parading in your undies might be frowned on normally, but it was just exactly right for the Globe Knitting Works in its participation in "Grand Rapids on Parade," which concluded a three-day exhibit at Ramona Park Saturday night.

+ + +

TWO OF THE machines in the Globe exhibit are shown here. Mrs. Julia Greenwalt is shown at an automatic tubing machine. Its two needles knit 4,000 stitches per minute. One operator can turn out 500 garments a day on this type of machine.

W. R. Luerhs is standing next to a rayon tubular knitting machine. With 1,200 needles making 240,000 stitches a minute, this machine turns out a yard of fabric every 7½ minutes. The fabric forms a 14-inch cylinder and makes possible seamless garments.

+ + +

GLOBE HAS 125 machines of this type and other machines that knit cotton, wool and combination fabrics. The exhibit at Ramona also showed four stages in production of nylon hose at the Grand Rapids plant.

R. W. Clements, president of Globe, said, "I believe this is a wonderful opportunity for Grand Rapids residents to become acquainted with Grand Rapids manufactured products, and Globe Knitting Works is happy to participate."

Story that accompanied a Globe Knitting photo in the *GR Herald*, Sept. 8, 1946

View of the interior of Ramona Gardens and two of the companies which participated: Globe Knitting and Rapids-Standard (Rapistan)

Note the marks in the floor made by skates.

Sunday Was Twosday as Twins Closed Convention

Sunday, September 1, 1946 marked Twins' Day at Ramona Park. Host to approximately 200 sets of twins, Ramona provided a day of fun for persons attending the ***International Twins Association*** three-day convention in Grand Rapids. This was the first international meeting for the group since the war. The city did not have its own arm of the organization at that time, but was represented by thirty sets of twins. As a side note, 8 sets of twins were born in Grand Rapids the week prior to this event.

Besides holding meetings and whatever else twins did when they convened, many participated in a scientific study conducted by Ohio State University professor, Dr. David C. Rife. The object of the various examinations such as blood tests, fingerprints, eye examinations and pain threshold tests, was to add data to the developing theories regarding the influence of heredity in transmitting various traits.

Added to the fun at Ramona Park was the conferring of prizes on winners in various classifications. The categories were most and least identical in three age groups, most attractive by gender, youngest, oldest and farthest traveled. Grand Rapids twins fared well in taking 8 of the prizes.

OFFICIAL GREETERS—On hand to greet members of the International Twins association at Ramona park Sunday afternoon will be Louie, left, and Larry DeLamarter, 5-year-old twin sons of Mr. and Mrs. Louis J. DeLamarter, jr., West River-rd. They will be representing their father, a park executive. A contest for 11 classes of twins will be held at the park, part of the program of the association's 3-day convention beginning Saturday.

Proud grandparents pose with their adorable twins in front of Ramona Gardens

Seeing double, twice, in front of the entrance to The Derby Racer.

Part of the history of Ramona Park was its connection with the military. Whether during wartime or peace, each of the two entities made contributions to the other. While this association is not of great significance to the total picture, it is an interesting element in the portrait.

In Entertainment

Considering the fact that Ramona was primarily a vaudeville theater, it is puzzling to imagine that military activity also enticed visitors to the lake. There was something about the military theme that drew great crowds. Such was the case in 1908, for example, when theater audiences saw the Great Military Spectacular Sensation of Kronau's "Our Boys in Blue" stepping through intricate drill maneuvers staged as an attack on a warship.

On a much more grandiose scale, reenactments of famous battles were the themes of various productions put on in the Ramona Athletic Field. In 1905, a spectacle called "The Fall of Port Arthur" depicted the recently fought battle by the same name in the Russo-Japanese War. Displayed on a huge stage in the center of the field, spectators viewed dramatic scenes of the war including a naval attack and destruction of Russian warships by Japanese torpedo boats. Fireworks came at the end, concluding the performance.

"Our Boys in Blue" on stage

"The Battle of Santiago" was another exhibition which re-created the largest naval engagement of the Spanish-American War. *"Cannons boomed, rifles cracked, men fell and soldiers cheered."* This production was staged for the benefit of the Grand Rapids Battalion building fund and used some local boys in the dramatization. What began as a mimic of the battle ended in tragedy when one of those boys stepped in front of a cannon as it fired and was killed instantly.

To celebrate July 4th in 1912, crowds were entertained by real soldiers as was stated in the GR Press: *"CROWD SEES MIMIC WAR AT REEDS LAKE - Ramona Has Greatest Day in the History of Grand Rapids' Resort.*

"Mimic war and games of peace each had their share in yesterday's local celebration of the Fourth of July. It was but natural that the game of war should be the most exciting feature of the day. The crowds which thronged Ramona, estimated at 20,000 were thrilled by the rattle of musketry and the roar of the field gun. As the khaki clad soldier boys carried out the battle maneuvers in true veteran steadiness and precision they were greeted with roars of appreciative applause.

"Five militia companies participated, including the four from the local battalion and a company from Grand Haven. There was the section of field artillery from Lansing and the local hospital corps. The most interesting feature of the battle was the work of the field gun. In all 125 rounds of ammunition were fired. After the battle there was a dress parade in the field back of the roller coaster and the companies returned to the city at 3 o'clock. Prior to the engagement the field gun from Lansing was the center of interest. The Grand Haven company and a company of infantry from Ionia, which arrived here last night, will practice at the rifle range today. "

284

Topping the list of military spectacles was the 1919 ordnance and vehicle exhibition at Ramona. Originally assembled by the United States War Department for a tractor show in Denver, this great collection was subsequently secured for viewing by the American Society of Automotive Engineers at Ottawa Beach. Grand Rapids was extremely fortunate that the ordnance department decided to send the exhibit on a tour of the west due to its immense popularity with civilians. From Ramona it went on to Duluth and then down through the Mississippi Valley. Among the personnel traveling with the exhibit were recruitment officers.

According to the account in the GR Press, July 5, 1919,

"Eighteen carloads of ordnance, used by the American army in comprising massive war machinery in France, will arrive in Grand Rapids Sunday from Jenison Park, [Ottawa Beach] where the equipment has been exhibited. Authorization from the war department to bring the war equipment here has been received. The equipment will be exhibited on a field near Ramona Athletic park and will remain during the coming week. It is expected public demonstrations will take place during five days at least.

"Two officers and 25 men comprise the personnel of the outfit. Three tanks, the Mark V., one of the largest made during the war; a six-ton tank, and a three-ton tank, all of which have been under German fire, and three big guns, one of them a self-propelling mounted eight-inch Howitzer, will arrive with the exhibit."

And, on July 10,

"Saturday's big show at the army ordnance exhibit at Reeds lake will include such features as the firing of the big guns in the exhibit and a display of the climbing and pushing qualities of the tanks. The big Mark V British machine will be used to knock down two large trees in the park back of the ball ground, each as large as a telephone pole. One of the smaller tanks will be run into the big ditch near the exhibition grounds, and Capt. Booth, in charge of the demonstration, guarantees that he will present the tank to the city if it can't crawl out again. Every piece of ordnance in the entire exhibit will be in complete operation throughout the Saturday show.

"The exhibit is giving interesting demonstrations of the various machines daily, a popular feature being the complete repair train which lights the exhibit with its own power through a string of electric lights running through the trees and along the wall of the athletic park, beside doing welding, sawing and repairing work of all kinds."

The show drew such great crowds that it was held over for an additional day's viewing which included a tug-of-war between the captured 22 1/2 ton German Lanz tractor and the American 10-ton tractor. As interesting as the demonstrations were, the re-loading of the equipment on the flatcars held equal fascination. It was done through the use of the German Lanz tractor. A winch was attached to its powerful engine, the tractor was loaded on the foremost car and all the other pieces except the tanks were snaked aboard the train by a long cable.

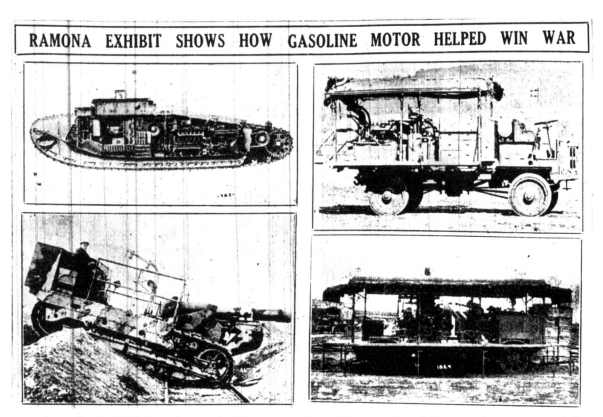

RAMONA EXHIBIT SHOWS HOW GASOLINE MOTOR HELPED WIN WAR

Upper left: Mark V British tank; Upper right: One unit of the ordnance mobile repair shop; Lower left: Eight-inch howitzer on self-propelled mount; Lower right: Milling machine tractor

In Service

The contribution of the military as entertainment for Ramona visitors was only a part of the association. On the other side of it, military efforts also benefited. Soon after railway tracks completed the connection to Reeds Lake from the city and before the railway company owned property at the terminus, there was a military presence on the very grounds that would become Ramona Park. In August of 1876, just a few weeks after General George Custer lost his life in the Battle of Little Big Horn, the Second Regiment of the Michigan State Troops set up an encampment on the shores of the lake. The gathering was known as Camp Custer, and retained that title when the troops returned to Reeds Lake in 1877 and 1879. The assemblage marched from downtown Grand Rapids out to the lake hauling all the gear they would need for the five day encampment. During those days, the men slept and ate on the grounds, held battalion drills, dress parades, guard mounting, and target practice.

There were more encampments on these grounds, after Ramona was in place, in 1897, 1914 and 1915. By this time the troops were identified as the Grand Rapids Battalion of the Michigan National Guard. For all of these events, the public was invited to come out and view the proceedings.

See the Soldiers
UNITED STATES REGULARS
.. IN ..
Encampment and Drill
.. AT ..
Masonic Home Addition, Reeds Lake
ALL DAY TODAY

Above, 1912; Right, 1915

GUARDSMEN TO DRILL AT LAKE

G. R., Ionia and Muskegon Companies to Spend Three Days in Heavy Work for Practice

Buy Thrift Stamps and Help Win the War

In the effort to secure funds through the War Savings Stamp program in 1918, Ramona Park did its part. Booths were set up whereby people could purchase the stamps, and the Ramona Theater stage was used as a venue for the appeals. *"With brisk and breezy speeches on the war savings stamps, a song on the Liberty Loan, a playlet based upon the subject of the draft and the flags of the allies, brought out one by one and left waving at the side of the stage, the popular summer theater has an inspiring 'Star Spangled Banner' atmosphere. The lighted Flag-decorated globes also are new."* When 5-year-old wonder-boy orator, Kenneth Hughes of Saginaw, made his appeal on the stage, the Thrift Stamps were completely sold out to the tune of $290. If the unprecedented sale had been anticipated, it was felt that at least $500 worth could have been sold. Official British war pictures were also shown in the movie portion of the shows.

Amusements War Time Necessity
—— By the Associated Press. ——
Washington, D. C., May 20. --- The Council of National Defense, in connection with a movement which it is formally inaugurating, looking to conservation along all necessary lines, has gone on record officially as favoring the continuation of theaters, motion picture shows and other forms of proper amusements as one of the essentials of war times.

This "official" statement of approval by the United States Government, published in June, 1918, expressed the importance of keeping up the spirits of the American citizenry.

In 1912 the grand dance hall was opened at Ramona Park. Strict rules were in place regarding acceptable dress and behavior. When a group of U. S. Soldiers entered, they were refused admittance for not wearing coats and white collars. However, in the absence of Manager DeLamarter, railway President Benjamin Hanchett came to the rescue and *"issued an order allowing the soldiers to enter the dancing pavilion and to remain as long as they conducted themselves properly."*

In 1917, the dancing "casino" was opened to soldiers as guests of the Park, and included a special carnival night. Also that year, a field day event was held in the park to raise funds for the soldier's comfort fund. This involved the efforts of the local chapter of the D. A. R. who took up the collections while the soldiers of the Grand Rapids Battalion competed in various events. Special events for soldiers continued in 1918 when soldiers visiting the theater were admitted without charge.

The theme, "Cheer Up, Ramona Will Open Soon," used first in 1912, was very apt when used during the war years. The photo below shows members of the railway company, ready to serve.

When the second world war was in progress, Ramona Park provided an escape for local people who needed cheering up, needed recreation and needed to get away from the daily grind and bombardment of bad news. With the option of traveling in automobiles curtailed by gas rationing, the park, with its easy access provided by the motor coaches, was readily available for all comers. With so many adult males being called into service, the park also provided employment for school-aged fellows who would not have received the nod during peace-time.

Remarkable Ramona Park provided an oasis for so many during troubled times.

Finale

The die was cast, the handwriting was on the wall, the demise of Ramona Park was inevitable and foreseen as early as 1949, when the theater was demolished.

The Last Days
Reeds Lake Preview

Ramona Park

"The Rendesvous of Refined Amusement Seekers"

CAR LANDING AT REED'S LAKE.
(WEALTHY AVE. AND TAYLOR ST. LINE.)

RAMONA, REED'S LAKE, GRAND RAPIDS, MICH.

From Crowded. . .

Waterfront merging with the Ramona Park grounds.

Entering with great anticipation and exiting with great satisfaction.

. . . to Deserted

No more skating at Ramona.

No more sounds of buzzes and bumps and sparks.

No more round and round, up and down, organ music.

No more strolling the midway, winning prizes, eating fries.

No more climbing to heights, dropping to depths, screaming.

Good bye, Derby Racer. So long, Ramona Park.

Remarkable Ramona Park

A place where the multitudes gathered for fun and frolic, a place where memories were made, a place that could never exist again, except through those memories.

SOMETHING DOING AT RAMONA

—Grand Rapids Press Photographer.

THIS WAS RAMONA PARK—Razing of buildings at Ramona park, where a shopping center and apartments will be built, is gaining in tempo. The derby racer is about half down, and many concessions on the north side, above, have been razed. In this group was the fun house, one of the larg and popular concessions that entertained hundreds of persons in seven decades. In the background the building housing the roller rink.

The End

Ramona Park just before the demolition of the theater in 1949.

After the construction of the apartments on Lakeside Drive, and Gaslight Village stores; before Jacobsons and parking ramp.

REEDS LAKE
OUR OWN RESORT

Neither space nor time permits the inclusion of the history of Reeds Lake in the same volume as Ramona Park. While the two were inseparable in actuality, it is natural to make such a division of material for the purpose of publication. Some of the topics which will be covered in the Reeds Lake tome are shown here.

Boats and Steamers

Small Craft

Florence

Belknap

Major A.B. Watson

Hazel A.

Ramona

Boat Clubs

O-Wash-Ta-Nong
and Lakeside

Boat Builders: Truscott, Gere, Seidel

Reeds Lake Naval Wars

Bathing Beaches

Manhattan
Beach

Rose's
Swimming
School

Fishing, Ice Skating and Ice Boating

Businesses

Ramona
Athletic Park

Hotels

Ice Companies

Sanitarium

Masonic
Home

Resorts

Leland Park

Ross' Pavilion

And: Lake Park, Miller's Landing, Poisson's, Alger Park

Saloons, Restaurants

Huber's Summer Garden

Phoenix Club

And: Jimmy Fairs, Thompson's, Lakeside Tavern

Also: Fisk Lake, Hodenpyl, Woodcliff, Bonnell, Pioneer Club, Reeds Lake Blvd, Airplanes, Fireworks and more.

Sources

Bibliography

Billboard Magazine, Michigan Tradesman, Popular Mechanics

Grand Rapids Newspapers:

Daily News

Democrat - Daily, Morning, Weekly

Eagle - Daily, Weekly

Herald and Herald Telegram

Leader - Daily, Evening, Weekly

Post - Saturday, Evening

Press and Evening Press

Times - Daily, Weekly

Images

Postcards, unless otherwise designated, are from the collections of David Bisbee and Tom Dilley

Abbreviations used:

EGRPL   East Grand Rapids Branch, Kent District Library, History Room

GRCA   Grand Rapids City Archives

GRPL   Grand Rapids Public Library, Photo Archives

GRPM   Grand Rapids Public Museum, Photo Archives

Top, **Bot**tom, **Mid**dle, **L**eft, **R**ight; **PC** - Postcard

Front Cover		GRPL	22	bot	Gerald Muir
Pub. page		EGRPL	23	top	EGRPL
Foreword		GRPL	23	bot	GRPL
Preface		GRPL	25	program	Mary Verwys
1	top	PC, Ed Bawden	26		EGRPL
2	top r	GRPL	27	mid	PC, Ed Bawden
5		GRPL	28	bot	GRPL
6	ad	1870 GR City Directory	29	top	GRPL
6	photo	GRPL	29	bot	EGRPL
7	photos	GRPL	30	photos	Lib. of Cong. Detroit Publishing
8	map, photo	GRPL	31	bot	Cooley 1912 Appr, Hildebrandt
9	top	GRPL	32	photos	GRPM
9	bot	Steve Ophoff	33	mid l	GRPM
10		GRPL	34	bot	GRPL
11	brochure	John Kamstra	35	top, mid	GRPL
12	top	Margaret Kimber	35	bot	Gerald Muir
13	top	GRPL	36	all	GRPL
14	top two	GRPL	37	all	GRPL
14	mid	Donna Kruizenga Boelema	38	top l	Gordon Hubenet
15	photos	GRPL	38	top r, mid, bot	GRPL
18	top	EGRPL	38	coin	Dick Ryan
18	bot	Margaret Kimber	39		PC, Chris Byron
19		GRPL	42	photo	GRPL
20	map, photo	GRPL	43	photo	PC, Robalyn Rose VanSolkema
21		GRPL	45	photo	Gordon Hubenet
22	top	GRPL	46		Gordon Hubenet
22	mid	EGRPL	48	photo, poster	Ron Pesch

179	mid	GRPL
180		GRPM
181	ticket	Dick Ryan
181	photo	GRPL
182	top	Karin McElwee Westdale
182	bot	EGRPL
183	top	EGRPL
183	bot	GRPL
184		GRPL
185	top r,l	GRPL
185	mid, bot	Donna Kruizenga Boelema
186	top	Hap Hecker
186	bot	GRPL
188	top l, bot	GRPL
188	mid	Mary Ellen Miklas Siegel
188	top r	EGRPL
189	letter	Jeff McElwee
191	bot	GRPL
192	bot	EGRPL
193	top, mid	GRPL
194	bot	Cooley 1912 Appr, Hildebrandt
195	top	EGRPL
196	top	GRPL
196	map	GRCA
197	top	GRPPL
197	bot	Hap Hecker
198	top	Hap Hecker
198	mid	GRPL
198	bot	Mary Ellen Miklas Siegel
200	brochure	John Kamstra
201	map	GRPL
201	bot	GRPM
202	token	Marian Szudera
202	bot	Rockford Historical Society/Snow
203	top	Gerald Muir
203	bot	Karin McElwee Westdale
204	top	GRPL
204	bot r	GR Patent Office
205	top, mid l	Donna Kruizenga Boelema
205	mid r	Fred Elliott
205	bot	GRPL
206	map	GRCA
206	mid	GRPL
206	bot	Donna Kruizenga Boelema
207	bot	Donna Kruizenga Boelema
209		Chip Rogers
210		Graves Family
211	top	Graves Family
211	mid, bot	Chip Rogers
212	top	Graves Family
212	bot l	Bud Vierson
212	bot r	Snow
213	top	Graves Family
213	mid, bot	Snow
214		Snow
215		Snow
216		Snow
217	pamphlet	Margaret Kimber
218		GRPM
219		EGRPL
220	top	Karin McElwee Westdale
220	left	GRPL
222	top r, bot r	GRPL
222	bot l	Cooley 1912 Appr, Hildebrandt
223	top l, bot r	GRPL
223	top r	Hap Hecker
224	top r,l, bot	GRPL
224	mid	Gordon Hubenet
225	top, mid	GRPL
225	bot	EGRPL
226	top, mid	GRPL
226	bot	EGRPL
227		GRPL
228		GRPL
229	bot	GRPL
230		GRPL
231		Jim Budzynski
232	photo	Fred Elliott
232	tickets	John Kamstra
234	top	GRPM
234	bot	EGRPL
235	top	GRPM
235	mid	EGRPL
236	ticket	Gordon Hubenet
236	mid	EGRPL
236	bot	GRPM
237	top	EGRPL
237	bot	GRPM
238		GRPM
239		GRPL
240	mid	Cooley 1912 Appr, Hildebrandt
241	mid, bot	Marcia VanNess
242	photos	Jim Chrysler
243	top l, mid l, bot r	GRPL
243	top r	Larry Baer
244	top l, r	GRPL
244	mid	Nancy Nichoson Myers
244	bot	Colleen Barr VanPuttan
245	top	Nancy Nichoson Myers
245	mid	GRPL
246	top	Paula Worden Naujalis
246	bot	Mary Ellen Miklas Siegel
247	bot	Margaret Kimber
248		GRPL
250		EGRPL
257	top	Hap Hecker
257	mid	Mary Ellen Miklas Siegel
257	bot	Donna Kruizenga Boelema
258		Hap Hecker
259		Hap Hecker
260		Hap Hecker
262	photo, map	GRPL
263	photo	GRCA
264	top	EGRPL
264	bot	Margaret Kimber
265	mid	Lynn Rae Teter
265	bot	Snow
266	top	GRPL
266	mid	Snow
267		GRPM

303

268	bot l	GRPL
269		GRPL
270		GRPL
271		GRPL
273		GRPM
274		John Kamstra
277		EGRPL
278		GRPL
279	bot	PC, Karin McElwee Westdale
281	top	GRPL
282		GRPL
283	bot	GRPL
287		GRPL
288		GRPL
289	top	Margaret Kimber
289	bot	PD, Tom Dilley
290	top	Ron Strauss
290	bot	GRPM
291		EGRPL
292	top	Karin McElwee Westdale
292	bot	EGRPL
293		Karin McElwee Westdale
295		GRPL
296	top l	GRPL
296	top r	EGRPL
296	bot	John Kamstra
297	top l	Dick Ryan
297	top r, mid 2	GRPL
297	bot	Robalyn Rose VanSolkema
298	bot	Robalyn Rose VanSolkema
299	top l	Margaret Kimber
299	top r	GRPL
299	mid l	Peter Walsh
299	mid r	PC, Tom Dilley
300	top l	John Kamstra
300	top r	GRPL
300	bot l	EGRPL
304		Karin McElwee Westdale
Back	top l	GRPL
Back	top r	GRPM
Back	bot l	EGRPL
Back	bot r	Fred Elliott

Derby Racer Construction, 1914

Index

Performers in the Ramona Theater and Ramona Gardens, who were not from Grand Rapids, appear in a separate index. Photos are indicated in **bold.**

306

Performers

Performers in the Ramona Theater and Ramona Gardens, who were not from Grand Rapids.
Photos are indicated in **bold.**

Postcard of
Ramona Theater
at Night

311

About the Author

Now that Gail Marie Snow is retired, she spends most of her time surrounded by antiquities. Her collection of family memorabilia birthed an interest in genealogy and seeking out the stories of her ancestors. In doing so, she gained an appreciation for history along with valuable research skills. She does volunteer work in the archives of the Grand Rapids Public Library and she is the historian and a Bible study leader at Cascade Christian Church. She belongs to the West Michigan Post Card Club, Daughters of the American Revolution, West Michigan Genealogical Society and The Grand Rapids Historical Society. She is also a member of Questers, an international organization that promotes an interest in antiques and preservation of historical landmarks.

This Grand Rapids native graduated from Ottawa Hills High School, then Michigan State University. After that, she married, and moved to Grand Blanc, Michigan, where she taught mathematics and German, and then had two sons.

In 1979, Gail and her boys moved back to the Grand Rapids area to live in the East Grand Rapids school district. She worked as a programmer analyst for Rapistan where she met her husband Charles Snow. Together they enjoy ballroom dancing and riding in their classic cars. When they travel, they like to visit transportation and maritime museums, battlegrounds and other historic sites. They have been enjoying retirement since 2004, surrounded by wildlife in their home in Ada Township.